The Oxford Internship Scheme:

Integration + Partnership in Initial Teacher Education

Edited by Peter Benton

Calouste Gulbenkia

Published by Calouste Gulbenkian Foundation
98 Portland Place
London W1N 4ET
Telephone: 071-636 5313

© 1990 Calouste Gulbenkian Foundation
ISBN 0 903319 53 5
Designed by The Upper Room

Trade distribution:
Turnaround Distri

Contents

Preface

Of the innovatory developments that the Gulbenkian Foundation's Education Programme supports as a matter of policy, some stand out as being especially timely. By addressing issues of common and pressing concern, they suggest a way forward that others in the field may usefully consider or emulate. In such circumstances the Foundation may offer to publish an account of the work, so that a greater number of people may come to hear of it.

So it was with this publication. The initiative it describes was grant-aided by the Foundation in 1987. Two years later, when the project had already assembled a collection of essays on its work and was shortly to seek a publisher, the Foundation offered to publish the manuscript. In so doing, we believe that the lessons of the Internship scheme, the subject of this volume, will make a valuable contribution to the current debate on teacher education at a time when there is a particular need for carefully considered and balanced thinking on the subject.

Simon Richey
Assistant Director (Education)
Calouste Gulbenkian Foundation, UK Branch

July, 1990

Chapter I

The Reform of Teacher Education

Harry Judge

Harry Judge was Director of the Oxford University Department of Educational Studies for 15 years until 1988. He was previously principal of Banbury School, a large comprehensive in Oxfordshire. As will be clear from later chapters, the conceptual framework of the Oxford Internship scheme was his and he was personally responsible for its presentation to headteachers and to the Local Education Authority. He was instrumental in securing support for the scheme from the outset and its wide acceptance was in no small part the result of his efforts.

Dr Judge is now Visiting Professor at Michigan State University with a particular interest in researching and writing about teacher education in an international context. It is with a view to setting developments in Oxford in this cross-national perspective that he has contributed the following chapter. Appreciation is expressed to the editor and to Georgia State University for their willingness to allow much of the material in this chapter to be taken from the author's chapter in Edgar B Gumbert (ed.), Fit to Teach: Teacher Education in International Perspective *(Atlanta: Center for Cross-cultural Education, Georgia State University, 1990).*

A. This a book about a specific and local reform in teacher education, written by those who achieved that reform and commented on by experts who are able to place these local developments in a broader national and international context. The present label of that reform is 'Internship' but its history is a long one. Internship represents a commitment to the school-based training of teachers. It is grounded in a partnership of skilled practitioners in the schools with university academics. It exploits the analogy (but not the model) of the teaching hospital in medical education. Fundamentally, it requires the integration of theory and practice. This introduction sets Internship against its appropriate background, in terms at once geographical and historical. It is not a coincidence that this book is, in large measure, a story about Oxford and Oxfordshire. Oxford University has been preoccupied with teaching for some seven centuries and with the formal training of teachers for one. Preparation for the professions is as much part of its historic as of its contemporary mission. Its more recent, but hardly novel, engagement in teacher education has reflected a public and increasingly political concern with the improvement of teachers - a concern which now rides high upon the agenda of many developed and developing countries. That engagement, in its various forms, also reflects changing concepts of schooling and of the criteria for good teaching. The Oxford University Department of Educational Studies (OUDES) was for much of its life concerned exclusively with the training of teachers for independent and academically selective secondary schools. For the past two decades it has addressed itself rather to the making of teachers for all kinds of schools and all varieties of pupil.

The University of Oxford sits at the heart of the County of Oxfordshire, although for long the story of the relationship of town (and county) with gown was one of coolness often degenerating into hostility and violence. It is not always easy for an international university to be a local university as well. More recently, the tale has been a happier one - especially, perhaps, in medicine and in education. The details of my own career, unimportant in themselves, illustrate this. I came to Banbury in Oxfordshire as headmaster of one of those local grammar schools designed exclusively for more able pupils beyond the age of eleven and for which the university departments of education prepared, on a national scale, many of the teachers. That grammar school became part, in the turbulence of the 1960s, of a new comprehensive school and in such places teachers became critical of the style of preparation offered in the traditional establishments of teacher education. As a representative critic of that style I became a member of the Committee of Enquiry (the James Committee) into teacher training appointed by Mrs Margaret Thatcher, during her vigorous tenure of the office of Secretary of State for Education and Science. More is written below of the James Committee, but in the year after the publication of its Report I moved to Oxford as Director of OUDES which was a decade later to become the nursery of Internship.

Unsurprisingly, therefore, a new urgency was given to building new relationships between the teachers and the trainers, between the university at large and the schools of the county in which it was set. Already, and during the lifetime of the James Committee itself, the Department of Education and Science (DES) in London had established in Banbury a pilot scheme for a Professional Tutor and yet another new term was added to the educational lexicon. Even sooner than that, a nationally funded research project linking Oxford University and Banbury School had been established to study the contentious matter of ability grouping and streaming in schools. The science tutors in OUDES were in the 1970s the first to establish sharply defined and effective links with local schools and in a short time all teaching practice (or student-teaching) was concentrated within Oxfordshire schools. The Oxford Educational Research Group, under the successive chairmanships of Professors Jerome Bruner and A H Halsey, undertook a series of school-based investigations and action projects.

These were some of the foundations on which Tim Brighouse chose to build when he came to Oxfordshire as its Chief Education Officer. He tells part of his own story later in this book, and from that clearly emerges the central importance of the imaginative programme of seconding the best among his serving teachers to OUDES for courses of full-time study. In a few years many of Oxfordshire's teachers had themselves been advanced students within the university, which learnt at least as much from them as they did from it. These men and women were behind Internship as the next wave of reform - a wave that had its own parochial origins but which was to coincide with a national, indeed international, urge towards new and better focused forms of teacher preparation. It is that international concern which gives Internship a particular significance to the 1990s.(1)

Within Britain itself the teaching force represents a massive educational investment, and is therefore certain to attract continuing and often unfriendly public attention. Although its size, at about 440,000, has shrunk a little in recent years, the salary bill for those teachers represents some 70% of the annual current cost of primary and secondary schools. The critical task for the rest of this century will be to match the output of the teacher education system (or systems) to the needs of those schools, as well as to retrain the teachers already working in them. It is precisely that matching of the structures of teacher education with those of the schools that has been so difficult to achieve for much of this century: indeed, the match has probably never been so neatly symmetrical as it was during the nineteenth century. The structures of both sub-systems (teacher education and schooling) have been continuously modified during the twentieth century, but the modifications have been imperfectly integrated. More particularly, there has been a significant and dangerous lag between the introduction of changes in patterns of schooling and appropriate adjustments to those of teacher preparation; this lag does much to explain both the continuing sense of unease and disorder in teacher education, and the predictably imperfect outcomes of many efforts at school reform.

The current state of teacher education can therefore best be explored through its speculatively predicted future and its recorded past. Current developments, and their likely outcomes, will bring new pressures to bear upon that state and so reveal much of its true nature. A greater measure of governmental responsibility for the content of teaching will tighten the disciplines of planning, as teachers will need to be produced (and shown to exist) if a national curriculum is indeed to be delivered. A highly probable shortage of adequately qualified recruits to teacher education will at the same time in the mid-1990s bring severe pressures to bear upon the undoubted determination of government to preserve high standards in the recruitment of teachers. The pressures for higher standards, for matching the curriculum needs of schools, and of finding enough teachers of any kind will interact and conflict. A new urgency will thus be given to the antique problem of maintaining an effective relationship between the structures of teacher education and of schooling. That relationship has in the course of its complex development moved through three phases - *elitist, comprehensive* and *efficient*. In each of those phases the principal themes have recurred and interacted with one another, and these in their turn are in this chapter characterised as *content, location* and *control*. Issues of content concern primarily what it is that is taught to students in teacher education, and in particular the balance between academic studies and practical or professional work. Issues of location concern, of course, the relationship of teacher education to the mainstream of higher education (epitomised by the university) and to the so-called lower schools. Issues of control obviously relate to the powers and responsibilities of central government, of the religious and voluntary bodies as the historic providers of much of teacher education, and of local governments as (although not for very much longer) the principal employers of teachers and providers of most of the non-university institutions of teacher education. The themes resonate through all three historical phases, and the argument of the rest of this chapter may best be introduced by a simple grid:-

	ELITIST	COMPREHENSIVE	EFFICIENT	
Content				1
Location				2
Control				3
	A	B	C	

B.Teacher education in England and Wales is a product of history rather than of logic, although much has been achieved in the past 20 years to give it more shape and coherence. Although it is now in consequence more of 'a system' than ever before, it is still marked by curious inherited divisions, both between curricular patterns of teacher education (and underlying ideologies) and between types of institution. These divisions were created in the nineteenth century, and can only be understood in that historical context. They are not without analogies elsewhere in Europe, but stand in marked contrast to the present situation in the United States. They are rooted in patterns of schooling, and specifically in the sharp distinction throughout the last century and well into this between public elementary education on the one hand and on the other the secondary education provided only for a privileged minority. Serious and vocational teacher education was for long confined to the preparation of teachers for those public elementary schools.(2)

Those schools were until 1870 provided exclusively by voluntary religious bodies, albeit with a growing measure of support and intervention from the state. Many of the teachers in them were in no sense qualified or licensed, but both the providers of the schools and the state as the source of finance had an obvious interest in raising the standards of teaching. This was attempted by an array of measures, including financial incentives for teachers who chose to seek certification, and the control of that process of certification by public examinations and by the monitoring functions of Her Majesty's Inspectors (HMI). Throughout the second half of the century the main source of teachers was the pool of pupil-teachers, who in return for modest payments and some free tuition worked as apprentices to more experienced practitioners. Such teacher training as existed was therefore undertaken for the most part within the culture of the elementary schools themselves, and for the majority that was for long generally deemed to be sufficient.

For a minority of the more able and determined, post-school training was provided through one or two-year courses in the handful of training colleges which the religious bodies had provided for their own teachers, again with varying measures of state support justifying government intervention in their management. By mid-century a score of such colleges existed. Those pupil-teachers who did not secure scholarships to them could nevertheless continue to teach as uncertificated teachers or submit themselves, without having attended a training college, to the national examination provided by the government as the one gate to certificated status. These colleges owed much to Scottish and continental examples, and became both more significant and (given their monopoly) more anomalous after the introduction to England and Wales in 1870 of secular public elementary schools, under the control of elected School Boards.(3) There was (with the important exception noted below) no secular alternative to these denominational colleges, which depended for their survival both upon financial support from the government and upon a supply of students from the pool of pupil-teachers. By 1900 there was only one certificated teacher for each 75 pupils, and only one trained teacher (who had, that is, attended a college) for each 128 pupils. Moreover the pupil-teachers themselves provided a significant direct contribution to the workforce: of 139,818 teachers in service in elementary schools in 1902, 30,785 were pupil-teachers.

From the beginning of this century, the public local education authorities were encouraged to build their own training colleges, although only a score of such institutions had been established before 1914. Public and political pressures upon an untidy system became stronger, and opposition to the pupil-teacher system more articulate. The minimum age for admission to pupillage was raised, and the roots of teacher training in the elementary school weakened. Scholarships were provided for intending teachers willing to stay on in secondary schools, and teacher education took a further step towards what was later to be defined as higher education. By 1914 most of the pupil-teachers had disappeared, and most intending teachers began their professional training after leaving secondary school (or its equivalent) and in one of the colleges. Those colleges, while not neglecting vocational concerns, were often marked by a strong academic bias in their curriculum and many students in them sought to combine their regular programme with contemporaneous study on university courses. Public authorities generally resisted this tendency, for example by withdrawing recognition from colleges which allowed students to combine a two or three-year course with work for a university degree. But it was long before attendance at a college, and subsequent success in an examination, became a necessary condition for employment as a teacher: as late as 1926 there was one uncertificated teacher for three that were certificated, and in many rural areas the numbers were equal.

The training of elementary teachers was therefore an important item on the policy agenda: not until very much later was that true for secondary school teachers. Even after the spread of public secondary schools in the early years of this century, the possession of a university degree was thought to be a sufficient guarantee of competence as a teacher. Indeed, such legal provisions survived into the 1970s, and the attitudes underlying them still longer than that. The universities became involved in the business of teacher training almost by accident. In the late nineteenth century all the training colleges were religious establishments, and this monopoly was offensive to many. Several universities therefore gladly accepted the government's invitation to establish what were known as Day Training Colleges, to provide a secular alternative to the conventional residential colleges for elementary teachers: 16 such colleges existed at the turn of the century. Their contribution to the training of elementary teachers represented nearly one-quarter of the total provision. Some of them quietly developed secondary departments, which responded in time to the general view among the associations of secondary teachers that the appropriate pattern of education and training for their members should be a bachelor's degree followed by a one-year university-based professional course. Early in this century this became the norm for those graduates who attached importance to any kind of formal training. The average annual number in this category for the whole country in the years before World War I was only 200, and of these 160 were women. In 1938 only 60% of the male graduates teaching in secondary schools had received this or any other kind of formal training; even in the 1960s, and until such training was made compulsory, nearly half of all the graduates going into teaching received no kind of training.

The universities therefore became the home of a particular kind of teacher training, possibly well adapted to the particular needs of secondary schools, and - partly because they successfully insisted on a four-year course as a minimum if a degree and professional training were both to be achieved - they were distanced from the larger but less prestigious business of preparing elementary school teachers. The training colleges outside the universities became the home of the two-year course, combining (often uneasily) academic and professional work. Teacher training gradually became the normal requirement for elementary school teachers, but not for their secondary cousins. Management of the training colleges, now separated from the structures of elementary and secondary schooling but still distanced from the universities in higher education, was exercised by the local education and denominational authorities. Central government exercised a tight control over the logistics and curriculum and examinations of the colleges; the universities depended upon it for recognition, but thereafter (strengthened by the voluntary nature of the training provided) enjoyed a considerable measure of autonomy, conferring for example their own diplomas as alternatives to the state certification examination. Between the two World Wars an attempt, which proved to be of largely symbolic significance, was made to draw the two separate sectors a little closer together by establishing Joint Boards to conduct the examinations for teacher candidates in the colleges, and so limit the influence of government upon the content of courses. But at the end of the *elitist* phase (marked roughly by the passing of the great Education Act of 1944) a very sharp dichotomy had been established between voluntary training within the universities for the academic secondary schools and an effectively compulsory one within the colleges for the elementary sector. These divisions still have geological importance, and the comments - on content, location, and control - made in this Section can now be incorporated in the grid displayed at the end of Section A.

C.There are two reasons for attaching to the second major phase in the development of British teacher education (from 1944 to 1972) the convenient label of *comprehensive*. The key, it has already been argued, to understanding the purposes and structure of teacher education - and not in Britain alone - lies in the relationship between the schools and the activities of teacher education itself. During the years under review the structure of British schooling changed dramatically: first, by the introduction after 1944 of universal secondary education, albeit of a bipartite variety and, secondly, by the acceleration during the 1960s towards the introduction of the comprehensive secondary school designed to incorporate the academic and general secondary schools which had preceded it.(4) The symmetrical relationship between a dual system of teacher education and a dual system of schooling was destroyed, but the necessary adjustments to the former made only slowly and painfully. Meanwhile, the national system was becoming more comprehensive in yet another sense as efforts were doubled to bring the untidy business of teacher education firmly and unambiguously within the mainstream of higher education.

Major changes were outlined in the year of the 1944 Act: from an early date only Qualified Teachers (the new technical term) were to be employed and qualification would depend (except, still, for university graduates) upon attending an approved course of training. The gates seemed to be closing upon an emerging profession. A new relationship was attempted between the universities and the colleges through regional forms of organisation which assumed responsibility, not always exercised with firmness and imagination, for the procedures leading to qualified teacher status, for the courses of study in the colleges and for examinations. In principle, the central government had yielded a great deal of its historic control; even in practice the system became a great deal more liberal and decentralised than it had been (or was again to become). The legal minimum school leaving age was raised twice in these years and contributed - along with the successful demands for smaller classes - to an impressive increase in the number of teacher training places and of institutions (as well as of their size and effectiveness). The output from the colleges in 1939 had been 6,000; by the early 1970s, when the peak was reached, it was 40,000. Even so, the length of the course had been extended from two to three years at the beginning of the 1960s, and by the end of that decade some 10% of all students were completing a fourth year in order to qualify for the newly introduced degree of Bachelor of Education (the BEd).

The colleges therefore came to resemble more closely other establishments of higher education. Not only were their courses of study more academically serious, but there was a marked shift towards laicisation: this had taken place rapidly after 1944. In 1939 there had been 63 voluntary (mostly denominational) colleges and only 28 maintained by the local education authorities; by 1951 the former category had shrunk to 56, while the latter mushroomed to 76. They were shortly to acquire a greater measure of responsibility for their own affairs through the reconstitution of governing bodies, and the representation upon them of faculty members. The universities themselves preserved their interest in the one-year course of training for graduates, which was not made compulsory until the early 1970s (and even then with significant loop-holes).

These years were also marked by expansion and diversification within higher education as a whole. University teacher training related only to the academic grammar and independent schools and had existed comfortably alongside, albeit at a considerable distance from, teacher training in the colleges designed to meet the needs of a separate elementary school system. But, already in the 1960s, the universities had ceased to be the only nationally recognised establishments of higher education: alongside them grew with government encouragement the 30 polytechnics, indistinguishable in many ways from the universities although subject (as they will now no longer be) to control by local government.(5) A straightforward marriage between universities and colleges of education, although ardently desired by many reformers, had not proved possible to achieve: too many issues of power, prestige and finance were involved. But a higher education 'family', which now included polytechnics and some colleges of higher education alongside the older universities, would need to clarify its relationship with a training college system marked by increasing ambiguities of purpose and status. That status had itself been subtly modified in the mid-1960s by a simple and inexpensive change of title from training college to College of Education.(6)

The James Committee, appointed by Mrs Margaret Thatcher in 1971 when she was Secretary of State for Education and Science, therefore faced a rich crop of problems and questions. Changes in the school system meant that the machinery of training was now badly out of line with it: teachers could no longer be professionally classified as being concerned only with younger or less academically talented pupils, or vice versa. The College of Education system had come to maturity, in terms of size and the length of the courses offered. But its relationship to higher education as a whole remained uncertain and uncomfortable. Moreover, the startling growth of the past decade had inevitably raised problems of quality and stability. Perhaps most serious of all, the quest for academic respectability - associated in part with the lengthening of the course, and more directly with the BEd degree - was believed to have generated a neglect of professional concerns, and an insensitivity to the real needs of schools and of intending classroom teachers. It was objected, in terms reminiscent of the early 1900s, that the colleges were unduly preoccupied with conventional university standards of subject mastery and scholarship and, to make things worse, that the professional study of Education had itself been etherealised. These years were the hey-day of the study of the four disciplines of education: sociology, psychology, philosophy and history.

Many of these anxieties were doubtless misplaced or exaggerated, but the structural problems underlying the polemic were real enough. The solutions proposed by the James Committee - which, although not formally adopted, have in my opinion had no small influence on the evolution of the present arrangements - were integrated by an effort to dignify and clarify the term 'professional'. For that reason the strongest emphasis was placed upon the professional development of the teacher in service through a range of educational and training activities. The formal distinction between concurrent (as in the colleges) and consecutive (as in the universities) forms of teacher education was rejected as unhelpful. All intending teachers should first complete a well-planned phase of personal higher education (the so-called first cycle) before proceeding to a second and sharply professional cycle of teacher preparation, sited partly within higher education and partly in the setting of real schools. The degree to be awarded after these two stages was to be a BA(Ed), and was conceived as being a degree in teaching rather than in a subject called Education. The intention in many of these details was to imply a flattering analogy with the professional and practical education offered (or so it is still fashionable to suppose) in medicine. The dependent relationship of the colleges upon the universities was to be terminated, and in effect a third sector of higher education created, based in large measure upon the existing colleges, many of which would wish to diversify their programmes of study. The Committee was sceptical of the advantages of teachers being educated in relative isolation from the rest of their contemporaries.(7)

The 1972 Report conveniently marks the transition from the *comprehensive* to the *efficient* phase. The phase which it concluded was marked, in terms of the explanatory grid, by a shift in content towards academic values and purposes, against which there was then a strong reaction. As for location, attempts to incorporate the colleges within the university sector were unsuccessful, but the growth of higher education itself opened up new possibilities for the future. As for control, central government preserved tight management of the funding and logistics of the system, while relinquishing much of the professional and academic responsibility for it. These very themes were to be given a new importance, and in some ways new definitions, in the succeeding (that is, contemporary phase) which has been dominated by an unexpectedly abrupt decline in the number of places required for teacher training. That decline, coupled with a new and vigorous determination by government to re-assert control of the values as well as the mechanics of the system, explains much in the present British pattern.(8)

D.The mid-1970s mark a watershed in the history of education in Britain. The Labour Prime Minister's speech at Oxford in October 1976 was widely and correctly perceived as a forceful attempt to break away from many of the conventions of the past. Standards were not high enough; the basics were being neglected; the educating professions had not been sensitive to public and parental anxieties; the needs of industry had been neglected; central government had not given a decisive lead and a great debate was needed. In spite of the contemporary disclaimers, it was clear that government proposed to intervene much more directly in the design and delivery of the school curriculum. The momentum in that direction was accelerated by the Conservative victory in the general election of 1979, and consolidated in the elections of 1983 and (even more clearly) 1987. There were, of course, profoundly important shifts of emphasis as result of these Conservative victories - notably in the attack on the powers of local education authorities, the new powers to be given to parents as consumers and the accompanying stress on privatisation - but there is now a well-established consensus in the corridors of power that more intervention is required, at least in the short term, to restore the educational system to a healthy state. A much more overt interest in the business of teacher education was therefore to be expected.

The pervading pessimism of the early 1970s was generated in part by the world-wide economic crisis caused by the rise in oil prices, and in part by the simple facts of demographic decline. Consistent falls in the birth-rate, in Britain as elsewhere, placed the system under great strain since contraction is nearly always more painful than expansion, even if the latter is inadequately funded. The effects upon the recently expanded world of teacher education were only too obvious. Government which had financed that expansion now found itself with wide and unchallenged powers in slimming down the provision, and used those administrative powers to produce significant changes in shape as well as in scale. In 1972, outside the universities which were sheltered from the storms that were about to break, there were 130,407 students in teacher training. In 1978 there were 36,000 and, although there have since been modest adjustments, the effects of that shock will be permanent. It is not simply a question of less of the same. The College of Education system has effectively disappeared, and only a handful of such single purpose institutions survive. The separate regional and national organisation of those colleges has been abolished. Many were brusquely closed; others were absorbed as going concerns by polytechnics or, in a few cases, universities; many more diversified their programmes of study in order to include a wider range of work for degrees and similar qualifications. These changes were part of a redrawing of the map of higher education, more than half of which is now conducted outside the universities.

The planning opportunity has been taken to redress the balance of the contributions made by the universities on the one hand, and on the other by the Colleges of Education (where they survived), the polytechnics into which some were absorbed, and the Colleges of Higher Education (which some became) - here referred to as a group, and for convenience, as 'the colleges'. 'The colleges' in this sense (now the polytechnic and college sector in cumbersome official parlance) were until recently oddly referred to as 'the public sector' in order to distinguish them from the universities which, although also publicly funded, have conventionally been regarded as enjoying a considerable measure of autonomy. In the early 1970s when enrolments were of course highest, teacher education was provided in 27 universities and 180 colleges. By 1983, when most of the surgery had been accomplished, it was provided in only 56 colleges - and 27 universities! Within the colleges, the last admissions to the three-year certificate course were in 1979, and all teacher candidates in those colleges now proceed to the BEd degree. More surprising, perhaps, has been the marked shift within the colleges from the concurrent to the consecutive mode - from the BEd to the one-year postgraduate course, the PGCE. This shift, from the longer to the shorter courses of the type advocated by the James Committee, has further tilted the university/colleges balance towards the former. It has also had the effect, intended or not, of securing that the universities continue to concentrate - albeit not exclusively - on the secondary schools, whereas most intending primary (that is, elementary) school teachers are trained in the colleges, which nevertheless make a substantial contribution to the staffing needs of the secondary schools. In a curious and incomplete sense, the much sharper divisions of the nineteenth century still influence the shape of the system.

These features of present British teacher education can be illustrated by the figures for admission to courses of teacher education in September 1987.(9) They are:-

| | PGCE | | BEd | | |
	Primary	Secondary	Primary	Secondary	TOTALS
Universities	946	4582	447	349	**6324**
Public sector	2308	2658	6888	1717	**13571**
TOTALS	**3254**	**7240**	**7335**	**2066**	**19895**

The total university share of admissions is therefore 32%, contrasted with a tiny 4.4% in 1972. 48% of secondary teachers are nevertheless trained outside the universities. The universities, to the tune of 78% of their total admissions, are predominantly concerned with teachers for the secondary schools. 54% of all students are on the one-year graduate, consecutive, course. These changes, taken cumulatively, are of great force: a much higher proportion than ever before of future teachers being trained in the universities, and a much higher proportion on courses where the focus, at least in principle, is on professional preparation rather than academic study. Here, then, are marked changes in the readings on the explanatory grid for the two themes of *content* and *location*.

But the current *efficient* phase of teacher education differs even more profoundly from its immediate predecessor. Government in the 1960s placed most of the expansion of teacher education outside the universities, although it may be doubted whether in the circumstances of that decade any real alternative was open to it. But, unlike government in the *elitist* phase in its relationship to the college sector, it purposefully abstained from seeking to direct the nature of the courses provided: this was the business of universities, the regional organisations grouped around universities, or the colleges themselves. This is why 1976 represents a watershed in the British educational polity, for no government which cares publicly about the curriculum of the schools can be indifferent to the curriculum of those establishments which produce teachers for them.(10) Nevertheless, few observers in (say) 1979 anticipated the lengths to which a British government would go in asserting, or in some senses re-asserting, its right to control such matters. The Secretary of State for Education and Science, who has the undoubted legal authority to confer or deny the status of Qualified Teacher, has ruled that access to that status shall normally be through courses of preparation approved by him. That approval is secured only if a number of conditions, or criteria, is satisfied and it is conferred or denied on the recommendation of a Council for the Accreditation of Teacher Education (CATE), the members of which are appointed by him. Universities, unlike the colleges, have been exempt from the visits of HMI, although they have always been free to invite such visits. That position has not been altered legally. But

CATE can make a recommendation only if it has access to a report written by HMI: every university in England and Wales offering courses of teacher training has now received such a visit.

What is clear from the criteria is that government has strong views about the proper nature of teacher training. There is firm and unsurprising emphasis, at present of particular importance for students for the BEd, on the importance of academic subject studies. This emphasis has been publicly regretted by some who argue that it is not in the best interests of intending primary school teachers: in that sense, the debate on content is far from dead. Equally marked is the concern with pedagogy, a word if not a concept that had ceased to be much employed in the 1960s. Those who teach teachers should themselves have had recent experience of teaching; teaching practice must be extensive and well organised; experienced teachers must themselves be involved in the selection of students for courses, and in the preparation of them. Similarly, students on courses which are to win approval must be introduced to the importance of multicultural education, of pupils with special educational needs, and must have a good understanding of the social context in which they are to work. All this represents an overt and principled attempt to give teacher education, of whatever type and wherever located, a sharp professional and practical focus.(11) What has been devalued, in colleges and universities alike, is the study of educational disciplines in the styles which had become orthodox in many establishments. The political and demographic changes of the later 1970s and the 1980s have produced many of the intended effects of the James Report: a second cycle (although not in those terms) for the majority of intending teachers, and a sharp emphasis upon the professional imperatives of that cycle. Moreover, the segregated colleges of education have all but disappeared, and the distinction between university and college substantially diminished. Although the primary/secondary distinction is of course still important, it no longer corresponds either to a simple difference of location or to variation in the type, graduate or not, of programme. University and college are engaged in fundamentally similar work, and unambiguously subject to the same controls.

Some critical questions nevertheless obtrude. In the *efficient* phase, the question of *content* has been decisively resolved: for all intending teachers the stress is to be upon knowledge of basic subject matter (mathematics, a foreign language, or whatever) and upon professional pedagogy: 'abstract theory' has been beaten upon the head. This clarity has been achieved by government *control*, exercised not only upon the colleges (as previously in the elitist phase), but also upon the universities. The issue of *location* has been redefined, with a growing similarity of programme structure (the consecutive mode), a much larger share of the market for the universities, and a softening of the historic distinction between the university and the college sectors. Under the Education Act of 1988 the two sectors will be similarly managed, with the removal of all colleges (including, of course the polytechnics) from local authority control and the creation of twin funding councils at national level, designed to apply government policies.(12) One critical question therefore relates to the rationality of any continuing distinction between provision by the universities, and the rest of teacher education. It is simplistic to suppose that the universities will automatically preserve some inherent commitment to teacher education based upon research: indeed, the requirements of the new criteria (including a significantly longer teaching year) make it more difficult than ever before to pay serious attention to scholarly as distinct from vocational responsibilities.

It may well be that dilemmas of this kind will oblige the institutions, and not just the universities, to devise new patterns of teacher education in which the legitimate demands of utility are integrated with an open and enquiring approach to the tasks of teaching and the roles of the teacher: the Internship is of course one example of such an effort. Such efforts are more readily deployed within the consecutive pattern of graduate teacher training, protected from the competitive internal pressures of the BEd, within which the objectives of a subject-based academic education and of professional preparation can be reconciled only with difficulty. In any case, as the table for 1987 admissions implies, there seems now to be no clear rationale for the BEd as a concurrent form of training, with its historical origins in the old training college model operating within a very different universe of secondary and higher education. Students themselves seem likely to prefer forms of higher education which allow them to defer final choices of career and to acquire Bachelor degrees which have wider currency than the single purpose BEd.

Postgraduate teacher training is, for such reasons, likely to become the dominant form of teacher education in Britain in the twenty-first century. Developed forms of the Internship may well become the preferred model of such training. But this pair of probabilities raises paradoxes and dangers. There is an unpleasant possibility that the stress on school-based teacher training will be misinterpreted and distorted. In particular, the critical and autonomous role of the university may be threatened by being eliminated. If the stress upon practical competence is excessive or exclusive, it may be falsely assumed that the whole of the responsibility for teacher training can be taken by the schools themselves or by the employers. Nothing could be more destructive of the dignity or of the independence of the teaching profession, upon which a healthy and critical democracy depends. Internship, by challenging the arid monopoly of a theory-based university, deploys the language of partnership. But partnership is reciprocal and without a major part for university or college teacher education will become, as it was a century ago, unimaginative, docile and repetitive. In 1988 the government announced its intention of introducing a scheme under which some intending teachers of mature years would be recruited to the schools and given by their employers modest on-the-job training in which universities and colleges might play little or no part. In 1989 it decided to introduce a pilot scheme, of potentially wider scope, under which intending teachers would be given a two-year period of combined employment and training during which responsibility for their preparation would be shared by their employers and, less substantially, the training institutions. This latter scheme is much closer to the spirit of Internship and, indeed, to a two-year pattern of teacher preparation for which the James Report argued and which I was happy to advocate some years ago.(13) Much will depend upon the contribution to be made by universities and others and upon the freedom allowed to them to behave with reasoned autonomy.

The Education Reform Act of 1988 has changed much in the British educational landscape, and probably more dramatically than any previous measure.(14) In particular, it has changed the relationships between government and other elected agencies and between schools and teacher education. It is the same central government which now regulates what must be taught and in what amounts that has the parallel responsibility for demonstrating that a sufficient supply of appropriately trained teachers is delivered in order to meet those legal requirements. If more mathematics and science and foreign languages are now to be taught by government order, then government must deliver the necessary teachers. Such a responsibility has in the past been weaker and more dispersed and the relationship between teachers and curriculum more flexible. The pressures on government to intervene powerfully in the mechanisms which control the supply of teachers through higher education will be irresistible. And those pressures will come to bear most oppressively in the mid-1990s when for demographic reasons the conventional supply of teachers will be most at risk and the school population is rising.

There are already plain signs of pressure on teachers and on their sense of worth and professional style. They have lost and not yet had restored their rights of participation in the processes by which salaries and conditions of service are determined. Acts and regulations now determine in unprecedented ways the details of what shall be taught. Appraisal and the techniques of human resource management erode traditional, and not always erroneous, ways of thinking and feeling about teaching as a way of life. Such factors are likely to discourage the intelligent and well-motivated men and women who are needed in the schools from committing themselves to teaching or from undertaking rigorous courses of professional preparation, if easy means of access to the responsibilities of a teacher are proffered. In such times it is all the more important that teacher education should be confident, soundly based in established and autonomous institutions able to resist successive changes of political mood and yet rooted in the real world of schools and the pupils they educate. Internship may not be all that important in itself but this book must surely demonstrate the fundamental value of the solid principles on which it is based.

References

1. See, for the United States, Jonas F Soltis (ed.), *Reforming Teacher Education* (New York: Teachers College Press, 1987). For several other countries see Edgar B Gumbert (ed.), see page 1 of this chapter.
2. Much of the information used in the following paragraphs is taken from H C Dent, *The Training of Teachers in England and Wales, 1800 - 1975* (London: Hodder and Stoughton, 1975) and P H J H Gosden, *The Evolution of a Profession* (Oxford: Basil Blackwell, 1972).
3. Marjorie Cruickshank, *History of the Training of Teachers in Scotland* (London: University of London Press, 1970).
4. Harry Judge, *A Generation of Schooling: English Secondary Schools since 1944* (Oxford and New York: Oxford University Press, 1984).
5. Tony Becher (ed.), *British Higher Education* (London: Allen and Unwin, 1987).
6. William Taylor, "Robbins and the education of teachers", *Oxford Review of Education* (XIV,1 1988):49-58.
7. *Teacher Education and Training: A Report by a Committee of Enquiry appointed by the Secretary of State for Education and Science, under the Chairmanship of Lord James of Rusholme* (London: Her Majesty's Stationery Office, 1972).
8. Harry Judge, "From Quantity to Quality: Teacher Education in Britain" in Thomas J Lasley (ed.), *Issues in Teacher Education* (Washington, DC: American Association of Colleges of Teacher Education, 1986) vol.II, pp.55 - 64.
9. *Education Observed, 7: Initial teacher training in universities in England, Northern Ireland and Wales.* (London: Department of Education and Science, 1988) p.45.
10. *Teaching Quality: Presented to Parliament by Command of Her Majesty, March 1983* (London: Her Majesty's Stationery Office, 1983).
11. *Initial Teacher Training: Approval of Courses, Circular 3/84* (London: Department of Education and Science, 1984).
12. *Higher Education: Meeting the Challenge: Presented to Parliament by Command of Her Majesty, April 1987* (London: Her Majesty's Stationery Office, 1987).
13. *Qualified Teacher Status: Consultation Document* (London: Department of Education and Science, 1988). Letter from Department of Education and Science to Chief Education Officers and others, "Articled Teacher Pilot Scheme", 27 June 1989. Harry Judge, "Degrees of Certainty", *Times Educational Supplement,* 3 March 1981.
14. On the new Act see Stuart Maclure, *Education Reformed: A Guide to the Education Reform Act, 1988* (London: Hodder and Stoughton, 1988).

A Note on Internship

Internship was part of the quest for what Harry Judge has earlier described as "new and better focused forms of teacher preparation". The basic structural outline Harry Judge first proposed to the tutorial staff of OUDES in 1984 and later to the Oxford headteachers in June 1985 has since changed in detail but not in essence. He suggested that

* a new kind of partnership between schools and university department was essential.

* teachers in schools were best placed to assist the development of young teachers in training, therefore the course must be school-based but closely coupled to the university contribution which was also valuable and distinctive.

* concentration on a smaller number of schools was necessary if true partnership was to be achieved.

* concentration of students (to be known as 'interns') in those schools would achieve the necessary 'critical mass' for them to be recognised as a significant group with a genuine contribution to make.

* pairing of interns would help achieve this larger group and would be beneficial in other ways such as offering added security, providing a partner to work with and creating a recognisable and effective unit to work with a designated subject teacher in the school.

* a commitment to one school over the greater part of a year would allow a gradual and controlled induction of the young teachers to a complex system which would provide a single rich case study of educational issues.

* there would be a close identification of one tutor with each particular school and a partnership between that tutor and the school's professional tutor would be established for the purposes of co-ordinating and overseeing the non-subject specific components of interns' work and study.

* there would be an agreed programme in curricular areas and an agreed general programme concerned with educational issues which would be school or university-based as the situation demanded, for one of the central beliefs was that the different parties should undertake those aspects of work for which they were best fitted.

* the programme would provide opportunities for teachers' INSET (In-Service Training) as well as for the training needs of interns.

* all parties - teachers, interns, tutors, school pupils, LEA - should benefit from the operation of the scheme and it should be a positive contribution to staff development rather than a burden to be shouldered.

These, briefly, were the key proposals that the schools, university and LEA agreed to develop as the Oxford Internship scheme. More detail as to the process of initiating and carrying through the changes that the new scheme implied are given in Chapter III, and a fuller treatment of its operation appears in Chapter IV. Before moving on to these concerns, however, it is important to articulate the ideas and principles guiding the Internship scheme, the shared understandings on which it is based.

Chapter II

Ideas and Principles Guiding the Internship Scheme

Donald McIntyre

The author of this chapter, Donald McIntyre, is Reader in Education at the Oxford University Department of Educational Studies and has a long-standing interest in how teachers - and particularly beginning teachers - learn. His thinking has shaped Internship from the time of the scheme's adoption, providing an invaluable theoretical perspective that has constantly informed developing practice. Apart from engaging in research into teacher knowledge, he is also a general tutor in the Internship scheme with responsibility for the work of one particular school group of interns and is thus in daily contact with the way the scheme is operating; like the interns themselves, he is continually testing theory against practice.

This chapter is concerned with the main ideas which informed the planning of the Oxford Internship scheme. These ideas are presented as falling into three main categories. First, there were the teacher education goals to be attained. Second, there were the endemic problems of teacher education which needed to be solved. Third, and most important, are the principles of procedure of the scheme, directed towards the attainment of the stated goals and formulated as solutions to the identified problems. It is these principles which have directly guided the planning and practices of the Internship scheme and which indeed are embedded in these plans and practices.

A. Goals to be Attained

The agreed goals towards which the programme is directed are the following:

On completion of the PGCE (Postgraduate Certificate of Education) year, interns should

1. be able to cope effectively in the classroom (ie have attained sufficient fluency in classroom management and control, and in the skills necessary for effective use of a variety of classroom teaching strategies, including all those widely used within a defined area of the secondary school curriculum);

2. possess a critical understanding of the curriculum and pedagogy of their subject(s) (ie they should have reconceptualised their subject(s) from university to school level and have attained an understanding of the different ways of organising the curriculum for their subject(s) - both within the subject(s) and in relation to the whole-school curriculum. They should be aware of the rationales which may be offered for the adoption of such different approaches and of different pedagogical strategies. They should have critically considered a range of evidence related to these varied approaches and strategies, including that derived from their own personal experience. In examining these approaches and strategies they should have applied diverse relevant criteria of subject knowledge, of personal benefit to the pupil, of social value and of professional practicality).

Within the wider context of their own teaching and of the education system generally, interns should

3. appreciate the potentialities and the problems of achieving social justice in their own teaching (ie they should have acquired the understanding, the commitment, and some initial plans for minimising in their work as a teacher - and for taking positive action to counter - injustices in relation to differences among pupils in (a) social class, gender, ethnic origins; (b) culture, religion; (c) current aspirations and current attainments);

4. be able to cope effectively with aspects of being a teacher which extend beyond the bounds of their own subject area(s) (ie they should be well informed about current practices and developments in secondary education generally and should, where appropriate, possess basic skills relevant to these practices and developments, eg in relation to assessment and certification arrangements, established curricular patterns and new curricular initiatives, current ways of organising and managing secondary schools and their own administrative role and relationships with colleagues, and current ways of providing pastoral care including relations with parents and their own role within that system, curricular and careers guidance, social education, and educational experience beyond the normal curriculum. They should have learned to think in critical and theoretically informed ways about the social and educational functions of these practices and developments).

In order to contextualise, strengthen and support the achievement of the goals expressed above, interns should also

5. be able to see schooling in relation to educational ideas (ie they should understand and appreciate different theoretical conceptions of education and see the contrast between the practicalities of schooling and theoretical ideas of education. They should be aware of the necessary tensions between such theoretical conceptions and the various practical and selfish concerns of those concerned with schooling - for example, teachers, administrators, parents, pupils and potential employers. They should be conscious of their own needs and of their own attempts to adopt viable compromise positions between their own educational ideals and the practicalities of schooling which they face);

6. be able to understand pupil characteristics and the differences among pupils (ie they should have attained a good understanding of the various alternative ways of considering the learning difficulties of pupils, deviant behaviour of pupils and more generally differences among pupils in their perceived characteristics, their behaviour and their attainments. They should also be able to relate this understanding to their own classroom activities, to the options available to them and the decisions they might take in their own teaching).

In order that interns may progress from the development of good teaching habits to the self-conscious analysis of such skills, they should

7. have developed a conscious awareness of practising teaching habits (ie they should have acquired unselfconscious habits of teaching which are sufficiently routinised and compatible with practical realities to sustain them through the first few years of their professional careers. They should be aware that the acquisition of these habits may have meant the suspension of some judgments related to educational values, theories of learning and teaching, curriculum plans, organisational arrangements etc);

8. have developed their own criteria for evaluating themselves (ie they should have learned to monitor their own teaching, not only in relation to the criteria specified by others, but they should also have articulated their own criteria for personal self-evaluation. They should have justified the choice of those criteria and generated valid ways in which evidence could be collected and evaluated in relation to these criteria);

9. be able critically to examine and subsequently make decisions about aspects of their habitual teaching (ie they should have acquired the capacity to bring any aspect of their teaching into their consciousness, examine the assumptions underlying it, investigate the validity of these assumptions with reference to the nature of the teaching behaviour itself, the contexts in which it is employed, and the impact of the teaching on pupils, and where necessary devise and test hypothetical ways of improving that aspect of their teaching).

These goals have been formulated with great care and as a result of extensive critical debate and negotiation. Their articulation was important in the planning of the programme. Nonetheless, we make no claims to be trying to achieve anything especially novel in our Internship scheme. We do claim however to have confronted the fact that neither we nor others have in the past adequately attained such a combination of goals. Part of the difficulty, certainly, has been a lack of explicit agreement among all those involved about the importance of each of these goals. More fundamentally, however, there have been several fundamental problems in teacher education which, not having been adequately confronted, have prevented the attainment of the central goals to which most teacher educators have been committed. It is to these problems that we now turn.

B. Problems to be Overcome

Among endemic problems in teacher education, and especially in PGCE programmes, the following were identified as especially important and as potentially soluble:

1. Student-teachers are marginal people in schools, without the status, authority or situational knowledge to be like 'real teachers'. In most teacher education programmes, student-teachers spend at most a term in any one school. Much of this time is necessarily spent in learning about the pupils and classes they are teaching, about the rules and conventions which have been established in the schools, departments and classrooms in which they are placed, and about such things as what resources are available, where they are stored and how to get access to them. Such situational knowledge is important for all teachers, but student-teachers, not knowing how to select, organise and use it, take much longer than experienced teachers to acquire it. By the time they have done so, there is often little time left for practising teaching in a way that makes adequate use of such knowledge. Other problems are that pupils frequently make life difficult for student-teachers, who are recognised as vulnerable and easy targets, and that supervising teachers are often unwilling to have well-established routines or carefully planned programmes disrupted in order that student-teachers can try out their own ideas about teaching.

Perhaps even more important than these objective problems of the student-teacher's position is the subjective use which student-teachers often make of it. Faced with classroom difficulties such as pupils' lack of motivation, indiscipline or incomprehension, it is all too easy to believe that things would be different 'if this were my own class' or 'if I weren't a student'. Real problems of inadequate skills or inappropriate strategies are thus neglected and in effect postponed, to be faced again in the more difficult circumstances of full-time employment in the following year.

2. 'Educational theorising' is often experienced as largely irrelevant to the tasks facing student-teachers in schools. For much of this century, perhaps the most serious and certainly the most widely recognised problem of teacher education has been student-teachers' inability to find significant practical usefulness in much of what they are taught in their teacher education courses. The precise nature of the problem has changed over the years: Mr Kenneth Baker's formulation of it in terms of the lack of apparent relevance of PGCE courses on philosophy, psychology, history and sociology may be recognised as a fair description of a problem of the 1960s but was an astonishingly ignorant characterisation of the general situation in the 1980s. Nonetheless, the concern of teacher educators to discuss issues which go beyond the giving of practical advice about classroom teaching, together with their need to talk in generalised decontextualised terms has consistently given student-teachers a difficult task of relating what they have learned in college or university to the problems of classroom teaching. For many, indeed, the task has been too difficult and has been rejected as not worthwhile.

3. There is often little opportunity to try out in schools even the practical advice given in college or university. Not surprisingly there are often quite substantial differences between the modes and strategies of teaching promoted by teacher educators and those practised in schools. One may say that the contrast is between good practice and actual practice, or alternatively that it is between idealised plans and realistic practice. However the contrast is described, where it exists student-teachers will not observe the practices which their tutors have encouraged them to adopt, and may well not have the opportunity to try out these practices for themselves. Such opportunities will in most circumstances depend on a good match between the thinking of tutors and the practice of supervising teachers; and it has generally proved difficult to ensure such matching.

4. Little value is generally attached to the observation of experienced teachers, with apparently little learning resulting from such observation. It is abundantly clear that the craft of teaching is highly complex and subtle, and that the majority of experienced teachers have developed this craft to a much higher level than would be apparent from their generalised talk about it. Yet student-teachers' observation of experienced teachers at work tends to be concentrated at the early stages of their school experience, when their own understanding of the task of teaching is so limited that they do not know what to note or to ask questions about. Too soon both they and their supervising teachers tend to believe that it is time to concentrate instead on 'the real task' of learning to teach from experience. Very little of the knowledge that is implicit in the teaching of experienced teachers is passed on to beginners.

5. Little help is given to student-teachers in critically examining the range of practice they observe in schools. Although student-teachers may learn little from experienced teachers about the subtle complexities of their craft, they are likely to be influenced by the general patterns of teaching which they find experienced teachers using. Inevitably such practice varies in its quality, and in its distinctive strengths and weaknesses. Although most student-teachers will have opportunities in seminars back at the university to discuss the relative merits of different approaches, in the school context they are not likely to have much help in looking critically at the practices they find there. The collaboration of teachers who voluntarily welcome student-teachers into their school departments and classrooms is something for which tutors must be grateful, and which they need diplomatically to sustain; and the constraints of diplomacy make collaboration and a critical perspective uneasy bedfellows.

6. There tends to be wide variation in the quality of supervising teachers' diagnostic assessment of student-teachers' teaching and their discussion of that teaching. Being a good classroom teacher does not imply that one will be skilled at assessing the teaching of beginners, at discussing their teaching with them, or at giving them appropriate guidance. There are relatively few teachers who are experienced in fulfilling such a role, and even fewer for whom it is a salient aspect of their work. Yet the task is clearly a difficult one if all aspects of a student-teacher's teaching are to receive careful attention, if idiosyncratic preferences are not to be confused with necessary requirements, and if advice is to be given in ways which are useful to student-teachers at the stage they have reached. It is not surprising that the quality of supervision varies considerably.

7. School visits from tutors are often seen primarily as occasions for the testing of student-teachers' classroom competence. Like other relationships in educational contexts, relationships between student-teachers and their tutors have tended to become much less formal and more friendly in recent decades. Nonetheless the objective reality that visiting tutors do have the task of judging the adequacy of student-teachers' teaching has not changed; and the relative infrequency of tutors' visits, their lack of contextual knowledge, and the understandable inclination of supervising teachers to cast themselves as student-teachers' friends, with visiting tutors as their judges, all combine to promote the view that the prime purpose of these visits is one of assessment, not of guidance and support.

Furthermore, the quality of help which tutors can give on these occasional visits is indeed constrained by their lack of knowledge of student-teachers' particular situations. In these circumstances it is not surprising that student-teachers often view their tutors' visits more as occasions to be survived than as opportunities for learning.

8. Student-teachers often learn to meet the different criteria of school and university staff separately, with different performances for different audiences. The different positions of university tutors and schoolteachers impose different demands upon them in their work, and lead them to have systematically different concerns and to emphasise systematically different criteria. University tutors are obliged and also well placed to concern themselves with research evidence, theoretical coherence, general ideas of good practice, and the educational and social values implicit in different practices. Schoolteachers, on the other hand, are obliged and also well placed to concern themselves with the feasibility of different practices, taking account of political, resource, expertise and time constraints, and with the effectiveness of practices within their own distinctive contexts. While neither group has a monopoly on any particular kind of concern, these systematic differences are clear, inevitable and not in themselves problematic. A successful teacher education programme must be one in which student-teachers learn to recognise the validity of both these contrasting sets of concerns, and learn to judge their own developing practices against both these sets of criteria.

Experience and research evidence suggest, however, that that is a very difficult demand to impose upon student-teachers, and that it is a demand which they are often not adequately helped to meet. On the other hand, it is a demand which student-teachers can usually avoid, because of the separateness of their work for university tutors and their work for supervising teachers. In school contexts, with supervising teachers, they can demonstrate their readiness and ability to use established teaching procedures, their concern with practical issues, and the toughmindedness of their attitudes. For university tutors, on the other hand, they can show their readiness to adopt innovative approaches to teaching, their concern with theoretical issues and ambitious educational values, and their idealistic and tenderminded attitudes. Most established patterns of teacher education appear to give student-teachers the opportunity, which they generally accept, of avoiding the challenge of relating their educational thinking to their acquisition of teaching practices.

9. In contrast to the habits of scholarly reflection which graduate teachers have learned in relation to their subjects, much of their learning about teaching is a semi-conscious trial and error kind of learning. Understandably and properly, learning the practical craft of teaching is generally seen by both experienced teachers and student-teachers as very different from the learning of academic subjects in universities. The contrast is, however, greatly and damagingly exaggerated. Established approaches to graduate teacher education have in general failed to excite student-teachers' intellectual curiosity about the task of teaching or to give them much help in taking a disciplined analytic approach to learning how to teach. Much of the university-based work in teacher education programmes has not been directly concerned with the task of teaching, or has not been found helpful in school teaching contexts. On the other hand, arrangements for learning how to teach in schools frequently consist largely of the handing over of classes to student-teachers for them to gain 'experience'. The anxiety which such responsibilities frequently evoke and the complexity of the tasks being confronted encourage student-teachers to seek oversimplified ways of construing the tasks, reassuring ways of explaining what happens, and solutions of any kind to their most pressing problems. Thus their most formative learning experiences tend to be in contexts which strongly discourage analytic reflection, even should the tools for such analysis be available. In these circumstances the dominant kind of learning is likely to be the shaping of patterns of activity by rewards and punishments from supervisors, and probably, even more, those from pupils. That people should learn to teach in this way is scandalous not only because of its inefficiency, its demoralising painfulness for many, and the unsatisfactory habits which are learned, but also because it encourages teachers in the longer term to have anti-intellectual attitudes towards their own craft and it leads them to have difficulty in bringing to consciousness for examination their own teaching habits.

10. Since graduate student-teachers, subject tutors and supervising teachers all tend to be primarily concerned about subject teaching, there is a danger that such cross-curricular concerns as multicultural education, equal opportunities, pastoral care, special needs, home-school relations and information technology may be marginalised. In the attempt to ensure the relevance of teacher education to schooling, many secondary teacher education programmes have in recent decades been increasingly focused on the classroom teaching of subjects, and have been structured in ways which reflect that major focus. Since it is surely undeniable that the most important task of beginning secondary teachers is generally that of subject teaching, it is not difficult to justify this kind of emphasis in teacher education programmes. Nonetheless, even beginning teachers in contemporary schools are asked to undertake some duties beyond those of classroom teaching, for example those of form tutoring; and in addition many necessary and important concerns for classroom teachers derive not from the subject or its pedagogy but from wider educational and social considerations. Subject specialists inevitably vary in their knowledge of, and concern for, such other aspects of teaching; and where total reliance is placed on them, student-teachers tend to be given very uneven introductions to these issues. On the other hand, general programmes provided specifically to deal with these wider issues, but lacking the immediate subject teaching link with schools, are likely to seem less relevant and of secondary importance to student-teachers. Either way, the important cross-curricular concerns can be marginalised.

11. What largely determines each student-teacher's learning about teaching is his or her own individual agenda of concerns, an agenda which may well not be closely related to the official agenda of a PGCE programme. Student-teachers bring with them not only their diverse reasons for becoming teachers but also varied and usually well-established ideas about what being a teacher involves and about what they need to learn. From their own personal educational experience, they are each likely to have developed understandings of their subject, of what learning that subject implies, of desirable and undesirable teacher-pupil relationships, and especially of what teachers should do for, and demand from, their pupils. Interacting in various ways with such direct learning from formal educational experience will be social and intellectual commitments, insights and felt needs developed in other contexts. In most cases, student-teachers' agendas for learning and for teaching are not very explicitly articulated, but instead form part of the commonsense which they take for granted in approaching the task of learning to teach.

The basic problem for the teacher educator is that it is each student-teacher's own agenda which determines the tasks of learning and doing upon which his or her energies will be focused; and this is especially a problem because the teacher educator has a responsibility to ensure that the beginning teacher develops the skills, attitudes and understandings necessary for professional competence. The problem is exacerbated by the complexity of teaching, by it not being an explicit body of knowledge like an academic subject but rather a practical expertise not easily accessible to explicit formulation, by the fact that there is legitimate scope for diversity of approach and difference of opinion, and by the implicit nature of most student-teachers' agendas. Furthermore student-teachers vary among themselves quite widely in the nature of their agendas. The effectiveness of teacher education programmes must depend upon greater account being taken of these differing agendas than has generally been the case in the past.

C. Principles of Internship

What pattern of teacher education might overcome these problems? To know how to answer that question we needed to look more closely at the source of the problems. To what extent did they arise simply because the generally prevalent organisational arrangements were inappropriate? To what extent, in contrast, might they have arisen from more fundamental sources, such as the conceptions of the knowledge required for teaching or of the processes of learning to teach which underlay the design of programmes?

Examination of these questions can be simplified by noting that most of the problems outlined can be grouped into two main categories. The first of these is concerned with problems of continuity between university and school contexts, while the second set of problems relates to the conditions of learning which student-teachers experience in schools.

1. University - School Continuity: Problems of discontinuity between university and school learning contexts are of critical importance for universities because the inclusion of university elements in teacher education programmes can only plausibly be justified in terms of their impact, sooner or later, on their students' activities as teachers in schools. If what student-teachers do in universities as part of teacher education programmes does not relate closely to what they do in schools during these programmes, then it becomes difficult to argue for the later relevance of these university activities. Yet there has been widespread evidence over many years that student-teachers do experience discontinuity at many levels between the school and university parts of their programmes. Among problems outlined above were those concerned with discontinuities in the kinds of knowledge, the particular practical

ideas, the attitudes, the concerns, the criteria and the ways of learning which are valued and adopted, even in the personnel who are experienced as having useful ideas to contribute. Could these discontinuities be removed simply by having a programme better organised to avoid them? Or do they represent a more fundamental and necessary tension between the concerns of university teacher education programmes and the realities of schooling?

A major concern of the Oxford programme has been to achieve more effective organisational continuity. Three aspects of this may be highlighted. First, the subject curriculum courses, which deal with all classroom teaching issues, are planned in detail by the subject teams of university tutors and schoolteacher mentors who are responsible for guiding interns' learning experiences in the university and in the schools. Interns' activities in the university and in the schools are thus jointly planned as one closely integrated programme.

Second, to allow this partnership and integration to be operationally effective, the course is structured so that for the greater part of the year interns spend two days each week in their schools, these days being sandwiched between two days of university classes, with a day each week for reflection, reading and preparation.

Third, a similar close integration of university and school work is achieved organisationally for wider whole-school and societal issues through groups of interns in the same school working together throughout the year. The significance of these issues can thus be studied in contextualised as well as more general ways, with the support in each school of a professional tutor from the school staff and a general tutor who is associated with that particular school but is a member of the university staff.

These organisational arrangements to overcome discontinuities are of great importance for the operation of the programme. They are, however, of little value in relation to some of the discontinuities noted above. It is certainly possible for curriculum tutors, visiting interns in different schools and meeting mentors regularly to plan and monitor the programmes, to become known, trusted and respected as partners by the mentors and other subject teachers in these schools. Since, however, they cannot for example get to know all the pupils in these schools, and since they do not have to do the day-to-day teaching jobs which the teachers do, they necessarily cannot offer the same contextualised knowledge or perspectives which these teachers can provide. The jobs which the tutors do have to do, on the other hand, both require and allow them to concern themselves with different kinds of knowledge - through reports and discussion of good practice nationally and internationally, of research evidence, of different theoretical positions and their implications, and of problems and possibilities of realising various educational and social values in the practice of schooling. Their university positions also require and allow them to concern themselves with appropriate academic kinds of criteria in judging the validity and value of the claims to knowledge embodied in what they study. The work of mentors and other schoolteachers, on the other hand, enables and requires them to give priority attention to what is 'practical' what is feasible, socially acceptable and effective, at least in the short term, within the specific contexts within which they work.

In these circumstances it would be very surprising indeed if the same ideas for thinking about teaching and learning tended to seem valuable to both schoolteachers and university tutors or if the same norms of good practice were generally upheld by these two groups. It would be even more surprising if teachers' actual practices consistently reflected tutors' ideas of good practice. The different opportunities and demands arising from the positions occupied by the two groups of people should lead one to expect them generally to have different perspectives and frequently, therefore, to have different opinions on specific issues.

It is thus evident that several of the most serious problems of discontinuity that have been experienced in teacher education have stemmed from an unrealistic and unhelpful assumption that a straightforward continuity of perspective was possible and desirable. The implicit model underlying most initial teacher education programmes, and perhaps especially one-year postgraduate programmes for intending secondary teachers, is that there ought to be a straightforward theory-into-practice continuity between the ideas discussed and approved in university contexts and those practised and approved in school contexts. (Some more recently planned programmes, taking a more inductive practice-into-theory or reflection-upon-practice approach, make the same unhelpful assumption of straightforward continuity.) Lack of such continuity has been problematic, to be blamed upon the unrealistic theory of the universities, or on the inadequate practice of the schools, and also on the failure of student-teachers themselves to demonstrate the desired continuity in their own thinking and practice.

Fundamental to the Oxford Internship scheme is a firm rejection of this theory-into-practice model. Before discussing appropriate alternative models, however, it is necessary to examine the second main category of problems, and the sources of these problems.

2. Conditions of Learning in Schools: Whereas schools are (let us assume) designed to promote learning by pupils, they are certainly not designed to promote learning by teachers or by student-teachers. Several of the problems identified earlier were concerned with unhelpful aspects of school contexts for thoughtful learning by student-teachers. Such problems of professional learning in the most obviously relevant of contexts would surely seem important for almost any model of teacher education, but they become increasingly important as one relies less and less on continuity or transfer from learning in a university context.

The most general of the problems identified was that of the heavy reliance on 'learning from experience' in an unguided and non-analytic way. As frequently diagnosed, the problem is one of dependence not only on student-teachers' unaided learning by trial and error from their own practice, but also on such learning in contexts which are so demanding or anxiety-provoking that what is learned tend to be strategies for surviving. The ethos which emphasises such learning from experience correspondingly militates against other ways of learning, whether by the explication of what experienced teachers do in their teaching, the trying out of ideas from sources outside the school, the critical examination of different practices, or systematic analyses by supervising teachers of aspects of student-teachers' own teaching.

Once again it is apparent that some of the sources of these unhelpful conditions for learning are organisational; and again, a major concern of the Oxford programme has been to organise the school-based element so as to improve these conditions. One important step has been to move initial teacher education from its very marginal position in the work of schools to a rather more significant place by concentrating the placement of student-teachers on a small number of schools, with an average of ten student-teachers, in five pairs, in each school. Closely related, and even more important, has been the placement of the student-teachers as interns, each attached to the same school for virtually the whole year, from October until June. By allowing the interns thus to get to know the school, the teachers and the pupils well, and by making them more like full members of staff, this is intended to enhance their opportunities to learn and to allow them to learn from a less vulnerable position. A major endemic problem for teachers is that of finding appropriate time for any activity. The Internship scheme aims to provide the necessary time for mentors in two ways: first, by the second half of the year, interns should by their contribution to teaching be creating considerably more time for their mentors and others than they take, thus to some extent recompensing for their heavy dependence on mentors' time during the first half of the year; and second, there are substantial and distinctive professional development benefits to be gained by mentors and others from involvement in the scheme, and the provision of some extra time for mentoring may justifiably be made as a valuable investment for this purpose alone.

As with problems of the continuity type, however, several of the problems of conditions of learning for student-teachers cannot be seen as soluble simply by improving organisational arrangements. Instead, they have to be seen as deriving from more fundamental characteristics of the task of classroom teaching, of teachers' conditions of work, and of teachers' professional cultures. Thus, for example, the commonsense of experienced teachers frequently treats what they do in their teaching as 'obvious' and not worthy of detailed explication, what their colleagues do in their classrooms as private and not a proper matter for discussion, and protected time for analytic, reflective discussion of teaching as an academic kind of self-indulgence which cannot be justified in a busy school. Such commonsense is entirely comprehensible, given the conditions within which teachers work; but it is not a commonsense which facilitates rational learning on the part of beginning teachers.

Discussion of conditions of learning for student-teachers in schools leads appropriately to a consideration of the most obvious and the most popular alternative to the theory-into-practice model of teacher education, the apprenticeship model. One of the great attractions of the apprenticeship approach is that it would virtually avoid all the discontinuity problems, simply by making university studies into a kind of theoretical background to the practical task of learning to teach, rather than an integral part of it. This seems to be the thinking underlying the New Jersey and French approaches recently publicised by HMI (1) with the obvious approval of the then Secretary of State for Education.

A good apprenticeship scheme would also have other attractions: it would highlight the expertise implicit in the classroom practice of most experienced teachers, and the potential value of this expertise to beginning teachers, as has not adequately been done by teacher education programmes in recent decades. A good apprenticeship programme would also ensure a sensitively judged progression in the tasks set for the apprentice teachers, so that the challenges with which they would be confronted would help them to learn the craft of classroom teaching, not be tests to be passed or ordeals to be survived. These two latter characteristics of an apprenticeship approach are indeed major elements of the Internship scheme.

There are, however, three major arguments against adopting an apprenticeship model. One is the set of problems examined above concerned with conditions of learning for student-teachers in schools: although there is massive professional teaching expertise embodied in the work of schools, it must be doubted whether the conditions and professional cultures of teaching are such that individual schools on their own could or would make adequate use of this expertise to help beginning teachers to learn the craft of teaching. A second argument is that any one school, or even a group of schools, is likely to be able to provide a much more restricted range of kinds of knowledge relevant to practice, and also a more restricted range of ideas for good practice, than would be possible in collaboration with a university department of education. Thirdly, and perhaps more crucially, the criteria in terms of which apprentice teachers would be encouraged to judge practices could at worst be idiosyncratic criteria of their individual mentors but at best would be likely to be heavily biased towards 'practicality'; and they would be unlikely to develop skills and habits for rationally evaluating and developing their own teaching.

Thus, although the concept of apprenticeship had implicit in it some valuable ideas for initial teacher education, as an overall model it was much too limiting to be an appropriate framework for attaining the goals of Internship. Apprenticeship was not the required alternative to the theory-into-practice model.

We could not indeed find any established model which seemed well calculated to facilitate the attainment of our stated goals or which would be helpful in overcoming the problems we had identified. We had to develop a new model. Since, however, our new model was conceived in the matrix of persistently experienced problems of teacher education and the apparent impossibility of generating solutions to these problems within the frameworks offered by established models, the foundations of our new model are implicit in the arguments already advanced. In summary,

(i) many of the major persistent problems in teacher education programmes are concerned either with discontinuities between

university and school components of the programmes or with poor conditions for student-teachers professional learning in the schools;
(ii) while some of these problems can be overcome by better organisational arrangements, others stem from more fundamental problems;
(iii) some of the major problems of discontinuity result from a misguided expectation of simple continuity and consistency between knowledge, concerns, and criteria emphasised in university contexts and those emphasised and used in school contexts; theory-into-practice (or practice-into-theory) conceptions of teacher education necessarily lead to fundamental problems of discontinuity;
(iv) avoiding problems of discontinuity by utilising an apprenticeship model of teacher education would not be a solution, because some of the problems of conditions for student-teachers' learning in schools would be exacerbated, and because important sources of knowledge, kinds of learning and goals of teacher education would tend to be neglected.

We are thus led to the need for a model of teacher education in which:
- there are strong contributions from both university and schools;
- the relationship between these contributions is recognised and planned in more complex terms than those of simple consistency between theory and practice;
- and a close partnership between university and school staff leads on one hand to a coherence experienced by interns between university and school elements, and on the other to a common understanding of the conditions needed for effective learning of various kinds in both contexts.

What relationship should be planned for between university and school contributions? Our thinking about this was influenced by reflections on research into teaching and into the processes of learning to teach.(2)

Reflection on research into teaching suggests first that there are many different kinds of valuable knowledge about teaching. At one extreme, for example, there is a growing body of knowledge based on process-product research, in which consistent relationships have been shown between the kinds of actions which teachers take in classrooms, and the behaviour and learning of their pupils. Increasingly useful generalisations are suggested by such research about the kinds of teaching activity which are likely to promote different kinds of learning. At the other extreme, research has also demonstrated something of the complex and sophisticated judgments which are embedded in the day-to-day practice of experienced teachers, indicating for example the subtle ways in which they transform the content knowledge they teach to make it accessible to their pupils, and the ways in which they take account of a multiplicity of factors in choosing the means they will use to achieve their immediate purposes. Intermediate between these two contrasting kinds of knowledge are various kinds of reflective distilled wisdom about classroom teaching and learning, much of it related to the teaching of particular subjects, and much of it reflecting commitments to distinctive goals or processes. It is evident that many very diverse kinds of knowledge about teaching could be accessible to beginning teachers and could be of substantial value to them.

Second, however, it is also clear that none of this available knowledge is totally reliable or universally applicable. Even the knowledge which is most clearly articulated and thoroughly investigated is of unknown generalisability across different kinds of content, contexts, teachers or learners. Wise beginning teachers, therefore, will take none of it on trust, but will carefully examine and test it for themselves.

Third, as has been noted already, the kinds of criteria likely to be emphasised in examining ideas or practices of teaching tend to vary systematically between contexts. University tutors are in positions which enable and encourage them to apply criteria relating to theoretical coherence, research evidence, and long-term educational implications and values. The positions of schoolteachers enable and encourage them to apply criteria of feasibility, in relation to constraints of time, resources and expertise, of social acceptability, and of effectiveness in their specific situations. Different kinds of test seem important in different contexts.

Research on the processes by which people learn to teach indicates that most learners start from their own ideas and commitments, and only gradually modify these in the light of experience and of ideas from other sources. If the teaching tasks which they are set are not too complex or threatening, they tend to judge their teaching in terms of its effects on pupils' classroom responses and activities, and to make sense of the outcomes of their teaching in terms of hypotheses which they test in later lessons. They tend to welcome information and ideas from a wide variety of sources and of a wide variety of kinds, to help them make sense of their teaching experiences.

What then did these research-based ideas suggest about the general pattern of relationships between school and university elements of the Internship programme? One conclusion was that it was important for interns to have sufficient security and support to be able to approach the task of learning to teach in a realistic, rational and exploratory way. It was also important that they should have access to different kinds of knowledge about teaching from different sources, and that they should treat that knowledge as tentative and in need of several kinds of testing. The problem here was not of persuading interns to do this, but of ensuring that this was also the generally agreed official agenda. Thus tutors in the university and mentors in the schools needed to agree, and to make clear to interns, that they not only would make available to the interns the kinds of knowledge they were best placed to provide, but that they would also expect the interns to test that knowledge for themselves. In particular, knowledge from university sources would especially need testing, with the help of mentors, against practicality criteria in the schools; and knowledge from school sources would especially need testing, with the help of tutors, against more academic criteria in the university. In this way interns should be encouraged to develop their personal thinking through synthesising knowledge acquired from various sources and tested against diverse criteria. Instead of learning that the academic concerns of the university and the practical concerns of the schools offered two discontinuous agendas to which they had to conform at different times, they should instead learn that, for example, ideas and practices which might be highly educationally desirable would be less useful, in some practical circumstances but not necessarily all, than other more educationally limited ideas. They should also learn to explore the limits of practical possibilities in a given context without permanently abandoning as unrealistic more ambitious aspirations.

Nonetheless, primary importance has to be given to interns' attainment of a basic competence in classroom teaching. This is so both because of our obligation as teacher educators to ensure it and also because many interns themselves need to be convinced that they are competent, and are recognised as being competent before they can have the sense of security necessary to examine their teaching objectively and openly in relation to their own aspirations as educators. It is therefore necessary that during the earlier part of the year interns' investigations of teaching should be primarily concerned with finding effective ways of doing things that are specified in advance as necessary aspects of competent teaching. Then, in the second part of the year, they are asked to articulate and explain their own criteria for some important facets of their teaching, and to gather evidence and look critically at their teaching in relation to these criteria.

The idea of a dialogue between, and a synthesis of, different sources of knowledge and different criteria for examining ideas and practices, is at the core of the Internship scheme. It embodies a respect for, and a questioning of, both the craft knowledge and practical wisdom of practising teachers and also the more systematised and abstract knowledge of university tutors. It is through this process of questioning dialogue and attempted synthesis that the model seeks to overcome the problems of discontinuity between university and school components.

The viability of the model is however dependent on both sides of partnership being able to help interns to gain access to the knowledge that each is best placed to provide, and to help them apply the criteria that each is best placed to apply. This is a demanding challenge for both sides of the partnership, but given the problems of learning conditions for student-teachers in schools that have been discussed, it is especially a challenge for the schools. It is through the development of effective partnerships between university and school staff, with increasing understanding being developed of what is possible and what is necessary, that this challenge will increasingly be met.

D. Conclusion

In conclusion, the main principles of the Oxford Internship scheme may be summarised as follows:

1. Concentration of student-teachers in particular schools, so as to raise the profile of initial teacher education in these schools, and to make it a significant task for the teachers involved.

2. Extended involvement of the student-teachers as 'interns' in the schools, so that they can become established, with situational knowledge of the students, teachers, resources, norms and ethos of the schools, and have more of the status of junior members of staff.

3. Partnership between university and school staff in joint planning of the programme, with agreement on issues to be dealt with, their ordering, and the respective tasks to be undertaken by staff and interns in school and university.

4. Integration of the programme, so that there are clear, explicit relationships, and relatively short time intervals, connecting university classes, workshops, reading and assignments with school observations, discussions, teaching and other tasks. In effect there is one coherent programme, with closely interconnected elements in school and university.

5. Secure learning environments, with learning tasks (especially those of teaching in school) being carefully graduated in a flexible way so that interns are not overwhelmed by the complexity or other anxiety-provoking characteristics of the tasks, but can instead approach them in calm, rational, analytic ways.

6. Explicit encouragement for interns to use ideas from diverse sources (in recognition that privately they will do so in any case), including their own personal histories as well as university and school sources, to inform their thinking and their teaching.

7. Explicit assertion, by both university and school staff, that consensus is not expected, either between university and school, or between interns and staff, about many aspects of good practice or about useful ways of thinking.

8. Emphasis on testing all ideas against various criteria including 'academic' criteria of theoretical coherence, consistency with research evidence, consistency with espoused educational and social values, and 'practical' criteria of feasibility in relation to constraints of time, resources and expertise, acceptability to relevant others, and effectiveness in context.

9. Division of labour according to clear principles:
(i) help and advice of any kind welcome from any quarter;
(ii) university staff especially responsible for help with generalised, decontextualised ideas and criteria, and school staff especially responsible for help with contextualised school-related ideas and criteria;
(iii) assessment of interns' teaching competence by school staff, moderated by university staff;
(iv) wherever a task could be equally well undertaken by university or school staff, it is the university staff's obligation to undertake it.

10. Two major stages of initial teacher education, the first focused on the development of interns' classroom competence, conceived in terms of consensual professional criteria, the second focused on the development of their abilities in articulating their professional aspirations as classroom teachers, in evaluating their teaching in relation to their aspirations, and in exploring and testing ways of more adequately realising their aspirations.

11. Contextualised study of under issues of schooling, so that issues of whole-school policy and of school-society relations are studied, like classroom teaching, both in terms of general principles, theories and evidence and also in relation to the specific school in which an intern is working, and especially as they impinge on the practices, opportunities and constraints of classroom teaching.

References

1. 1989a *Teaching - it's a vital profession. The Provisional Teacher Program in New Jersey.* Her Majesty's Inspectorate (London: Department of Education and Science, 1989).
1989b *Initial Teacher Training in France. The training of secondary teachers in the Académie de Toulouse.* Her Majesty's Inspectorate (London: Department of Education and Science, 1989).
2. Donald McIntyre, "Designing a Teacher Education Curriculum from Research and Theory on Teacher Knowledge" in J Calderhead (ed.), *Teachers' Professional Learning* (London: The Falmer Press, 1988).

Chapter III

The Process of Change

Anna Pendry

Internship implies change of many kinds and, however much they may know about theories of institutional change, it is not always easy for the participants - even those willing the change - to adapt to new roles and relationships and to accept the loss of a certain degree of autonomy.

The writer of this chapter, Anna Pendry, Tutor in History at the Oxford University Department of Educational Studies, was perhaps more keenly aware than anyone of such problems. As co-ordinator of the Development Group of seconded teachers during the year prior to the launch of Internship, she was placed precisely at the point where the interests of teachers and tutors met, and, inevitably sometimes, conflicted. Anna Pendry is both a curriculum tutor and a general tutor in the Internship scheme and is currently engaged in research into the development of history student-teachers' pedagogical content knowledge in the scheme.

This chapter seeks to trace the process of the development of Internship, relying heavily on a chronological review of the period from the mid-1970s to 1987, with particular emphasis on the years 1985 to 1987. The earlier period is characterised by an increasingly close relationship between OUDES, Oxfordshire LEA and Oxon secondary schools which created the preconditions necessary for the development of Internship. The final two years involved intense development work for the changes in teacher education we were proposing. The value of a chronology is that history establishes what was done, when it was done and something of the relationships between events. Hence chronology can describe the complex process of change experienced here, and particularly that part of the process that Fullan, in his work on innovation in education (1), characterises as the adoption stage.

In an attempt to explain this process, as well as describe it, use will be made of certain key ideas seen as central to understanding the process of development. Of critical importance are themes related to the theory of change, notably meanings of change, the factors affecting the adoption and implementation of change, the role of commitment and the dilemmas of rational planning. Other ideas which will be explicated are derived from our specific context - the history of relationships between OUDES and Oxon LEA; the strong teacher involvement in the development; the history of autonomy within OUDES. Finally, two more general ideas to be addressed are nature and sociology of professional knowledge about teaching and teacher education, and the role that action research has played in the development process.

By drawing on specific chronology and on more general concepts it is intended that the chapter will both illuminate the idiosyncratic elements of the Oxford situation and suggest ways of thinking about change in different contexts. It is also hoped that these complementary approaches will resolve some of the methodological problems posed by the position of the writer - an active participant in much of the process of development, and central to it in the period January 1986 to June 1987. The time that has now elapsed, the richness of the data related to all aspects of the development and the use of theoretical constructs should all enhance the external validity of the interpretations offered.

The complexity of the process of development and the scope of the change that this was designed to effect have themselves both generated and validated the explanatory ideas employed in this chapter, and the nature of each of these will be discussed before introducing the chronology of the development. It seems reasonable to suggest that any account of change in education will owe much to the ideas of Fullan, and this account is no exception. Although the contexts and changes of which he writes - notably those related to teaching in North American schools - are very different from a context involving Oxford University, Oxfordshire LEA and Oxfordshire secondary schools engaged in a collaborative venture to change teacher education in fundamental ways, his concepts can both illuminate our experience and perhaps be extended by them. Fullan's identification of several phases in the change process, characterised as initiation or adoption, implementation, continuation and outcome (2) enables us to describe what was happening in Oxford as the adoption phase of change - although the period prior to 1985 is probably most appropriately seen as providing the preconditions for adoption. As Fullan says "It is during the adoption phase that the direction or content of change is set in motion. Decisions are made about what is to change, at least in terms of goals and sometimes substance. The process of adoption can generate meaning or confusion, commitment or alienation, or simply ignorance on the part of participants and others to be affected by the change."(3) The adoption phase at Oxford was certainly concerned with both negotiating what changes we wanted in teacher education, and how we would achieve those changes. It also generated the variety of responses indicated by Fullan! An apparently simple idea presented by Fullan is that "change is a process, not an event".(4) Our experience certainly confirms this, and also suggests that the necessary time span for successful change is even longer than he anticipates. We spent 18 months fully immersed in the process of adoption, and this period was preceded by several years of relevant developments. The first two years of implementation can also be seen, in part, as a continuation of the process of adoption - both by those involved since the inception of Internship and by those who have joined the scheme since it commenced in September 1987.

Acceptance that implementation may also mean a continuation of the adoption process, particularly in an innovation on the scale of Internship, also allows an acknowledgement of Fullan's central thesis concerning the meaning of change. "All real change involves loss, anxiety and struggle...and the meaning of change will rarely be clear at the outset and ambivalence will pervade the transition. Any innovation cannot be assimilated unless its meaning is shared."(5) Our experience confirms this, despite the length of time we spent in planning and development, suggesting that whilst time is an important factor in assisting adoption, so too is adequate recognition of this fundamental characteristic of change. What was not fully understood by me and others centrally involved in the development work was the need to recognise the significance of subjective meanings of change, and this was certainly one of the factors leading to the alienation of a number of departmental tutors during part of the adoption phase. The range of factors which it is necessary to take into account when considering the initiation of change does, as Fullan says, make the mind boggle (6) and evidence for many factors that he cites can be found in the Oxford context. He himself suggests that the overview he presents of the change process is simplified and that the reality is much more "snarled".(7) Certainly our experience would suggest that several of those factors which he associates specifically with implementation were also relevant in the period of adoption - particularly those related to the characteristics of the change itself: in our case the principles and proposed practices of Internship. The extent to which these were understood and valued was a significant variable during the period 1986-87.

A particularly interesting issue raised by Fullan, and yet another of the dilemmas inherent in change is the role played by commitment. "The more the planners are committed to a particular change, the less effective they will be in getting others to implement it if their commitment represents an unyielding or impatient stance in the face of ineluctable problems of implementation."(8) Our crucial development phase was centred around what was, certainly, a highly committed group of 12 seconded teachers (the Development Group) whose work was co-ordinated by me and the Reader of the Department. The perception of others must have been that we presented both an unyielding and impatient stance (the language of documentation certainly suggests this), and yet we saw our commitment as crucial - we viewed ourselves as the engine driving Internship. However, we were certainly in grave danger of losing many of the carriages!

The final aspect of Fullan's ideas seen as particularly helpful in understanding our process of development is what is implied by his statements of what needs to accompany commitment. At the time of development we had no adequate theory of change. Our understanding of how best to enable all the potential participants in Internship to contribute to, understand and implement the ideas was inadequate. Fullan suggests the need to "be more sensitive to the possibility that our version of the change may not be the fully correct one, and to recognise that having good ideas may be less than half the battle (compared to establishing a process which will allow us to use the ideas)".(9) Although we made many attempts to involve all participants, and ultimately the changes have been extremely successful, we probably relied too heavily on a rational planning model, and gave too little attention to the complexities and idiosyncrasies of our context and circumstances as a means for facilitating the adoption process.

The importance of the development of relationships with Oxon LEA, through diverse means and in a variety of forms, cannot be underestimated. The chronological account will reveal how this occurred and how it enabled the preconditions for Internship to be established. A major consequence of the close relationship between the two bodies has been the financial support committed to Internship by the LEA - initially the secondment of 12 teachers to the Development Group and subsequently of the equivalent of 0.5 of a full-time teacher (0.5 FTE) to each participating school, used in part for secondment time and also to lighten the teaching commitments of mentors and professional tutors working closely with interns. This investment was made at a time of growing financial constraints in education and is testimony both to the quality of past relationships and the value of Internship as a means of enabling not only initial teacher education but also the professional development of all teachers involved in the scheme.

Related to the importance of the institutional links between the educational authority and the university has been the extensive involvement of practising teachers in all the major development work. School teachers have been contributors to the work of OUDES for over 15 years, but from 1986 they became active partners in the adoption phase, involved in both the decision-making as well as in advisory roles. Their involvement in every aspect of development - be it the principles of the scheme, the roles to be adopted, the nature of curriculum programmes, the form of the General Programme - has ensured that the plans have taken adequate account of the realities of schooling and of teachers' perceptions, beliefs and knowledge about teacher education and has been a major factor in persuading schools - in the initial stages - to become actively committed to the scheme. Arguably, their involvement would have been very difficult to achieve without LEA support, although it has also relied heavily on the goodwill and commitment to valuable ideas of many individuals - teachers already faced with a plethora of educational innovations (GCSE, TVEI, profiling...), and, in 1985-86, industrial action. Ironically, it is probably teacher involvement that has been the single most important factor in ensuring the successful adoption of Internship, and yet it was also their involvement which made that process as complex and difficult as it was.

A significant consequence of both the principles of Internship and the engagement of non-university staff in its development was the attack on university autonomy that these represented. The traditional autonomy of university teachers is a valued and valuable characteristic of any university department. At OUDES it has been most evident through subject specialisms, with individual or very small groups of tutors responsible for planning and teaching within their own curriculum areas. What to teach students, how to teach them and, to some extent when to teach, have all been subject to autonomous decision-making within OUDES. The changes that Internship entailed, and the process of adoption itself, required OUDES to operate in many ways as a unit. General principles related to teacher education needed to be accepted and form the basis of curriculum programmes; negotiations with schools had to be conducted at a departmental level; there needed to be sufficient similarity in the ways tutors carried out their roles for schools to understand the nature of Internship. It is not surprising that such changes were fiercely resisted by some tutors - the objective reality of the changes proposed did mean a weakening of autonomy for tutors who were already engaged in a very successful PGCE programme. One of the desirable freedoms of higher education was being threatened and yet, in the adoption phase, it was not apparent what would compensate for this loss.

It has been suggested that ideas drawn from the sociology of professional knowledge may be helpful in understanding some of the tensions we encountered during the adoption phase. From October 1986 until June 1987 the Development Group of seconded teachers and OUDES tutors held regular joint meetings to both discuss progress and make decisions about future plans. These meetings, and their aftermath, were often characterised by uncertainty, confusion and alienation - exactly the sort of responses that Fullan suggests are likely during the process of change. Such responses may have been generated by a context in which teacher educators and teachers were discussing the nature of a new PGCE programme - one that sought to draw upon the different kinds of knowledge that each group could bring to teacher education. In the joint meetings the teachers were commenting and advising on the knowledge and work of the tutors, often in abstract and theoretical terms. It may well be that people are more likely to talk in these terms about the work of others; that people resist abstract knowledge about their own work as it is perceived as irrelevant to their craft knowledge and that the knowledge people use in their own work is characterised by short time-scale, specificity and the extensive use of contextual information with a major emphasis on the how rather than the why. If such hypotheses are valid (and there is evidence in Schön's work on the nature of professional knowledge that they may be (10)) then the discussion by teachers, with tutors, of the tutors' own work and expertise was extremely likely to lead to tension.

Action research played a major role in our development work, with most members of the Development Group, and myself as its co-ordinator, engaged in action research investigations. The decision to employ this methodology was made by the OUDES tutors and it was seen as appropriate as we were faced by a development task of achieving a desired state of affairs ie putting Internship principles into action, and yet also wanted to find out how it was possible to do this. The scale of our enterprise made it impossible to research all its aspects in only one year but action research potentially would enable us to extrapolate to areas of the programme not considered in the investigations undertaken. It al-
offered the possibility of generating new theory about In+
as testing the theory we had already formulated. 1
decision were both positive and negative. Action r
imparted rigour and extensive theorising both to th
Development Group as a whole, principally througl
and to their individual research projects. Of those re
are still in progress (as M Litt or D Phil theses) and th

offered have been invaluable in securing the adoption of Internship. Two have been used as models for all the subsequent development work in particular curriculum areas, and others have formed the basis of critical aspects of Internship. However, we were very dependent on the Reader's expertise in action research methodology and his long absence due to illness during the development year did create difficulties with the supervision of the studies. There was also concern that the small scale of study necessitated by rigorous action research would leave too many gaps unexplored. Finally, my own research focusing on my role as the Development Group co-ordinator emphasised the principles of Internship - the characteristics of the change we were proposing. Hence in the context of the Development Group I tended to concentrate on only one of the factors which affect adoption. In restricting the scope of my research, I also restricted my role. This may well have been appropriate, but there were factors related to implementation which were ignored by me and not taken up elsewhere until a very late stage in the adoption process.

The discussion so far has concentrated on the key ideas seen as central to understanding the process of development. What follows is an attempt to explicate the chronology of the period from the mid-1970s to 1987. It has already been established that an important characteristic of the years up to 1985 was the increasingly close relationship between OUDES and Oxfordshire LEA. This was achieved through a number of initiatives, but perhaps the most significant event of the period was the appointment of Harry Judge, the headteacher of Banbury School (a large, state comprehensive school) as Director of OUDES in 1973. The designation of local schools as Associated Schools, particularly closely linked to OUDES and to which all our students were to be attached for their teaching practice, was another feature of the 1970s, a major shift from the early years of the decade when students were spread all over the country. Within the associated schools, the role of Professional Tutor became increasingly important, with a senior member of staff assuming responsibility for the student's school experience in conjunction with the subject supervisor for each individual student. Changes were also taking place in OUDES staffing: increasingly appointments were of subject specialists who had had successful school teaching experience. The number of local schoolteachers seconded to OUDES to engage in the Special Diploma in Educational Studies increased, and a wide range of options was offered by tutors working in collaboration with local advisers. Research within Oxfordshire schools (and others) was also facilitated by the foundation of the Oxford Education Research Group, an initiative led by H Judge, J Bruner and C Halsey. By the end of the 1970s it was evident that working with local comprehensive schools and focusing on classroom teaching were critical elements in the work of OUDES.

The establishment, in 1982, of the first of four joint appointments between the university department and local schools can be seen as a bridge between these early years of development, which provided the preconditions for Internship, and the more intense adoption phase of the 1980s. These appointments involved much more than the buying in of schoolteachers' time - they represented a contractual agreement between the university and the authority within which half the week would be spent teaching in school, and the other half as a curriculum tutor within OUDES. Such an arrangement would not have been possible without either the previous close relationship between authority and university, or the vision and political skills of both Tim Brighouse (then Chief Education Officer for Oxfordshire) and Harry Judge. As a product of the 1970s the joint appointments are further evidence of OUDES' commitment to state education, and to the central importance of classroom teaching and the skills of classroom teachers in the training and education of future teachers. The nature and existence of the joint appointments (or associate tutorships as they became known) were also very significant in the adoption of Internship. I held the first of these posts, in History, from 1982-1986, and my initial understanding of and commitment to the principles of the new model derived almost entirely from my experience as an associate tutor. Increasingly during the four years I was aware of the tension between my knowledge and expertise as a classroom teacher, and what I should be offering the students as a curriculum tutor. Different institutional positions gave me two very different perspectives on teaching, each of which generates its own criteria against which ideas about teaching should be tested. To espouse both perspectives and operate within each was no easy task, and my instinctive (it can only be described as that) recognition of the dilemmas this posed was the most significant motivating factor for my initial involvement in the development of Internship. However, the importance of these posts extends far beyond the personal. They were further evidence of how both schools and OUDES could benefit from close collaboration, and of how OUDES valued practising teachers. As the planning for a new PGCE gathered momentum they ensured that, at least to some extent, the views of schoolteachers were represented - something which was certainly significant to the schools in the later stages of adoption.

Serious attempts to reformulate our PGCE programme began in 1984, concurrent with but not led by Circular 3/84.(11) The Circular was an important part of the context within which we were working, but the intention of OUDES, as expressed by the Director, was to reform the programme as we wished and not simply to conform to external criteria. Discussion focused around two key issues: the structure of the PGCE course, and its content - particularly the relationship between curriculum work (ie that related to classroom, subject teaching) and General Professional Studies (GPS) - more general educational issues. A limited amount of progress was made in relation to structure, with support for divided weeks (ie between school and OUDES), for teaching practice in two schools, for a teaching practice across two terms in one school all being expressed but no decisions made. Much more heated were the discussions related to content. The excellence of curriculum work in the past was seen as under threat by proposals to extend the GPS components, and for the first time the importance of autonomy was espoused by some. An historical perspective suggests that the debate (and dispute) about what themes should be included in GPS, their status and their relationship with subject work was a necessary part of the change process. At the time the debate appeared to achieve little beyond the agreement that the PGCE curriculum as a whole needed to be more cohesive and that one way of achieving this was to ensure that the GPS programme would be the same for all students, with them all studying the same themes at the same time. Although this could hardly be described as a revolutionary step, arriving at it had necessitated extensive consideration of what we were trying to do as a department. In some ways the painful process of change had begun, although at that point there was no clear way forward.

This deadlock was broken by the Director at the end of 1984 with a short paper on a possible restructuring of the PGCE course.(12) It proposed many of the structural features that OUDES was to subsequently adopt - split weeks, blocks of time in school, concentrations of students in schools, mentors responsible for pairs of students. It also cited the importance of the long established principle of close relations with Oxfordshire schools, and the potential "for preserving some of the existing freedoms which are an essential feature of a university teacher's life".(13) Initial reaction, from both a small group of headteachers and OUDES staff, was favourable; and this paper provided the basis for renewed discussions in early 1985.

The details of the structure were progressively elaborated, and in June 1985 a formal proposal was made to headteachers and LEA representatives to adopt this new model as a means of "changing the basis of the training of graduates as teachers".(14) As Dr Judge stated "much more than that is envisioned. It entails new roles for professionals in the university as much as in the schools, new relationships between the two, and enlarged opportunities for co-operative inservice development and for research". The paper essentially addressed the organisation of a new programme, and whilst details (eg exactly what the year would look like in terms of who would be where, when and for how long) were to change, it provided a blueprint for the essential features. It also recommended that there should be 12 or more full-time secondments for 1986-87 to "ensure that the launch of the scheme is flawless".(15) The paper ended with the words "I believe that this is the right direction and pace at which to move. I want to go. Is anybody else coming?" The Director's personal commitment, his charismatic presentation, the history of the previous decade and the quality of the proposals were an irresistible force - the headteachers, the authority and OUDES committed themselves to the adoption of the Internship model.

At the time we were unaware of the extent to which the adoption phase would involve shaping the content and direction of change. As we understood it our priority was to recruit a Development Group of seconded teachers for 1986-87 who would help to translate the general arrangements described in June 1985 into a fully elaborated PGCE programme. We also envisaged 1986-87 as a year in which we would be able to make some structural changes as a transition phase to full implementation in September 1987. Hence our immediate concern was to locate teachers with the relevant interest and expertise for an as yet unspecified development task. The Director asked me to co-ordinate the work of this group and hence to relinquish my joint appointment in July 1986. By February 1986 the Development Group had been identified - 12 teachers who all held posts of responsibility in their schools, mostly senior positions, and who between them represented all the curriculum areas offered by OUDES. They also included several professional tutors and had a great deal of experience of working with beginning teachers. By now, however, Donald McIntyre had joined OUDES as Reader and his knowledge and expertise in teacher education were to be crucial in articulating the development task. The six months from January 1986 were of fundamental importance in recognising what new conception of teacher education might be represented by the structure we had adopted.

This new debate was initiated by a discussion paper presented to OUDES staff in January 1986 which postulated three very different conceptions of the new structure as a framework for teacher education. The first of these, a centre-periphery model, suggested that we use the new structure to extend the school-based element in our current PGCE course and hence that teacher education should involve the application in schools of a body of knowledge and skills that are principally acquired within a department of education. The second conception was an apprenticeship model, making the classroom and its practitioners the focus of teacher education. The third possibility (which became known as Model C) presented a reflective, questioning model in which ideas gained from school practical experience should be complemented by more generalised and abstract ideas presented in the university. Students would be encouraged to work in a critical, questioning and reflective mode, testing ideas about classroom practice against a range of perspectives, and testing more abstract ideas against the realities of classrooms. It was stated that "this model sees the student-teacher as an active agent in the construction of her/his own professional theory and does this in partnership with teachers and tutors, the school and the Department (OUDES), attempting to make appropriate use of all the expertise available".(16) Although advantages of the first two models were recognised, the third was presented unequivocally, even arrogantly, as the most appropriate to adopt, both to exploit fully the structure we had already accepted and because it encapsulated an innovative conception of teacher education. Given the radical reconceptualisation of teacher education implied and that the paper was written and presented by a temporary associate tutor it seems surprising that the proposal was accepted as readily as it was. Subsequent events were to show that it was certainly not a result of acceptance of all the ideas.

A possible explanation is that in real terms the proposal meant nothing to many people. It said that a re-definition of roles would be required, but neither the subjective nor objective reality of change was apparent, at this stage, to its participants. The erroneous assumption that tacit consent was the same as acceptance and commitment was to prove problematic in the development work ahead.

This apparently consensual position was maintained throughout the period from January to July 1986. Throughout this time, the staff of OUDES met regularly (in a forum known as the PGCE Advisory Group) to advance and extend the ideas implicit in Model C. The discussion centred on the three areas identified by Donald McIntyre in his paper - "the teacher education goals to be attained through the PGCE programme, the endemic problems of teacher education which needed to be solved and the principles and procedures of the scheme, directed towards the attainment of the stated goals and formulated as solutions to the identified problems".(17) The expressed purpose of these discussions was to provide a framework within which the Development Group would work - their role was principally to be with how to implement the new PGCE rather than with what that PGCE would consist of. Inevitably, such distinctions are difficult to maintain in practice but without them the task facing the Development Group would have been far too broad. The product of this period was the Commissioning Paper - a document intended "to outline a design which will maximise the productivity (of the Development Group) for the year, provide a basis for rigorous research and evaluation, and minimise confusion and frustration".(18) The paper included sections on the three areas identified above, and also sections on the responsibilities of curriculum tutors, mentors, general tutors and professional tutors, the implications of Internship for INSET and the issues raised for the assessment of the professional quality of interns. By July 1986 it appeared that OUDES had adopted both the structure and principles of Internship, and that the following academic year would be characterised by hard work rather than tension.

What of direct teacher involvement during this period? To ensure that this could be accomplished several curriculum groups were established, based around the major curriculum areas of this department. They consisted mainly of practising teachers, possible mentors of the future, and were led by OUDES curriculum tutors. Their discussions were to run parallel to those of the PGCE Advisory Group, and were to inform and be informed by the 'in house' debates. Initially it was intended that these groups would share common agendas, but this attempt at rational planning was not sustained in the following academic year. Desire for autonomy and more adaptive planning procedures resulted in them following a less centrally prescribed route than had been (probably inappropriately) initially intended. Nevertheless, they ensured the involvement of a wide range of teachers in the adoption phase, and were the forerunners of the subject mentor groups which meet regularly now that Internship is under way.

In September 1986 the Development Group began its work. Each member was to explore, through their own research, a particular aspect of the proposed programme. Four of these investigations were directly related to a particular curriculum area - problem solving in science teaching, the teaching of controversial issues in history, the development of pupils' oral skills in English and the use of different teaching styles in mathematics. One was concerned with special needs, a key cross-curricular theme in the General Programme. Two studies investigated the mentor's role - one examining the problems and possibilities in supervising and collaborating with a pair of interns, the other the task of a mentor as the manager of the diverse kinds of learning experiences sought for interns within the school subject department. Another study focused on the interns' own teaching and the feasibility and value of the kind of non-judgmental structured analytic discussion of it which has been described as 'clinical supervision' or 'partnership supervision'. The final action research study was one concerned with how interns can most effectively gain access to and use the professional craft knowledge being used by teachers they observe. Three members of the group investigated issues which could better be examined by surveys rather than in the first instance through action research. One sought to establish the extent and nature of any consensus among OUDES tutors and Oxfordshire teachers concerning the teaching abilities which it was most essential for interns to acquire. Another investigated lesson planning and how student-teachers' ideas and practices developed. The final investigation concerned the role of the professional tutor and what this might realistically and appropriately be within the new scheme. Each of these studies was to be supervised by an OUDES tutor, but they were also discussed within the group so that we could share our understandings of the possibilities and problems of Internship. In addition to pursuing their own individual research the group spent a great deal of time together, initially discussing the Commissioning Paper and subsequently aspects of the scheme such as the role of the curriculum tutor and how it could be introduced to all schools. The intellectual and social cohesiveness achieved by the group was one of its most distinctive characteristics, and this certainly contributed to tension within the adoption phase.

As the year progressed, this tension became increasingly evident; and particularly at the regular joint meetings of OUDES staff and members of the Development Group. These meetings were to provide a forum both for discussing all aspects of the PGCE (from administration to questions of principle), and to make decisions related to policy. The involvement of non-departmental staff in OUDES decision-making was one of the problematic issues, but perhaps more significant was the now increasingly evident objective reality of the changes. In addition, many of these realities were being expounded by teachers, rather than teacher educators, in what was certainly perceived (and sometimes intended) as a prescriptive and authoritarian way. There was little opportunity and often scant sympathy for participants to negotiate their own meanings of change. The situation was further complicated by the absence of the Director on sabbatical leave in the second term of the year, and the extended illness of the Reader, a key figure in the development process.

However, although the characteristics of change that Fullan describes were so painfully evident, considerable progress was being made. The extent of this became clear in January 1987 when an 'open evening' was held for all interested local schools. Participants included not only senior teachers, but also those most likely to be mentors, and their response was overwhelmingly positive. When, in the spring, they were asked if they would like to join the scheme when it was launched in September 1987, we received offers in excess of the number of PGCE interns we had accepted. Their commitment was not uncritical - appropriate questions were asked about resourcing, and particularly the potential workload of mentors. Recognition of the importance of these issues, coupled with their desire to join the scheme, suggested that they were aware of both the possibilities and problems of Internship and yet welcomed the opportunity to be involved in this innovation in teacher education.

At Easter the Director returned to OUDES and significant changes were made to the pace and nature of the development. It was evident that there were still important gaps in the programme for September - for example, the General Programme, whilst the subject of extensive discussion by teachers and tutors since January was nowhere near completion; the system of assessment had not yet been finalised and there were no final guidelines on the roles of curriculum tutor and mentor. Relationships between the Development Group and many staff were poor, and both I and the Reader had undoubtedly antagonised several of our colleagues. The Director's actions were designed to ensure that all staff who had become alienated from the development work (for whatever reason) were re-engaged in the process, and that the programme gaps were filled even if this would mean delaying the incorporation of all the theoretical understandings generated by the as yet incomplete research by the Development Group. The tasks for the group were much more pragmatically defined, and permanent members of staff assumed much more of the responsibility for the work which remained to be done. Key issues relating to both adoption and implementation had been addressed, and whilst the Development Group had tended to concentrate on factors related to the quality of the change itself, the Director emphasised the involvement of all and a clear route to the time of implementation.

The culmination of the year, and indeed the adoption phase, was a weekend conference in July 1987 at which all the schools to be involved in the first year of the scheme were represented. Produced for this was *The Internship Handbook* (19), the outcome of the work by tutors, Development Group members and the curriculum groups over the previous 18 months. It elaborated the principles of the scheme, the structure of the year, the nature of the curriculum and general programmes, the roles of all those involved, and the ways in which interns would learn and how they would be assessed. The purpose of the conference was to inform and to induct, and finally to launch our new programme of teacher education.

The Internship scheme has now been in operation for three years, with the fundamental principles enhanced rather than changed as we find increasingly effective and sophisticated ways of translating them into practice. The process of change experienced at Oxford is in many ways typical, but it is certainly made distinctive by our particular context and the nature of the ideas we were developing. The majority of the difficulties we experienced were probably inescapable, although a more theorised understanding of the nature of change might have helped us to avoid some of the tensions, particularly those encountered in 1986-87. Certainly, with hindsight, individual decisions can be criticised. The wisdom of appointing a temporary associate tutor to a key role must be questioned, particularly when the Director himself was to be absent for part of that crucial year. However, change is suffused by dilemmas and there is a constant imperative to take account, simultaneously, of so many factors which often act in opposition to one another. Ultimately we achieved, and continue to achieve, our goal of fundamentally reconceptualising teacher education.

References

1. Fullan, M, *The Meaning of Educational Change* (Teachers College Press Ontario, 1982).
2. Fullan, ibid, p.40.
3. Fullan, ibid, p.53.
4. Fullan, ibid, p.41.
5. Fullan, ibid, p.25.
6. Fullan, ibid, p.80.
7. Fullan, ibid, p.40.
8. Fullan, ibid, p.85.
9. Fullan, ibid, p.86.
10. Schön, D A, *The Reflective Practitioner: How Professionals Think in Action* (New York: Basic Books, 1983) and *Educating the Reflective Practitioner* (San Francisco: Jossey-Bass, 1987).
11. *Initial Teacher Training: Approval of Courses, Circular 3/84* (London: Department of Education and Science, 1984).
12. PGCE Colloquium Papers (unpublished paper, OUDES, 1984).
13. General Staff Meeting Minute 552.3 (internal minute, OUDES, 1984).
14. Judge, H, *Teachers and Professional Development: A New Model June 1985* (unpublished paper, OUDES, 1985).
15. Judge, ibid.
16. Pendry, A E, *PGCE Internship Programme: Discussion Paper* (unpublished paper, OUDES, 1986).
17. McIntyre, D I, 'Ideas and Principles Guiding the Internship Scheme' in the present volume.
18. Benton, P, Pendry, A E, et al, *The Internship Model: A Commissioning Paper* (unpublished paper, OUDES, 1986).
19. *The Internship Handbook* (unpublished paper, OUDES, 1987).

Chapter IV

The Internship Model
Peter Benton

As is clear from the previous chapter, the agreed structure for the Internship model of initial teacher education marked the culmination of a process of development spread over several years which was particularly intense in the two years immediately preceding the full, formal launch of the scheme in September 1987. This chapter seeks to provide what is in effect a blueprint for the organisation of Internship and to demonstrate how the principles outlined in Chapter II are embedded in the operation of the scheme.

Peter Benton was Tutor for the PGCE Course at the Oxford University Department of Educational Studies during the period from 1984 to 1988 and was thus very much concerned with the practical development of the Internship model, promoting its adoption in the schools and organising and running the new course in its inaugural year. He is a curriculum tutor for English interns and also has responsibility for a general tutorial group.

The basic structural outline of the Internship model was first presented by Harry Judge to the tutorial staff of the Oxford University Department of Educational Studies (OUDES) in 1984 and later to the Oxfordshire headteachers in June 1985. It is significant that a large number of those who were made aware of the proposed scheme - tutors, teachers, heads, LEA - were positively inclined towards it from an early stage. No doubt this was largely a direct result of Harry Judge's powerful presentation and the esteem in which he was held, but it was also the right idea at the right moment. As Donald McIntyre has pointed out in an earlier chapter, almost everyone concerned with teacher education had expressed concern over the shortcomings of initial teacher training. Even those courses that were school-based - as the Oxford course had increasingly been - lacked the degree of integration and close partnership offered by Internship. Whatever difficulties might lie ahead, it was clear from the outset that there was a shared belief that the principles of Internship made sense, were intellectually and educationally honest and embodied a professional approach to teacher training. There was perhaps also a sense that Internship represented a positive initiative at a time of considerably lowered teacher morale.

The demanding, sometimes painful, yet always ultimately rewarding progress of Internship from the basic structure as first proposed by Harry Judge to a working reality has already been related by Anna Pendry in the preceding chapter and it will be clear from her account that articulating the principles generally and coming to terms with what they meant individually was far from easy. Nonetheless, by June 1987 a highly detailed structure embracing the principles of Internship had emerged in the form of *The Internship Handbook* and was agreed as the basis for the new scheme by all parties concerned. That structure forms the basis for the outline of Internship which follows. It is, however, important to recognise that the model is continually being refined and that certain elements - notably those concerned with assessment, the General Programme, 'Chartered Internship' and the phasing of the year - have either already undergone or are in the process of undergoing some change. Fuller details of what such changes entail are given in Chapter X.

1. The Partners

The Oxfordshire Local Education Authority (LEA), one of 104 such covering England and Wales, is responsible for some 35 secondary schools in Oxfordshire - an irregularly shaped administrative area of central southern England of approximately 50 by 30 miles with the university city of Oxford at its centre. The LEA is statutorily charged with securing that efficient education shall be available to meet the needs of the population of the area. State maintained secondary schools in Oxfordshire are of three types. Most are 11-18 comprehensive schools, ie they cater for students from the age of 11 years when they leave primary education, to either 16 when they enter employment, vocational training or some form of further education, or to 18 years when they enter training, employment or higher education. Some are schools for pupils aged 11-16 years who then enter employment or vocational training or move on to further education at an 11-18 school or a College of Further Education. A number of the schools in Oxford City are Upper Schools which cater for students aged from 13-18 years, and apart from their not having students in the 11-13 age range, they are broadly similar to the 11-18 comprehensive schools. Although all Oxfordshire secondary schools are regarded as being part of the Internship scheme, typically only about 16 schools are actively involved in any one year. Rotation of active membership of the scheme, with some schools resting thus allowing others to join, has been envisaged from the outset.

The Oxford University Department of Educational Studies (OUDES) is one of a number of University Departments of Education (UDEs) responsible for the initial training of teachers. It takes up to 150 student-teachers annually spread across the sciences (Physics, Chemistry, Biology); Mathematics; English; Modern Languages (French and German); History; Geography. All the students are graduates holding a first degree in an appropriate subject and are embarking on a one-year course of initial teacher training geared specifically to the secondary age range ie to the teaching of pupils aged from 11-18 years. Successful completion of this course - the Postgraduate Certificate in Education (PGCE) - leads to their being recognised by central government's Department of Education and Science as qualified teachers. Although the PGCE course is the largest single commitment of the 18 tutorial staff of the university department, they also have a strong commitment to teaching for higher degrees and further professional qualifications, to in-service training, and to writing and research. In addition to the 150 PGCE students there are typically about 70 post-experience students following Masters or Doctoral programmes or working for the Special Diploma in Educational Studies.

2. The Partnership

As was stressed in earlier chapters, at the heart of the Internship scheme is the idea of a close partnership between OUDES and the secondary schools and teachers of the county of Oxfordshire. The Internship scheme means that school staff are full partners with their university colleagues in planning, implementing and evaluating the content, activities and procedures of the PGCE programme. Such a partnership implies not only a much fuller recognition of the part to be played by school staff than has been traditional, but also a far closer collaboration of the university staff with them. Thus, the second fundamental idea of the scheme is that the Oxford PGCE programme is much more fully integrated than is traditionally the case. The student-teacher's tasks and experiences, whether in the university or the school, are planned to complement and illuminate each other rather than being two different and separately planned agendas.

The third idea which is basic to the scheme is that PGCE students are each involved in the work of one school, and one subject department in it, throughout their training year. Rather as medical students, sometimes known as an interns, receive training in teaching hospitals, so this course bases PGCE students firmly in an attachment school throughout the year. Although the medical analogy should not be pressed too far, Oxford PGCE students are thus in a different position from those who undertake a traditional course. It was precisely to signal that difference and to impress the nature of the change upon all concerned that the PGCE students became known as interns - hence 'The Internship Scheme'.

For such a close working relationship between co-professionals to be developed and to be sustained over a period of time takes an act of will and of positive commitment from all concerned and it requires shared understandings, well-defined structures and agreed procedures. Inevitably therefore the setting up and maintenance of such a scheme requires an uncommon degree of openness and consultation at all levels. The membership and operation of the University Certificate Steering Group which was set up in the spring of 1984 to oversee the development of the new course, reflected very clearly the nature of the new relationships that were emerging. The Steering Group was an essential element in the new course gaining acceptance. It would be difficult to imagine such radical changes being adopted by so many different interest groups without the backing of a similarly constituted body.

3. The Steering Group

The composition of the group was significant: tutors representing the different curriculum areas in OUDES were matched by an equal number of subject teachers from schools in the LEA. The Director of OUDES was a member and so too were the Chief Education Officer (and later a senior adviser and education officer). There were representatives of the

Oxfordshire Secondary Headteachers' Association and of the Deputy Heads' Association. There was a teacher representing the Professional Tutors' Association within the county and a member of the Council of Oxfordshire Teachers' Organisations representing the interests of the teaching unions. Westminster College, the local college of education which also has a secondary initial teacher training course, was represented as also were nursing education and HMI. It was significant that the teacher representation outnumbered that of the university department and that the group was chaired by the head of modern languages at a local comprehensive school. These arrangements were rightly understood as outward and visible signs that the university had no intention of dominating the development it had initiated, that it wished to consult at every stage with those who had a legitimate interest and that all concerned were co-professionals. In itself it was a microcosm of all that Internship stood for, most notably integration and partnership. The steering group met regularly and often throughout the period before the formal launch of the scheme and provided an invaluable forum for discussion. Problems and criticisms were aired openly and honestly with the result that the group's members felt confident they could voice the views of those they represented and could influence policy. At a time of particular tension in the teaching profession, they were able to inform those whose interests they represented of what was being discussed, to solicit their views, and reassure them that no hidden agenda was being pursued.

4. Developing the Framework

Frequent consultation at all levels was and remains a characteristic and absolutely necessary feature of Internship. Partnership is meaningless without it. Thus, after the basic outline of the scheme had been agreed by the Steering Group, Harry Judge made his presentation to the heads of all Oxfordshire secondary schools. He extended an invitation to make a preliminary - but not binding - commitment to the scheme. heads were asked to consult staff and, if their view was favourable, to indicate how many interns they might wish to take and in what subjects. Only a very few schools felt unable to join the scheme and the university was offered over a hundred more places than it needed. A substantial number of heads felt their schools could offer ten or more places in five pairs and it was largely, though not exclusively, their schools that were regarded as being potentially the first ones to launch the scheme.

Over the months that followed, OUDES undertook a massive campaign to inform all secondary schools of what the scheme entailed. Tutors visited all secondary schools that had expressed an interest and held seminars in subject departments as well as addressing full staff meetings and groups of senior staff, bringing back comments and criticisms for discussion by OUDES staff, the Steering Group and curriculum groups. There were further papers, progress reports and meetings at OUDES and with the LEA. Most important, the LEA had agreed to the secondment of 12 teachers to form an Internship Development Group in the school year 1986-87, and the need to provide some guidance for this group's activities was a powerful force in concentrating minds on many unresolved issues. As Anna Pendry has indicated in the previous chapter, the Development Group played a crucial role in shaping the structure and direction of the new course. Painful though some of the joint staff/Development Group sessions may have been, they were essential in forcing us to confront basic issues in teacher education, to articulate the principles that underpin Internship and to negotiate our understandings of the scheme. A stronger scheme which was widely acceptable emerged as the result of the Development Group's work.

It was understandable that a number of the schools from which members of the Development Group were drawn should form the nucleus of the group of schools in which the full scheme would be launched in the autumn of 1987: these teachers had, after all, been actively engaged with developing, trialing and discussing aspects of the new course for over a year. Nevertheless, given that the scheme was oversubscribed, it was important that the final decision as to which schools would be invited to launch the scheme was taken by the University Certificate Steering Group as a fully representative body rather than by OUDES alone.

After all this preparation, what does the Internship model look like in practice? What follows is necessarily a simplified model and readers seeking more detail, particularly on the definition of complex roles such as those of professional tutor, are directed to Appendix A.

5. The Model

The 150 interns are each attached in subject pairs to one of the 16 schools with, typically, ten students in each school. (In fact, the two extremes are a minimum of four pairs and a maximum of seven pairs in one school.)

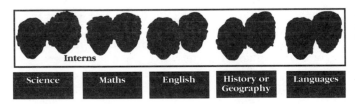

A group of ten paired Interns attached to one school: there are sixteen such groups in all

Interns work as pairs attached to a subject department in their school. This makes it possible for one experienced teacher, called a *mentor*, to co-ordinate their classroom-related learning experiences throughout the year and for them to have regular experience of planning, working and discussing together with others in the department to which they are attached as part of a team.

As one of a pair whose work is directed by a mentor, they are also able to work with small groups and individuals as well as with whole classes, to observe and be observed within a supportive environment. Their mentor gives them the protection and the individual guidance they are likely to need, particularly in the early stages and, as the year progresses, their mentor judges how to increase their responsibilities so that they can benefit personally and can also contribute most successfully to the work of their department. The schools themselves are responsible for the appointment of mentors, though the closeness of the relationship between school departments and university curriculum tutors means that there is inevitably some consultation. The advice of professional tutors in the schools is also likely to be sought by school management and university curriculum tutors alike. Given the demands of the mentor's role, heads of department, who have many other commitments, increasingly suggest a colleague as mentor. Typically this will be somebody who has sufficient experience to be an effective mentor and who may well be seeking further experience and additional responsibility with, perhaps, promotion to head of department in view. The role may be rotated (or occasionally shared) in subject departments both to increase knowledge of the scheme and also to spread the training benefits it offers.

The concentration of, typically, five pairs of interns in a single school means that each intern, as well as being a member of a curriculum group of interns all training to teach a particular school subject, and as well as being half of a pair attached to a subject mentor in a particular school, will also be a member of a mixed subject group of interns attached to that same school. Within each school a member of staff, designated as the *Professional Tutor*, has co-ordinating responsibility for this full group of interns and works closely with the five mentors. The professional tutor is also in close contact with the university general tutor (see below) and together they are responsible for the weekly school-based seminars on professional matters. The professional tutor is thus a key figure in the school and contributes much not only to the smooth running of the scheme but to the professional development of the interns. It is a complex task which is outlined more fully in Appendix B, but perhaps the simplest way of summarising the professional tutor's responsibilities is in the form of the six key processes which span the professional tutor's involvement in the scheme across the year: induction, integration, co-ordination, support, monitoring, and evaluation. All 16 professional tutors from the Internship schools meet regularly to co-ordinate and develop the scheme in conjunction with their colleagues from the university. Although the professional tutor was formerly often a deputy head, it is less frequently the case in Internship. As deputies have so many other calls on their time there may be benefits from allocating the role to another member of staff with some seniority. Certainly the opportunities offered by the post are attractive to many teachers looking to broaden their experience. It is however important that the professional tutor should be accorded a recognised status within the school hierarchy if s/he is to function effectively in relation to mentors and heads of department.

Attached to each school is a *General Tutor*, a member of OUDES staff, responsible, in consultation with the professional tutor, for co-ordinating the work of the interns in that school and for those aspects of their work not directly related to subject teaching.

Most general tutors will be responsible for work in a particular curriculum area as well as for a general tutorial role with their school-based group of about ten interns. Dual curriculum/general tutor roles are usual in PGCE courses and it is not uncommon to find that concern for whole-school issues is marginalised because both the student (whose immediate concerns centre on the teaching of a specialist subject and on classroom survival) and the general tutor (whose central interest may well be the teaching of a specific subject) perceive general issues to be of less importance. The role of general tutor in the Internship scheme gives *all* tutors a high profile in schools in areas other than their subject discipline and requires that they relate their subject expertise to a wider educational framework. Most importantly, it offers the opportunity to take on this responsibility in the setting of a real school which they come to know intimately. Thus, for example, the organisation of the pastoral care system, the workings of the governing body, the financial management of the school, the school's policy on information technology, the implementation of the National Curriculum, are just a few of the many areas with which the general tutor will become acquainted and where s/he has an opportunity to relate theory and practice.

6. The Curriculum Partnership

The PGCE programme is organised in two main strands which, where appropriate are closely interwoven. The curriculum strand, organised separately by each curriculum area, is concerned with classroom teaching and subject curricula and is the responsibility of curriculum area teams consisting of OUDES curriculum tutors and the mentors for that area. Thus, although the basic curriculum unit in any one school consists of say, an English curriculum tutor from OUDES plus two English interns, plus an English mentor from the school, the full English team - which meets regularly throughout the year to plan and monitor the English course - consists of all the English tutors from OUDES plus 15 English mentors from the Internship schools, plus the English Adviser or advisory teacher from the LEA. In addition, a wealth of daily experience is shared by the 15 pairs of English interns. A similar pattern operates in all the other curriculum areas in which OUDES trains teachers; thus there are 75 mentors in all. Two examples (English and Maths) of how curriculum programmes may be jointly planned and run are given in Chapter V.

One part of the curriculum strand consists of a common planned programme, agreed to be suitable for all schools, mentors and interns within the curriculum area. Complementing this planned element is the work which springs from mentors' response to the concerns and needs of their individual interns in the context of their school experience. Interns are helped and encouraged by their curriculum tutor to share and examine with the rest of their curriculum group, the problems and insights that they have experienced.

7. The General Programme Partnership

The second strand, the General Programme, or General Professional Studies, is concerned with whole-school issues. It focuses especially on the school curriculum, the forces that shape it, and such associated issues as the ways in which different pupils are catered for and the ways in which account is taken of the rights of different groups. Examples of general programme issues would be the pastoral and social education of pupils, gender issues, education in a multi-cultural society, the education of children with special educational needs, and schools/industry links. To a large extent this programme is planned centrally, with appropriate support materials being made available by OUDES staff who take responsibility for particular issues. Each general tutor works together with the professional tutor from the school to which s/he is attached to co-ordinate the general programme for a particular group of interns. Regular weekly seminars, specifically focused on whole-school issues, take place in each of the 16 Internship schools with the interns, university general tutor, school professional tutor and other teachers from the school as appropriate. It is not unusual to find this aspect of the Internship scheme being related to the schools' In-Service needs - for example, probationer teachers' induction programmes may, where appropriate, be linked to the Internship seminars; university produced support material has been used in staff training; the investigations carried out by interns into the schools' policies and provision in key areas have been used as the basis for reviews by the schools.

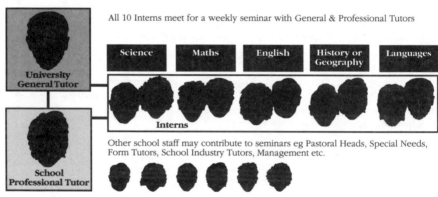

All 10 Interns meet for a weekly seminar with General & Professional Tutors

University General Tutor

Science | Maths | English | History or Geography | Languages

Interns

School Professional Tutor

Other school staff may contribute to seminars eg Pastoral Heads, Special Needs, Form Tutors, School Industry Tutors, Management etc.

In addition, the general group of interns from each school meet their general tutor on a regular basis at the university department for a substantial number of weeks in the year for joint lectures, presentations, workshops and follow-up seminars.

8. An Integrated Programme

Wherever whole-school issues are related to classroom or curriculum concerns, links are established between the general programme and the curriculum programme in both school and university contexts. Thus, for example, catering for children with special educational needs is both a *general* concern in terms of school organisation and provision and a *curriculum* concern in that interns will need to think specifically about how they, as teachers of Science or Maths or English or whatever, are going to meet the special needs of children in their own classroom. Throughout the year an agreed set of general, whole-school issues is programmed into the work of all curriculum areas and mentors and curriculum tutors have to take account of these elements in their course planning. Given that there are 16 schools active in the scheme and not many more university tutors, one of the curriculum tutors attached to a school more often than not doubles as a general tutor for that school. Thus curriculum tutors cannot be other than deeply involved in what have traditionally been seen as general issues and they encounter these not in a decontextualised way but in the rich context of a single case study which they have come to know well - their own Internship school.

The whole picture, which has been presented piece by piece above, is a complex interlocking set of relationships which help to sustain each other. In practice, it is not possible, and indeed it is contrary to the spirit of the scheme, to draw neat boundaries around each role, function or relationship: all participants are interdependent and committed to working as co-professionals, each contributing their particular skills in the context where they are most likely to be effective. An overall view of the scheme which puts together the elements described earlier might look like this and serve to show the close-knit relationship that exists within the Internship team in each of the 16 schools:

The model outlined above represents the basic structure of the Internship scheme in one school but the reality is more flexible, more adaptable and more dynamic than a diagrammatic representation can suggest. The network to which these professionals and intending professionals are given entry by virtue of their participation in Internship is a large one. There are 75 school mentors in all who meet regularly in subject groupings to plan and monitor the course with their university colleagues and who very often influence each other to introduce new ways of working in their schools and in the university as a result. There are 16 school professional tutors who meet regularly and whose concern for professional development has a similar broad and beneficial influence. The input from 16 university tutors - particularly in view of their larger national perspective in some areas and the support materials they produce to back up curriculum work and the study of whole-school issues - makes

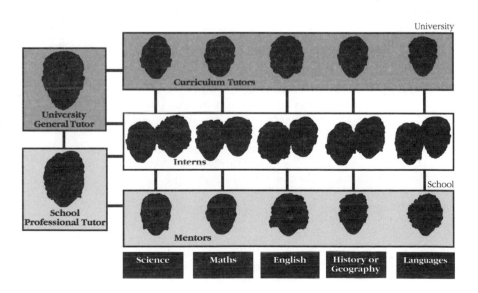

a valued contribution of a different kind. The LEA advisers likewise attend meetings and the scheme, schools and university profit from their knowledge and expertise. There is a Field Officer, seconded full-time from the LEA and based at OUDES, who fulfils a vital liaison function in visiting all schools regularly, and who knows every professional tutor, every mentor, every OUDES tutor and probably every intern. Most important of all, there are 150 highly intelligent and questioning intending young teachers, the vast majority of whom enjoy a growing professional relationship with those with whom they work and whose insights into the 16 schools are valued and often used in curriculum and staff development. At every level the very purpose of training new young teachers continually forces all participants back to first principles to ask themselves what it is that they do, why they do it and how it can best be done. Internship is intended to provide a real context for the continuing professional development of every one involved and to mark the end of the old and damaging theory/practice divide.

9. LEA Support

Internship's potential as a catalyst in schools, as a spur to professional development, and as a means of ensuring the continued recruitment of well-trained teachers, prompted the invaluable support offered to the scheme by the Local Education Authority. In Chapter IX, Tim Brighouse, who was the Chief Education Officer for Oxfordshire at the time, presents the case for such close LEA involvement. This support took several forms some of which are outlined more fully elsewhere in the book. The work of the Development Group of 12 teachers seconded full-time to help plan the scheme has already been related by Anna Pendry. The work of the Internship Monitoring Group and of the Internship Support Group, consisting of teachers from each of the Internship schools seconded one day per week during the first and second years of the scheme respectively is drawn upon by the authors of Chapters VII and IX. The Field Officer and author of Chapter VII was, as has already been mentioned, seconded from the LEA.

LEA support, then, has been vital at all levels and has been particularly significant in the recognition that time needed to be allocated in order for mentors and professional tutors to do their jobs. Each school active in the Internship scheme has been granted time equivalent to that of employing 0.5 of a full-time teacher to use in its support. Thus mentors are offered some time (never enough) to plan with their interns and to debrief them; professional tutors can get to know their interns and may choose to timetable the joint school-based seminars with the university tutor rather than hold them after school. The additional time means there is a chance for talking, planning, evaluating, investigating and reporting to take place in a more productive and professional way inside the school than had formerly been the case. Interns, mentors and, of course, pupils gain enormously from even the small amount of time that is made available to each mentor. It is highly prized not only for these reasons but also because it represents a formal recognition that there is a professional task of training to be done and that teachers have a central and valued contribution to make. That 0.5 FTE means that it is possible for there to be a continual educational debate, a rolling seminar, in progress in each of the Internship schools.

10. Self-evaluation and Reflection

Debate and continual reflection are key concerns and, as has already been suggested, it is not only the interns who are engaged in evaluating their practice: mentors and tutors are similarly involved. Relationships are significantly different as a result.

It must be clear that the Internship scheme cannot operate on the principle of knowledge invariably being delivered *de haut en bas* and the attendant power relationships that this implies. It will be recalled from the outline of the principles of Internship given in Chapter II that the scheme seeks actively to encourage questioning and to make a virtue of the inevitable differences of view which will be encountered by any intern in the course of working closely with a number of different professionals and fellow interns during the year. It is not intended to be an apprenticeship scheme, with the mentor cast in the role of expert teacher to be emulated uncritically by the intern. Equally, it is not a theory-into-practice scheme, with general ideas of good practice being taught in the university in the hope that they can be observed and practised in more concrete terms in the schools. Instead the aim is to put the emphasis on the interns, as active, intelligent and critical learners who, because of their abilities and their concern to make sense of teaching, should be given every assistance to sort things out for themselves. To achieve this end they need to take account of a variety of knowledge, acquired from different sources and offering different, sometimes apparently contradictory, perspectives. A basic principle of the scheme is that there are valid different points of view that interns should meet and consider.

It is such considerations that inform the dialogue and the relationship between the interns, the mentors, professional tutors and the general tutors. An awareness that all share common professional concerns and many - though not necessarily all - of the same goals, underlies the dialogue but there is no sense that there is only one acceptable approach. As a result, all concerned put themselves and their views 'on the line' much more than formerly and there is perhaps a greater sense of risk. If so, it is in the belief that the rewards of adopting this approach are correspondingly greater.

Not only is it intended that interns will think critically about the different concerns and ideas expressed: they should also have an opportunity to test ideas for themselves in the classroom. By reflecting on all they see, do and read, it is intended that they will develop their own personal insight to guide their teaching. This notion of testing and reflection linked to the development of a personal set of insights leads naturally to a recognition of the importance of an overt process of self-evaluation.

Inevitably all interns will have been engaged in a process of self-evaluation and in developing their own concepts of teaching since day one of the course. That conception of teaching is likely to take account of a number of different perspectives such as the practicalities and constraints which impinge on a teacher's work; the view the interns take of their own subject; the view they have of the purpose of secondary education; the roles and responsibilities they think it right for a teacher to assume; the way things are ordered in other departments in other schools; and their own personalities, skills and inclinations. On the basis of such considerations each intern gradually develops a sense of the kind of teacher s/he aims to be. It is important that a context should be provided in which these concerns can be surfaced, encouraged and questioned.

Although interns are encouraged to think along these lines from the outset, there is particular stress on self-evaluation in Phase Two of the year. One means by which self-evaluation is developed is through 'partnership supervision' of the intern by the mentor, the curriculum tutor or a paired intern. Here the intern asks for a specific aspect of his or her teaching to be observed by one of these, acting as a non-judgmental partner, and subsequently talks through what s/he was attempting and makes a personal assessment of what happened. A main task of self-evaluation is for the individual intern to articulate how, in the classroom situation, the success of his or her teaching should be judged. Other aids to this end include personal teaching diaries, lesson analyses and tape recordings of specific lessons.

On the basis of such practical activity, discussion, reading and reflection, each intern is required to produce a written self-evaluation towards the end of the year. A crucial task of the mentors at this time is therefore that of providing an environment in which, the intern having achieved a basic level of classroom proficiency, the emphasis is shifted from that of assessment and scrutiny of the intern's work to that of a collaborative partnership intended to take the intern beyond competence.

11. Assessment
Intern's progress is monitored and assessed continuously throughout the year. Key responsibilities are shared on the one hand by the mentor and curriculum tutor, on the other by the professional tutor and general tutor. These are formalised in reporting procedures which require judgments to be made by all four at three reference points in the course of the year and to be discussed with each intern. The concept of formally moving to Phase Two of the year (or gaining Chartered Intern Status as it was known for the first two years of the scheme) is a crucial part of the PGCE course and of the assessment process. A move to Phase Two is merited when the intern's performance shows a sufficient degree of competence when set against the List of Important Abilities which was developed and agreed jointly by OUDES tutors and Oxfordshire teachers. The list is concerned with interns' performance in six main areas: Planning of Work; Class Control; Clear Communication; Management of Learning; Evaluation of Pupils' Work; and Recognition of the Teacher's Role. The list will be found in full in Appendix B at the end of the book. Each intern must successfully complete Phase Two before the examiners will recommend him or her as a qualified teacher.

12. 'Chartered Intern Status' and Phase Two of the Year

The guiding idea underlying the notion of Chartered Intern status, as it was known for the first two years of the scheme, was that of providing a dynamic for professional development throughout the PGCE year. In the first two terms of the course the major emphasis was inevitably on the attainment of a satisfactory standard of performance in relation to the List of Important Abilities to which reference was made earlier. The first review related specifically to the award of Chartered Intern status took place at the end of the second term and a majority of the interns achieved that status at the beginning of the third term. Thereafter the thrust of school-based work was to take the intern on beyond competence. Interns who did not immediately achieve Chartered Intern status would receive additional support and focused practice from the mentor and curriculum tutor.

It was the view that the award of Chartered Intern status at a stage when it was clear that the intern had demonstrated a sufficient competence, would act as an incentive by announcing formally that teachers and tutors were agreed that - on present performance and unless there was some unlooked for falling off - the intern would be passed as a competent teacher at the end of the course. Far from causing interns to rest on their laurels, it was argued, the effect was likely to be highly positive and to encourage a more open relationship between all concerned. In particular it would mean that the partnership supervision of the last term could be more effective as the interns would know that improvement, not assessment, was the central purpose of the exercise.

As will be apparent from several references in later chapters, the idea of Chartered Internship and the purposes behind it were thought to have some merit but its practical application was seen as too rigid and the unwieldy appellation proved to be more of a hindrance than a help. (The title, rather like that of 'intern' or 'mentor' was chosen partly to signal that something new was happening and that new attitudes and relationships were expected). The key concept of moving to a second phase has been retained but its application is now more flexible. The title Chartered Intern has been abandoned.

13. The Structure of the Year

Having assembled the main elements of the course it may be helpful to relate them to the structure of the year as a whole as it unfolds. Though invariably very similar, the detailed arrangements for the Internship course are never exactly the same in consecutive years as there are no fixed school terms in the English system and they will vary in length from year to year largely according to the date on which Easter falls and, to a lesser extent, according to the idiosyncratic requirements of the LEA. Thus, the middle term of the three-term year may vary in length from a scant 10 weeks to almost 15 weeks with consequent adjustments in the other two terms to produce a school year totalling 40 weeks. The one fixed quantity is that the Department of Education and Science requires all PGCE courses to be at least 36 weeks long of which a minimum of 15 weeks must be spent by the students in schools.

A central aim of the structure that has been evolved has been that of providing a secure, supportive and phased introduction to teaching designed to meet the developing needs and capabilities of the interns throughout the year. Broadly, the structure of any year is very close to the following model though, for the reasons given above, the various activities may start and finish at slightly different points in the year:

Beginning in early to mid-September -
(i) 2 weeks of initial placement in a primary or middle school near the intern's own home.
(ii) 1 week of initial placement in a secondary or upper school near the intern's own home. It is considered important for this second placement to be in a school which is served by the school attended in the first week. These two periods of initial placement are arranged by the intern in consultation with the LEA in his or her home area. In the preceding June or July OUDES contacts the schools when alerted by the prospective intern, confirms the arrangements with the headteacher and sends details of the structured observation tasks that the intern will be requested to carry out during this placement. The intern also receives details of these tasks and appropriate support materials well before the start of the initial placement period. Schools are asked to complete a form detailing the intern's observation and teaching activities during this attachment together with any comments on the intern's time in the school that may seem appropriate.
(iii) 3 weeks of Induction. The first week is entirely university-based and involves meeting and working with university general and curriculum tutors and the professional tutor from the school to which they will be attached. It is also an important period for interns to meet and get to know the other half of their Internship pair with whom they will spend much time in the coming months. Interns are debriefed on their experiences of the previous three weeks and their perceptions are related to the Internship scheme and what lies ahead of them. The remaining weeks continue this process of familiarisation and induction. Interns spend an induction day in their school with their professional tutor and their general tutor and a second one with their mentor. There is a strong focus on what is to be learned from the craft knowledge of teachers and on acquiring appropriate strategies to observe and question tactfully, appropriately and effectively. This introduction to understanding and learning from the teaching of experienced teachers is fundamental to the course. There is evidence to suggest that it improves not only the interns' understanding but, indirectly, teachers' own perceptions of what they do.
(iv) 10 weeks joint school/university ('J' Weeks) with interns spending two days each week in the school and three days at OUDES. Typically, one-and-a-half of the three days based at OUDES are focused on curriculum concerns with interns working in curriculum groups with their curriculum tutors. About half a day at OUDES is devoted to an agreed programme of General Professional Studies with interns attending lectures and presentations and working in general groups with their general tutors. During the two days in school interns are working largely with the mentor

and from time to time with the curriculum tutor who will visit the schools regularly and may work alongside the interns. The mentor link is not exclusive, however, and interns are encouraged by the mentor to observe and work with other members of their departments in school. The mentor makes a point of spending time with the interns planning work and discussing lessons they have observed and in which they have participated relating these activities to the programme agreed between OUDES curriculum tutors and all mentors in that subject area. The mentor ensures that the group takes account of the concerns of the general programme of whole-school issues as appropriate. At some point in these two days each week there is a seminar for all interns which takes place in school and is organised by the OUDES general tutor and the school professional tutor. In addition to being closely involved with the work of a single subject department and with a wide range of cross-curricular issues in the school, all interns begin to develop an insight into the role of the form tutor and of the pastoral system through their attachment to a form or tutor group.

[These 10 joint school/university weeks are broken by the Christmas vacation with rather more before than after the break]

(v) 12 weeks of block school experience ('S' Weeks). These begin typically at the end of January after the last three joint school/university weeks and place the interns in their schools for five days a week teaching between half and two-thirds of a full timetable and taking a full part in the life of what is by now 'their' department and of the school. They team teach together and with their mentor, and are likely to work at various points with their curriculum tutor on lessons jointly planned and delivered. As well as teaching and planning together, the interns also take individual responsibility for whole classes; may assume responsibility for form tutoring activities; and continue to have planning and debriefing sessions on a regular basis with their mentors every week. The weekly school-based seminars organised by the general tutor and the professional tutor and attended by all interns in the school continue throughout this period.

One further study week, coinciding with the schools' half term holiday is university-based. It provides an invaluable opportunity for sorting out ideas, sharing problems and solutions with other interns and generally troubleshooting at just the right moment in the block school experience.

[The 12 weeks are split into two roughly equal periods by the schools' Easter holiday]

(vi) 6 weeks joint school/university ('E' Weeks) with interns spending two days each week in the school and three days at OUDES. This is a return to a pattern used earlier in the year but the emphasis and the intention are different because it occurs in the second phase of the year when self-evaluation is a key concern. By this time interns have already spent some 80 days in the school and 15 days prior to that in two other schools - well in excess of the minimum 75 days required by the Department of Education and Science. During this period the vast majority of interns have moved from novice status to that of a colleague whose work is known and trusted by their mentors and tutors and, after careful monitoring of their progress by means of continuous assessment, these interns will enter Phase Two of their course. Whilst still continuing as classroom teachers during this phase in school, a major concern for interns will be to concentrate on aspects of teaching they wish to improve and to focus on developing particular areas of expertise. Examples might be undertaking special needs work related to their own subject area; making a significant contribution to some aspect of curriculum development in their department such as developing materials for a specific purpose or spending time looking at the department's or school's resourcing and approaches with regard to a cross-curricular concern such as gender issues; carrying out a substantial project related to school fieldwork, open days, industrial visits etc. A main concern will be the writing and presentation of their self-evaluation and of their dissertation. Dissertations are usually school-based and are increasingly concerned with negotiated topics which both the intern and the school feel it would be valuable to investigate. As a result much small-scale research which is of use to the school has been undertaken.

One further study week, coinciding with the schools' half-term holiday and not long after the beginning of the joint school/university weeks, is university-based. As with the previous half-term, it provides an opportunity for interns to meet and discuss their progress with curriculum tutors and general tutors and to discuss the development of their dissertations, also to share ideas, problems and solutions with other interns. Above all, it provides the opportunity to reflect, read and write.

The year ends in early July after 36 weeks, of which the equivalent of 21 weeks will have been spent by the interns in school classrooms. The vast majority of the interns will achieve qualified teacher status and go on to teach in comprehensive schools the following September. Typically, 30 or more of the 150 interns will take up their first employment with the Oxfordshire LEA.

Chapter V

Learning to Teach:
Designing and Running Two
Curriculum Programmes

Chris Davies and Linda Haggarty
with Val Parkes and Jude Stratton

The focus of this chapter is on the planning and implementation of the Curriculum Programme in the Internship scheme. The authors start by looking at the theoretical underpinning of a curriculum programme and work towards a recognition both of the problems raised and of the opportunities offered by the scheme. In order to do this in a coherent and accessible way, they have chosen to divide the chapter into three sections.

In the first section Chris Davies, an English Curriculum Tutor, focuses on translating the theoretical perspective on becoming an English teacher to the working procedures which enable the application of the perspective within the scheme.

In the second section Linda Haggarty, formerly a Mathematics Curriculum Tutor at OUDES and now a lecturer at Reading University, looks at one way in which the university/school partnership has been realised and, at the development of a programme within that partnership which satisfies the principles of the scheme.

In the third section Valerie Parkes, the Mentor from a school English department, and Jude Stratton, the Mentor from a school mathematics department, explore their involvement in the development and implementation of the scheme. They offer a distinctive perspective which recognises opportunities and problems associated with the scheme from their points of view.

A. The English Tutor's Perspective

The planning of the English course within the Internship scheme is described here in terms of the theoretical perspective which structures the OUDES approach to the wide range of concerns that beginning English teachers need to understand. The aim is to exemplify the distinctive contribution that curriculum tutors can make in that part of the curriculum programme which takes place at the university, and the kind of thing we are talking about when we refer to the theoretical element of the programme.

Clearly, any respectable PGCE English programme must aim to make beginning English teachers aware of the current major issues within the subject, of what goes on in the teaching of the subject in schools, and of current innovative approaches to, practice in and thinking about the subject. This could, and frequently does, entail constructing an arbitrary route through a list of specific subject elements during the process of one year's PGCE course, ensuring that each of various major subject concerns receives the time and attention it deserves. Approaches to ways in which young people can be helped to develop essential abilities and capacities in reading, writing, talking, knowing about language and appreciating literature will all be dealt with in their turn, both individually and in various possible combinations. Theoretical perspectives on the writing process, the value of group talk, the centrality of imaginative literature, the place of popular culture within the subject, and so on, will be explored and practical experience of ways of dealing with such concerns in the classroom will be provided, and evaluated. It is possible that a coherent philosophical position of some kind about the purpose of the subject will underlie such a design, or will emerge during its unfolding.

When defining the English programme within the context of the Internship scheme, it might appear entirely reasonable on initial consideration that a fairly straightforward menu of subject issues could be organised, within one sequence or another, which could provide a rich and relatively unproblematic introduction to the many complex issues involved in English teaching. The Internship scheme's emphasis on exposing beginning teachers to diverse and possibly conflicting perspectives on a range of issues to do with teaching, especially in terms of possible mismatches between theory and practice, would simply increase the rigour and extent to which student-teachers scrutinise and explore the different elements of their subject.

Intuitively satisfying and desirable though such an approach might at first appear, it lacks the kind of guiding principle that is needed to help newcomers find their way into teaching a subject as ill-defined and amorphous as English. In terms of an underlying and theorised rationale, the menu model is flimsy: English is not just anything a particular practitioner wants it to be, it is a collection of diverse (but specific and identifiable) beliefs, theories and practices. Faced with a bewildering list of separate elements on a PGCE programme, and a tendency among its practitioners to philosophical imprecision, new teachers of English require some coherent way of thinking about where they stand, and what they ought to be doing. They need a theoretical framework of some kind. This is true of any subject, to a certain extent - when it comes to English, the problem is of some urgency.

A debate about the very nature of English has been taking place at the level of higher education for many years now. Without going into detail, the issues in this debate can be outlined as follows: for many years the study of English was seen as the study of English literature - literature was seen as being the body of work in which certain specially talented individuals communicated their particularly powerful insights about what it is to be human, using their particularly powerful resources of language. Other individuals applied their intelligences to appreciating the quality of the literature produced by great writers - appreciating and learning from the insights about life by appreciating and interpreting the extraordinary ways in which great writers use language. This involved the close reading of texts, the privileging of certain writers and certain kinds of writing above all others, and a certain kind of sensitivity to language and life.

Against this version of the subject, another version emerged during the last 20 years out of the work of more theoretically-minded critics. The origins of this work were in structural linguistics and in sociological, political or psychological perspectives on culture rather than in a humanist concentration on the individual. Under an overall heading such as cultural theory, or literary theory, this other version has drawn on a number of distinct theories all sharing a commitment to understanding the ways in which language and culture operate in society - the ways in which language and culture reproduce and reflect ideology. In this version, great literature loses its privileged position, and becomes just one of many significant forms of language and culture which are to be studied for an understanding of the way social meanings operate on people as social beings.

For a long time, certainly since the 1960s, secondary English has reflected the first version. English teachers in schools, and those writing about the subject, have seen English as dealing with the notion of *personal growth* - young people have been helped to develop as individuals by exposure to the humanistic concerns and sensitive language use of great writers, and by being encouraged to use language in similar ways. Caroline St John Brooks, in her study of one typical comprehensive school English department, describes this view very vividly:

The English teachers held strong ideological commitments and beliefs, central to which were a number of truths which were taken to be self-evident, but which were essentially unprovable. They held that pupils could and would enter a fuller, freer life through writing, discussing their own and other people's writing, and by the act of making the kind of judgments which are made by the writers of fiction, plays and poetry. These truths were the badges of the faithful. (Brooks, 1983).

Inevitably, though, just as the first version permeated into secondary education from university English (in that instance, through the inescapable influence of F R Leavis in Cambridge), the influence of modern theory, having established itself in higher education, began to make itself felt in secondary education. The arguments at the secondary level are somewhat more complex, and also involve questions of literacy and the demands of the outside world, but the essential conflicts of belief are identical to those in higher education: is it the job of English to engage with the emotional and personal growth of pupils by introducing them to the resources and possibilities of imaginative literature, or should it concentrate on the outside world's demands for literacy - for efficient and effective language use - or should it view language and culture as an ideologically loaded activity, empowering young people with the rhetorical and analytical resources that they need to cope with the dangerous discourses of the modern world?

For many practising teachers, such a characterisation of internal conflict between subject beliefs might seem unnecessarily contentious and, if such conflicting beliefs only surfaced in theoretical discussions of the subject, so it would be. For a number of reasons, though, it is not possible to sidestep this problematic perception of the subject - especially in the context of planning and running a PGCE English programme.

Firstly, there is a good deal of evidence to suggest that these different beliefs about the subject do indeed form part of the thinking of practising English teachers. Research carried out at OUDES into the attitudes of English teachers to different kinds of English subject philosophy does indicate strongly that - however the dominant version of the subject as it operates in secondary education is characterised - individual English teachers do vary widely in their beliefs about the subject. The evidence of this research certainly undermines the idea of a straightforward consensus as to the nature of English amongst secondary English teachers.

Secondly, the advent of the National Curriculum has raised questions about the nature of the subject more acutely than ever before. The Cox working party's report on English explicitly outlined different versions of the subject (which it claimed, perhaps more hopefully than realistically, should not be seen as mutually exclusive) such as *personal growth, adult needs, cultural heritage,* and *cultural analysis* (HMSO, 1988, paras 3.19 - 3.24). Precisely the same outline was later to be incorporated in the National Curriculum document (DES, 1989, paras 2.20 - 2.27). This diversity of beliefs closely reflects the diversity encountered in our own research.

Thirdly, and of immediate significance in the context of postgraduate teacher education, is the demanding process that graduates must go through in transforming their subject understanding from that of the higher education student to that of the secondary education teacher. This will involve, in any subject, a major shift from scholarly to pedagogical concerns. In English, a mainly academic debate about the nature of English translates into urgent questions about the place and value of the subject within the secondary curriculum, and any group of recent graduates will inevitably represent a wide range of conflicting perspectives on this issue. Student-teachers have to think about the nature of the subject they are planning to teach on a number of possible dimensions, therefore: how does their higher education understanding of the subject relate to the needs of secondary pupils, how does it fit in with the thinking of other English teachers, how does it fit in with the thinking of their fellow student-teachers; where do they stand in relation to the debate as it takes place in higher education, where do they stand in relation to the debate at secondary level? For those who come with an unproblematic perception of the subject, there are difficulties because the demands of secondary education are different from the demands of higher education; for those who are already conscious of conflicting versions of the subject, there are difficulties because the majority of school-teachers do not share that consciousness.

For all these reasons, therefore, it was felt essential that the English programme should provide more than a straightforward passage through an apparently consensus-based version of the subject, even if enlivened by an emphasis on innovative and ideal approaches within that. The notion of any stable consensus about the nature of English is hard to sustain and, if student-teachers are to be able to conceptualise the different ways that teachers think about English (and, crucially, to follow that thinking through into classroom practice), if they are to be adequately alert to the questions and demands posed by National Curriculum English, and if they are to be capable of transforming their subject understanding from that of undergraduates in higher education to teachers in secondary schools, it became increasingly apparent to us that the English programme should take the difficulty of defining the subject's aims and concerns into full and effective account.

The process of designing the English programme on such a basis has been gradual over a three-year period. Our starting point was, certainly, far closer to the arbitrarily sequenced menu of major items outlined at the beginning of this account. This had the major virtue of being determined in a fully collaborative way over many months, in several meetings between curriculum tutors and representatives from Oxfordshire English departments (transforming, during this period, into meetings of future mentors from the Internship schools). In addition, there was significant input into this process from one of the English teachers seconded onto the Development Group, who had investigated ways of approaching the specific element of oral work in English as one component on the English programme. Considerable time and effort was devoted to agreeing on the most effective way of sequencing the major components of the programme so that each component would inform the next in the most effective way possible, resulting in the decision to make the idea of *writing as process* the first major area of the English curriculum that would be dealt with. This would then be followed by concentrating on oral work within English, leading then to aspects of reading - comprehension, responding to literary texts and encouraging the habits of reading in various ways. Many other elements - such as working with the media, drama within English, special needs and so on - would also be dealt with along the way.

A fairly comprehensive English programme was outlined in this way, not radically different from what had preceded it, but certainly with a fresh and somewhat less arbitrary (because carefully thought-through by all those who would be involved in running it) sequencing of its separate elements than usually tended to be the case. But it was only when the issue of how to deal with differing and possibly conflicting versions of the subject was brought into play that an overall structuring strategy began to assert itself.

It had been the case, before this time, that attention was paid within the course to questions about the nature of English, to new theories and approaches within the subject, and to the perceptions of the subject that different student-teachers brought with them. Partly in response to the research being carried out at OUDES into this issue, partly in response to the vigorous interest in such matters of previous students, and partly in response to the enthusiastic agreement of the teachers involved in the planning, it became increasingly attractive at the final stage of planning that the overall structure of the course should incorporate such a perspective. The first version of the English programme that ran throughout the first year of the Internship scheme therefore took this perspective as its starting point, and its effectiveness was carefully monitored throughout the whole of this first year.

Thus, it was decided to begin the English programme by exploring the different individual histories of the interns as students of English, both in their own schooling and in higher education. The different subject contents and philosophies that they had encountered during their own educations were explored and compared, as a basis for investigating the different kinds of English that occurred within current secondary education. An overview of different approaches to the subject in schools was explored in early sessions at OUDES, focusing on the literature on the subject, and on policy documents of a local and national kind (eg school English department policy documents, and publications from sources such as HMI). Immediately following this, the interns' first task once in their different schools was to investigate the policies and beliefs operating in the departments that they would be working in throughout the year. This involved reading documents, investigating resources, talking to teachers and observing practice in the light of this perspective.

Their growing understandings of the different kinds of English that they perceived taking place in their schools were then examined in the context of OUDES seminars, providing a vivid and impressive picture of diversity, inventiveness and, to these new teachers, some confusion. For some, this was a bewildering experience because central verities about the subject were called into question; for others, it was equally bewildering to encounter a somewhat less problematic and theorised version of the subject than the one they had become aware of during higher education. For all, though, the notion of asking fundamental questions about the nature of the subject they were to teach was validated and emphasised so that all of the subsequent individual elements of the course could now - in addition to the specific considerations about each of these elements that would be explored in depth - be considered within the overall theoretical framework which forced them to address questions such as 'What kind of English does this approach imply? What alternative approaches are available, and what are the implications of these? How do these different approaches relate to my own beliefs about the subject?'

As the year progressed it was clear that those interns already familiar with an approach to English which questioned traditional beliefs about its content and aims felt most at ease in applying this kind of questioning to all aspects of their increasing involvement in English teaching. For some, this process merely led to a fairly rapid confirmation of their preference for the dominant form of the subject that they encountered, which in most cases was a literature-based personal growth version. For others, this process allowed them to explore and reflect on a wide variety of approaches (in terms of both content and aims). In all cases this overall theoretical framework did appear to assist them - to a greater or lesser extent - in working out their own philosophy and practice of the subject.

Subsequent to the first full operation of this programme, having carefully monitored its success (especially through the interns' self-evaluations, which provided many with an opportunity to explore the nature of their own beliefs about the subject in the context of their own classroom practice), it appeared to be the case that the theoretical framework had been of considerable value, but that a somewhat cautious application of it had resulted in a limited effectiveness for some interns. A more emphatic application of these ideas was therefore introduced in the second year of the programme.

The results have been immensely encouraging. The increased emphasis occurred by introducing more explicit and detailed accounts of the nature of different versions of the subject. This process was given a considerable boost with the publication of the first of the Cox working party reports on English teaching, with its account of different versions of the subject which more or less exactly reproduced the characterisations and terminology that had already been offered within the programme. As a result, virtually all the interns were confidently thinking about the subject, and developing their own ideas for teaching, within a conscious framework of exploring and questioning the nature of English, and had become highly articulate on these perspectives by the end of the first term (this became particularly apparent when each was interviewed individually about how they saw these issues, and where they felt they stood at this particular stage). In addition, a group of the English interns had themselves initiated a series of informal seminars under the heading of 'Versions of English', and had begun to produce papers on these issues for circulation among themselves. This can be illustrated most vividly by the following passage from an article by an English intern on the experience of becoming an English teacher published in the PGCE course newsletter:

English as a subject presents a unique trauma for its teachers which we were grappling with all last term - that is, when looked at closely, certainties crumble and all that remains visible is a series of contingent day-to-day unreflected-upon assumptions. Hence a large part of our time, when not greedily consuming US teen-fiction, has been devoted to teasing out the sneaky little contradictions which remain within our topic, whether we acknowledge them or not.

Experience of the first two years of the English programme so far strongly suggests that our theoretical framework has proved effective, and entirely in accord with the major principles of the Internship scheme. Our aim has been to provide a powerful stimulus and a supportive structure for thinking about, and developing expertise in, classroom English teaching. Certainly no less than other subjects, and perhaps even more than most, English presents very real difficulties as a secondary discipline in terms of identifying the most desirable and effective aims and content, and in terms of working out how to achieve and work with those in the classroom, for the benefit of all pupils in the comprehensive school. The theoretical basis of the English programme has been developed to achieve this aim above all, and not simply as a convenient structuring device. Whilst it certainly has assisted interns in thinking constructively about the different elements within the course, its most powerful effect seems to be, so far, in the way it forces interns to think long, hard and productively about the kinds of English teachers they might become, and want to become.

B. The Maths Tutor's Perspective

1. Content and Joint Development of a Curriculum Programme
In the summer of 1986, mathematics tutors from OUDES, local teachers, the LEA mathematics adviser and an advisory teacher met as a steering group to discuss how mathematics could move forward in the Internship scheme. An early decision was that I should produce some materials for mathematics which would satisfy the principles of the scheme, would exemplify those principles in practice and would form a model for future planning. Consequently, in the autumn term, I began to draft materials concerned with three quite different issues of concern to mathematics teachers: styles of teaching, pupil motivation and the underachievement of girls in mathematics. Each seemed to present its own set of challenges. The first required that interns should test a full range of styles of teaching in the classroom, as recommended in mathematics education publications, whilst recognising that many teachers themselves did not use that full range. The second was of a more theoretical nature with little explicit, practical discussion of the issue in schools and the third not only had to link in with a whole-school study concerned with rights of groups but was also likely to meet with criticism from some potential mentors.

We felt that these materials would have to be detailed so that everyone could understand what was taking place as interns studied the issues, and explicit in terms of each person's responsibilities, so that tutor, intern and mentor would know exactly what they had to do. At the same time we recognised that in order to trial these materials we would have to persuade the mathematics PGCE students in 1986/87 to trial the role of intern, and the subject supervisors in the schools to trial the role of mentor. Consequently, another group was set up for mathematics subject supervisors. All agreed to take part in the trialing as did the students on the course.

Another important reason for setting up the group was so that we could begin to work in partnership, creating a course together which was appropriate for the students, acceptable to teachers and tutors and manageable in its implementation. At an early stage in this creation of the programme both the steering group and the supervisors' group engaged in brainstorming sessions in which we listed what we considered to be essential elements of a PGCE mathematics course. A principle at that stage, and one which we have continued to adhere to, was that agreement had to be reached about what was essential. Every issue we deal with has been discussed and its place in the course agreed; it would not be appropriate to make any change to that programme without discussion and agreement in what has now become a single mathematics group.

Thus, in the spring term of 1987, we began the trialing of the three modules which I had developed. I considered it important that I should take responsibility for the writing of the modules and equally important that supervisors should have the opportunity to modify these modules at any stage of the development. As well as explaining in detail what the tutor sessions would involve, I also explained what the supervisor acting as mentor and the student acting as intern had to do.

For the supervisor it meant arranging for students to observe teachers, arranging for interns to teach small groups and whole classes and allowing students to discuss their developing ideas with them. It was - and continues to be - very important that mentors are not asked to do too much, that they are asked to do only those things they are in the best position to do and that once they have agreed to accept the recommendations in the modules, they allow those things to happen.

For the students it meant that they were expected to engage in certain background reading, carry out certain tasks in schools such as observation of particular aspects of teaching, discussing lessons and ideas with their supervisors, teaching in certain ways and then collecting all their thoughts on each issue and, after careful reflection, developing their own theories on those issues.

As the trialing progressed I was able to gather data in a number of ways from both supervisors and students so that by the end I was able to draw some conclusions which would help us in further development of the mathematics programme.

All the students and, with one exception, all the supervisors actually did what they had agreed to do before the trialing and were extremely positive about what had happened. The students found that by focusing on particular aspects of their teaching, they could begin to understand and develop their own ideas on those aspects. They all thought it had helped to enrich their PGCE year although I was amused to note two comments made at that time by students: *"I don't know if I reflected on the issues but I certainly thought hard about them"* and *"How can we be expected to think about pupil motivation when we have all these lessons to plan?"* The second had not quite worked out that theory can inform practice!

The subject supervisors were also very positive and wanted to continue with their involvement in the scheme. They particularly liked the detail included in the materials and felt that what they had been asked to do was realistic. Many said that they now had an understanding of what Internship was about and, using the three modules as models, would like to be involved in the production of further materials. It was also interesting just how many of them also commented on how discussions with students had helped them in their own thinking on the issues and that materials were being displayed in mathematics departments and discussed by other teachers as well.

Thus, by the summer of 1987, we had a mathematics group with a good understanding of the scheme, the knowledge that they already knew quite a bit about the role of mentor, three modified sets of materials, a draft programme outlined for the year and a willingness and enthusiasm to work together to develop our understanding and produce further materials. As it turned out, not all subject supervisors actually became mentors when the scheme was launched but most continued with their involvement when new mentors joined the group.

As a group we decided that our next module should be concerned with classroom management. Mentors had already made it clear that I, as tutor, should do all the writing and modifying but that together we should agree on the framework as well as the detailed input and the appropriate base -

school or university - for each aspect of the module. They also requested that the same amount of detail should be included so that I would once again write what I would be doing as well as what they as mentors should do and what interns would be doing. It seems essential that as new mentors join the group, and as experienced mentors run through the materials, we continue to discuss and modify materials, develop new materials and continue to share ownership for the scheme.

2. The Relationship between Curriculum Tutor and Mentor

I think it is vitally important in building relationships in the scheme for tutors in the university department to believe that partnership with teachers in schools is both desirable and essential; that practising teachers have a quite distinct contribution to make to teacher education and that the tutor's role is also distinct and complementary to this; that they are being paid to engage in teacher education and teachers are not and that tutors, as well as being 'players' in the implementation of the scheme, are also responsible as 'managers' of the scheme.

In mathematics, mentors and tutors are involved in joint planning, trialing, development and implementation of the scheme but in addition, the partnership has been strengthened as I have spent time working in school not only with interns and mentors in classrooms but also with mentors and other teachers before interns arrive both in and out of classrooms. By the end of the first year of the scheme, mathematics mentors were saying how positive they felt this relationship was and how good they thought the scheme was: *"the scheme is great and the maths modules are first rate", "working as a mentor has been a pleasure", "(the interns) should be aware they are doing one of the best PGCE courses in the country", "(the interns) seem to have got to a position which might have been reached at the end of the first year of teaching."* However, it would be misleading if I suggested that there were no problems in the relationships between mentor, tutor and intern and it is important to explore these.

On one level the mentor-tutor relationship, as I have already argued, is working well. Nonetheless, I am aware that each mentor is essentially doing teacher education a favour. They have a small time allowance to do the job but, particularly at the beginning of the year, this is not enough. Consequently, I find myself unable to question either their plans or their practice; if a mentor does not do what has previously been agreed, what can I as curriculum tutor say? As long as mentors continue to be provided with this level of support - or less - the partnership will really only allow challenges from mentor to tutor and not the other way round. Another tension exists if a mentor seems only to be encouraging interns who agree with their particular style or philosophy. The scheme should allow interns to test a range of ideas and develop and justify their own style and philosophy. I think, from the other direction, mentors also feel that they must agree with the theoretical perspective I provide. From conversations the interns have taped with their mentors, it would appear that the lack of consensus on issues is never really explored.

In addition, I think interns feel they have to keep everyone happy. All the group I worked with last year talked about *"keeping their mentor happy"* or *"being polite"* or *"looking interested"*. Many felt that questioning teachers about why they had done certain things in their teaching or why they held certain ideas about teaching was being *"impolite"*. That interns were able to question what they saw later, often with their partner intern, is to their credit but their experiences would most certainly have been enriched if they could have talked these things through with the teachers concerned. They were also very aware that they were taking up a great deal of their mentor's time, so were often reluctant to ask for time to discuss, for example, their developing theories.

I was also surprised to find that my own role needed some clarification during my visits to school. It became clear to me very early on that I should not try to be a 'subject teacher'; that I was not in the best position to discuss the practical realities of full-time teaching. Rather, I was the person in the best position to link the theoretical input in the department with the practical teaching activities engaged in by the interns; the person who could encourage interns to question what they saw in the light of theory and work out their own solutions. This in itself was not always easy. I think interns would have preferred me to tell them the 'answer' rather than ask them more questions but perhaps that is partly to do with the way they were taught themselves as pupils in school and the ways in which they expect to learn about teaching.

Another potential difficulty emerges as experienced mentors are replaced by new mentors. Relationships have to be established, and I am increasingly aware that ownership of the scheme could seem unreal to many; that time has to be spent thinking about fundamental ideas and principles and that materials, which must appear rather final and polished, have to be discussed, accepted and, if necessary, modified until new mentors are satisfied.

3. Divisions of Responsibility for the Interns' Learning

As mathematics tutor I take responsibility for the running of the mathematics component of the course. As well as producing materials for the course, the group has requested that I produce a detailed chart explaining week by week what each of us is doing; we all find this invaluable. Thus, I have a great deal of control of the planned part of the course.

What I am unable to do is to take account of the unplanned part of the course, the concerns of particular interns in particular schools at particular times of the year. An important aspect, therefore, of the planned programme is that it has built into it unplanned time when interns can raise issues of concern and share their ideas with the rest of the group.

The interns are given copies of the programme and materials so they know what is expected of them. It is becoming increasingly clear to me from recent research just how different each intern's personal agenda can be for the year and how different their experiences of school and mathematics teaching are from the ones we are asking them to try out for themselves. We are, in addition, asking them to become problem solvers, gathering information from a range of sources and, with the help of a range of criteria, to work out their own theories on various issues. This in itself is a difficult transition for them to make. An interesting and unanticipated extra problem arose at the beginning of the second year of the scheme when many mentors compared the new interns unfavourably with the ones who had just left, yet I was not aware of any significant difference between the two groups of interns. It made me realise just how much progress interns actually make throughout the year. In the scheme, therefore, the interns really do have to learn to take responsibility for their own learning and to take initiatives in the university and in the school.

Mentors have responsibility for the implementation of the scheme in their school and in their department. This requires a great deal of time and effort; the framework previously agreed in the university provides a starting point and sets of issues to focus on throughout the year. What each mentor has to do on their own is not only translate that into a reality given their particular school and its accompanying set of constraints but also take advantage of all the other opportunities their particular school can offer the interns - planned or unplanned.

Mentors obviously have other responsibilities in the school. In the first year of the scheme, one mathematics mentor was also deputy head, others were heads of department and about half were main professional grade teachers. Each brings its own problems: those with other responsibilities had problems balancing all the demands being made on them and, in terms of being mentor, some found it difficult to make regular time commitments to talk to the interns. Main professional grade teachers sometimes found it difficult to negotiate timetables for the interns and take initiatives on the interns' behalf. Mentors with only part-time teaching commitment in mathematics had the added problem of finding appropriate times when they could work with interns in their lessons.

Yet despite there being such a range of individuals, each with their own personalities and responsibilities and each in their own schools, and given that they operated in such different ways, there was not a problem. This was a reality of the scheme which could be recognised and accepted and I think one which suggests that the scheme could be successful elsewhere.

Mentor and tutor have joint responsibility for assessment of the interns although, once again, we recognise that one may be better placed than the other to assess aspects of the interns' work. Thus, the mentor is more likely to have detailed knowledge of the interns' classroom competence, with the tutor acting in a moderating role across schools, and the tutor is in a better position to assess and moderate written work done by interns, although mentors have access to that written work when (and more importantly if) they have time.

A responsibility which mentors have, and which has proved problematic, is that of devising an appropriate timetable for the interns working with them. This means, amongst other things, identifying colleagues to work with the interns. Two comments made by mentors at the end of the first year of the scheme give some indication of the problem: *"Choose the teachers that the interns go to with extreme care. It is not enough to be willing, it is important to participate in the spirit of the scheme"* and *"prepare the ground in the department first so that the majority of the people are supportive...the philosophy of the new scheme should be made clear rather than it just happening by chance".* That other teachers thought the scheme was a substitution method of initial training meant that many interns received less support than either I or the mentors wanted. Interestingly, mentors also tended to continue collaborative teaching through the year with interns and allowed interns to 'take over' other teachers' classes later in the year. This not only meant that mentors rarely created time for themselves but, also that some interns were not often observed because those other teachers tended to leave them to it. Indeed, a few interns suggested that I, as tutor, had observed them more than anyone else.

Since then, as well as alerting all mentors to this danger, I have also offered to join in departmental meetings to help explain ideas to other teachers.

4. Opportunities Offered by Internship

The Internship scheme seems to me to point the way forward for teacher education because it allows interns to explore systematically issues of concern in teaching and to work out their own realistic theories on those issues. The issues are not wholly practical or wholly theoretical but combine the two in such a way that each informs the other. In addition, in the second phase of the year, interns are able to develop their own conception of teaching and determine not only the extent to which they satisfy their own goals but also strategies which they can use to move even closer to that conception. The process of self-evaluation is helped as interns engage in partnership supervision either with another intern, their mentor or another teacher, or their tutor.

Thus, in mathematics, interns have had the opportunity to grow not just towards basic competence in the classroom but beyond this to become critical, reflective, self-aware teachers. The fact that several of them in the first year of the scheme chose to produce 50 A4 sheets of closely argued analysis concerned with the underachievement of girls in mathematics because, as one said, the assignment *"provided me with the opportunity to collect my ideas together"*; that even though they worked extremely hard they did not want the number of assignments reduced; that many talked of re-reading assignments before job interviews and that I received a letter months later from an intern who said she had been re-reading her self-evaluation assignment, all suggest to me that something very worthwhile and exciting has happened. I am also conscious that heads interviewing interns for jobs realised very early on that interns had an awareness, a competence and a confidence which other students simply had not yet managed to acquire.

It is obviously right to put interns at the top of any list when itemising opportunities offered by Internship but there are others also involved in the scheme who have benefited from it. As mathematics tutor I now know what my role is in initial teacher education and it is a role which is consistent with my wider role in the university. Now I do not have to take on the role of experienced practitioner, I do not have to set assignments in the first term on lesson planning knowing that the lesson may not take place, I do not have to discuss pupil motivation when students have spent only days in school. I now welcome the fact that I can discuss a range of styles of teaching with a group of interns knowing that they can try those styles out for themselves - maybe even the next day - discuss their experiences with their mentor and ask the mentor for their opinions, watch teachers using (or not using) a range of styles and learning from their experience. And perhaps, best of all, I do not have to give them tips or suggest there are correct ways of doing things. As active, intelligent learners, they are working these things out for themselves.

On a personal level, I feel that now I understand my own role better, I can more easily be honest about what I do not know and can learn from others. The simple fact is that teacher educators are not teachers. Teaching a full timetable week after week and year after year can only really be understood by those doing just that. I am well aware that taking a step away from that either within the school hierarchy or to departments of education not only removes credibility but also results in educators misremembering and reinterpreting classroom teaching. I have a great deal to learn from these teachers and there is no doubt in my mind that they are the expert practitioners when I am with them in classrooms. But they, in turn, now recognise my contribution, which is not the same as theirs but which is, nevertheless, important and valued. Working together in partnership has increased our mutual respect for each other.

However, teachers say more than this about Internship and their own development. What it has allowed them to do, amongst other things, is to put classroom studies high on the agenda. This might seem a remarkable, possibly unbelievable, claim in a school where one might have expected it to be there anyway but all those concerned with education recognise the truth in the statement. By discussing issues with interns, mentors have been able to talk about things which are important to them, have become aware of their own knowledge. In addition, many have changed their own classroom practice. One mentor said she was rethinking her own classroom approaches, introducing more investigative work in her lessons, as a result of discussions she has had with the interns. Another felt more confident working in the computer room with pupils...and so it goes on. The INSET potential for teachers and tutors is tremendous.

5. Problems Raised by Internship
The single biggest problem so far appears to be due to a shortage of time. In the first two years of the scheme mentors were allowed roughly one lesson each week for implementing their role. The fact is that very many mentors have spent much longer than this discussing ideas with interns or arranging teaching programmes for them but this cannot be acceptable.

Interns are also short of time. We ask them to work extremely hard throughout the year both at OUDES and in school not just in their teaching and seminars but in addition we ask them to read, reflect and write throughout the year. The pressures of a highly structured programme based in two quite separate institutions for many weeks of the year cannot be underestimated.

As a tutor I also feel under pressure because as well as spending far more time in schools working alongside interns and mentors, I also have other commitments as well as on the PGCE course. Administering, organising and steering such a venture whilst working in partnership can appear daunting at times.

In terms of the mathematics component of the scheme, there are a number of problems which remain unresolved and which I pose as questions.

(i) How can I persuade mentors and interns to be more honest with each other? A lack of consensus should be explored rather than ignored; at the same time, honesty can be threatening for both teachers and interns.

(ii) How do I persuade interns to use a range of criteria to help them formulate their own theories on each set of issues? At the moment many interns are happy to theorise without taking account of reality; unless they can do this their theories will fail to sustain them through even their early years of teaching.

(iii) How do we involve other teachers in the scheme? Indeed, how do we help them to understand the principles of the scheme?

(iv) How do I persuade each new set of mentors that the scheme is partly theirs; that we are working in partnership; that they own it and can modify it?

C. The Mentors' Perspective - the Combined Experience of English and Maths

1. Developing a Curriculum Programme Jointly
From the very beginning the curriculum programme was developed in an interactive fashion. Thus, for example, as the maths group widened and eventually became the group of mentors so the modules came under greater scrutiny for their relevance to the classroom and the feasibility of running them in the schools. This was an interesting time - we brainstormed what should be in a module on Classroom Management: this produced very different ideas and approaches, for we come from differing backgrounds. The module was then constructed by the curriculum tutor and discussed yet again. At every stage we had the chance to comment, change, revise. The interesting thing was to achieve a balance, a consensus as to what we, in our very different ways, could work with. This in itself was a process of learning - about the members of the group, and from each other. We felt involved, we knew what was going on, we had some power. With that power came the responsibility to ensure that we were happy with what was decided.

In order to understand the context of the curriculum studies we needed to learn something about the General Programme; this gave us an overview rarely held before on a PGCE course. Now at last we had some idea of what our students were doing whilst they were not with us and we could see that what we were doing was an intrinsic part of the whole.

2. The Relationship between Curriculum Tutor and Mentor
The basis of this relationship is a tricky one for it is fundamentally an unequal one. One half of the partnership is paid to do the work involved

in setting up and running the scheme. The university tutors consequently do a larger share of the work and bear the greater responsibility. The mentors are not paid for their involvement and for them it is a very small job; indeed it is not even defined as part of their job. The mentors therefore do the job through interest and a belief and commitment to the ideals of the scheme. It is a tribute to the scheme and those involved that this relationship appears to be so equal.

In the process of achieving this feeling of equality in the relationship a danger is that either side might be seen to be telling the other how to do their job. A careful balance therefore has to be maintained - curriculum tutors must not appear to be imposing their views on mentors, nor to be asking too much of mentors in terms of preparation for meetings or writing the curriculum programme. The relationship relies heavily on goodwill and the belief of the mentor that the scheme is worth working for.

The curriculum tutor has to get to know the departments that s/he is working with. It is important that this is done not just through the eyes of the interns. The fact that curriculum tutors are regular visitors to the school means that they become familiar with school policy and practice. This also means that the support they are able to offer to interns is effective, and that they are able to relate theoretical discussion in seminar groups to interns' practical experience in schools.

The curriculum tutors provide mentors with detailed information about the work undertaken at OUDES; this means that mentors can cover discussion of particular issues at the same time as they are being investigated at OUDES. Theoretical knowledge is therefore examined in a meaningful context, and interns have the opportunity to test suggested approaches in the classroom, and to discuss their discoveries afterwards with an experienced teacher.

The curriculum tutor's visit to schools helps to reinforce this important link between theory and practice, particularly if s/he is able to take part in the discussion that follows interns' involvement in a particular lesson. Interns find that post-lesson discussion is an extremely valuable activity, and learn a great deal from it, whether they are discussing their own involvement in the lesson, or what they have observed in activities led by the teacher. After the lesson, both teacher and interns have questions that they want to ask, or points to raise. If a curriculum tutor is present at such a discussion, s/he is able to relate what is discussed to questions and issues which have already been raised in seminar groups.

3. Divisions of Responsibility for Interns' Learning

It is a principle of the Internship scheme that the curriculum tutor and the mentor have *"a* distinctive *and* equal *contribution to make"* to the professional development of interns: *"the curriculum tutor from a base in the university and the mentor from a base in school"*.

It is the curriculum tutor's responsibility to provide interns with a much wider field of reference than that of one particular school. Curriculum sessions provide a theoretical framework for, and way of thinking about, the teaching of a particular subject. The curriculum tutor has a breadth of local practice, as s/he is responsible for pairs of interns in several schools. In leading sessions at OUDES s/he is therefore able to refer to the policy and practice of several departments. The fact that the curriculum tutor is a regular visitor to schools means that s/he is also able to refer to the work that individual interns are involved in. Particular successes can be shared with the rest of the group, so boosting the intern's confidence and enabling members of the curriculum group to learn from each other's experience.

The mentor's responsibility is to enable the interns to learn from their experience within the context of the one school. Discussion and analysis is focused on particular activities that interns have been involved in, or the individual approach of the teachers within the department. If the relationship between mentor and curriculum tutor is effective, then clear links can be established between work undertaken in curriculum group sessions and interns' experiences in school.

Mentors are fully responsible for organising interns' time within school, ensuring that they observe a range of activities and age groups. They are responsible for deciding when and how interns become more actively involved in lessons, through working with individual pupils, monitoring small group work, or teaching part or the whole of a lesson. The mentor works closely alongside interns in the classroom, and can therefore draw their attention to management techniques, disciplinary procedures and practical, organisational details which they can learn from. The curriculum tutor can help interns to learn from teachers' craft knowledge by providing them with detailed observation schedules, outlining what to look for, and what questions to ask of themselves and of the teacher, in order to benefit most from watching an experienced practitioner at work in the classroom.

4. The Problems Raised by the Internship Scheme

Time is at a premium during the school day and mentors and classroom teachers often do not have enough time to work with interns effectively. Mentors need time to discuss curriculum issues with interns, debrief observation activities or lessons taught, or to plan ahead for the coming week. They also need time to liaise with other members of staff in the department in order to discuss progress and to negotiate interns' timetables each week. Time must also be made available to see the curriculum tutor, the professional tutor and any colleague in school who has a particular problem or success to report. Sometimes it is not merely a matter of shortage of time, but shortage of time at the appropriate moment. Interns, too, often find it difficult to see a member of staff when they need to, as the teacher is not free when the intern has time to talk.

The mentor who is also a head of department faces a particular problem. When the interns are in school two days a week the mentor wants to devote full attention to them, which goes against the role of caring for a department. At its extreme, the mentor can be cut off from the rest of the department for two days a week.

In some schools, especially with the new pressures of GCSE, it can on occasions be difficult to accommodate two extra people. Some teachers are reluctant to give up their classes or to do the extra work of supervising.

Add to this new staff, changes of staff, and probationers, and the organisational problems become quite complex.

5. Opportunities Offered by the Internship Scheme

The first period of 'J' weeks - roughly the first third of the year during which the interns are in school for two days a week - allows interns to become gradually familiar with the school's policy and practice, and the opportunity to form relationships with classes before starting to teach them, so that pupils readily accept them as their class teacher as they move on to take full responsibility for classes during 'S' weeks - the second stage of the year when interns are in school full-time. Mentors work with interns in the classroom and gradually hand over more and more responsibility to them. Pupils hardly notice that their regular classroom teacher is no longer taking the lead; they accept the team teaching situation easily, and once interns begin to take full responsibility for the group, the occasional presence of the teacher in the room is not seen as something unusual. The nature of the course is such that interns have the time and the opportunity to think about teaching techniques *before* becoming responsible for groups.

The opportunities for learning support provided by interns are numerous. They can work with individual pupils and provide the extra attention that they need, and which the teacher is too busy to give. This may be going over a piece of writing that the pupil has produced and helping him or her to learn from their mistakes; it could be helping a pupil to select suitable reading books, and reading some of the book with them; some pupils need guidance with assignments that they have missed due to absence; others need advice when drafting and redrafting a piece of writing.

When interns take full responsibility for a teaching group, including the preparation of materials, planning lessons and marking written work, then the teacher has more time to spend on other administrative tasks. In some circumstances, this extra time may be used to work with other teachers either in the classroom or in the planning of new resources and developments. In this way, the Internship scheme may contribute to INSET in schools.

Anyone involved in appointing a probationer last summer was quickly convinced that the Internship scheme is the best PGCE course around. It prepares the interns best for schools, not just in the variety of ways of dealing with pupils both in and out of the classroom but chiefly by having addressed the relevant issues. The course allows them to gain far more of a whole-school perspective whilst at the same time becoming more part of the department they are working with. For us, as mentors, there is the challenge to defend our own views, to reflect on where we are now, to consider alternatives, to read the modules and (on the rare occasions when there is enough time) to return to the literature of education.

When we began writing this chapter, we were slightly nervous about whether we all had the same things to say! University and school perspectives might have made a sharp contrast and the cultures associated with English teachers and mathematics teachers might have meant that the ways in which the ideas were developed were along divergent routes. What we hope we have demonstrated (and we have succeeded in persuading ourselves) is that the theoretical underpinning has been such that it has allowed practical implementation of the scheme both in a number of schools and in two quite different disciplines in OUDES.

References

1. Brooks, Caroline St John - 'English A Curriculum for Personal Development?' in Hammersley, M and Hargreaves, A, *Curriculum Practice: Some Sociological Case Studies* (Falmer Press, 1983)..
2. D.E.S./Welsh Office - *English for Ages 5-11* (1988).
3. D.E.S./Welsh Office - *English for Ages 5-16* (1989).

Chapter VI

Being a Teacher: Whole-School Aspects of the Internship Scheme

Brian Woolnough with David Pell and Barbara Wynn

This chapter, written by a general tutor from OUDES and his professional tutor partner in school with the close co-operation of a second professional tutor from another of the Internship schools, relates how the 'whole-school' aspects of the Internship scheme - the rhetoric of the theory and the centralised planning - worked out in practice in a typical school. Inevitably and unsurprisingly the constraints of each particular school modified the original plans. Thus, although what follows does not describe exactly what happened in all of the schools, it is highly representative of the pattern of activity in them over the year.

1. Introducing Internship to Park Hill School

As was the case in all the schools involved, the Internship scheme at Park Hill School started well before the beginning of the academic year in September. Not unusually, there was already a considerable history of the school and OUDES working together. The general tutor, himself a scientist responsible for the curriculum work of the PGCE physicists, knew the science department of the school well through having had students at the school in the past and having worked with staff on post-experience courses. The school's professional tutor, an English teacher who continued to teach his subject as well as take responsibility for the students in the school, knew OUDES well through having worked with the English tutors and their students and having been seconded to work on a higher degree. Such a familiarity had many advantages but it also meant that many of the staff involved began the scheme with preconceived ideas rooted in the old tradition of teacher education.

Park Hill School is a large, split-site school which provides a comprehensive education for all secondary school pupils in the area. It is situated in an old market town of about 15,000 inhabitants serving both an agricultural community and large scientific establishments. At the time Internship was introduced, the school, with roots in a long established voluntary aided grammar school and two secondary modern schools, was in the throes of another internal reorganisation brought about by continuing falling rolls. One might be forgiven for thinking that the situation was traumatic enough for the school without the addition of 12 interns for most of the year and a commitment to Internship. Though some of the teachers not immediately involved had some understandable reservations about introducing the scheme at this time, in the event such apprehensions proved unjustified. The six pairs of interns, one pair each in geography, maths, physics and modern languages and two pairs in English, were welcomed into the school and proved a benefit to the school as well as benefiting enormously from it themselves.

The school was introduced to the scheme through a variety of means. The professional tutor had been involved fully with the development of the scheme, as a member of the Internship Development Group, and the mentors had been involved in planning the curriculum aspects of the work with the curriculum tutors at OUDES throughout the preceding year. The Development Group had produced full written documentation for the scheme and this was available for those most concerned. The general tutor and the professional tutor, who had both worked as part of the Development Group, met twice in the summer term specifically to plan the school-based activities at Park Hill. It was also arranged that the general tutor should spend two days at the beginning of the next term at Park Hill, sharing with the staff in their preparation for the term and shadowing a new pupil around for a day to get a 'feel for' the school from the pupil's perspective. The general tutor and the professional tutor were invited to speak to the whole of the staff in the summer term, and had explained the scheme and responded to their questions. Although much documentation had been circulated to schools earlier in the year, many of the staff not immediately involved with the scheme would not be familiar with it and their knowledge of Internship would be largely informal. Achieving a wider shared understanding of the scheme was important. Those most closely involved with launching the scheme in the school had attended a residential weekend conference organised by OUDES at the end of the summer term. This conference helped to clarify perceptions, to agree course content and individual responsibilities and to boost the sense of shared ownership and commitment by mentors, professional and general tutors, heads and the LEA. Commitment at the end of the summer term was strong. All was prepared: only the arrival of the first interns remained. There was a shared belief that the Internship scheme, whatever problems might emerge, was significantly better than previous patterns of preparing student-teachers, and everyone concerned was eager to see how it would work in reality.

2. Induction of Interns to Park Hill

The interns arrived at Oxford in September after three weeks' structured observation in both primary and secondary schools in their home area. Their next two weeks were based in the department, being introduced to the curriculum work through their curriculum tutors who had been responsible for their admission to the course, and to the whole school general programme with their general tutor. One of their first tasks was to debrief their experiences from their preliminary school observations and from their own schooling and this was done at OUDES by the general tutor and the school's professional tutor. This seminar enabled interns not only to share their insights about their experiences in schools, but also to become confident with the other Park Hill interns who were to be the group with whom they would explore whole-school issues, throughout the year. On two other occasions during this period at OUDES the interns met their professional tutor: at a welcoming party on their first evening, and at a seminar in which he talked to them about Park Hill.

In the second week the interns and their general tutor visited their school. The half-hour coach journey on the subsequent school days did much to bind the group together through providing an opportunity for informal discussion without tutors' involvement.

During this first induction day the interns were welcomed by the principal who spoke of his hopes for the school. They received a brief introduction to the curriculum of the school from a deputy head, met their mentors who introduced them to their departments and spent some time attached to a pupil for a part of the day. They were also given a brief tour and introduction to the catchment area of the school, and shown the widely different home environments of the pupils. The school underlined its welcome to the interns by providing a buffet lunch for them, their mentors and other senior members of staff. It was a gesture which was much appreciated and did much to establish the scheme in the corporate identity of the school. A brief plenary at the end of the day with the professional tutor and the general tutor enabled any queries that had arisen to be clarified.

The importance of the general tutor and the professional tutor working together both at OUDES and in the school, and being perceived from the outset by the interns as doing so, cannot be overstated for this conveys the underlying message of shared partnership and of joint responsibility for the course.

3. The General Programme

The general programme is concerned with issues which are not peculiar to one curriculum area and which impinge on schools as a whole. It addresses the characteristics of the learners served by the schools, the organisational structures which the schools adopt to enable them to carry out their functions, and their relationship to the society in which they operate. The content and organisation of the curriculum, aspects of its delivery in the classroom, and the professional, political and social factors which shape it are therefore at the heart of the general programme. The individual Internship school is thus, in some measure, a microcosm of the larger system. It provides a single, in-depth case-study and the various interlocking, and complementary, elements of the general programme were designed to allow the interns to focus on a number of different themes and to relate them to their own experience. School-based activities not only enabled the ideas introduced at OUDES to be grounded in the reality of schooling but also themselves generated ideas to be discussed and developed in seminars at OUDES. While the university-based elements of the course sought to give a theoretical rationale to the various themes, and the school-based activities provided a teacher-focused perspective, the co-ordination of the activities through joint planning and involvement avoided a simplistic distinction between theory and practice. It was sometimes possible for the professional tutor to attend the department-based seminars led by the general tutor. It was usual for the general tutor to be part of the school-based seminars, which the professional tutor led. The school-based seminars were held at the end of afternoon school on Wednesdays each week after two days of school-based activity. A small but important touch was that the school kitchens provided refreshment for these sessions. Such things may appear trivial but, like the welcoming party for interns, mentors and professional and general tutors at OUDES or the buffet lunch provided by the school when the interns first appeared, they are important in creating a positive atmosphere.

Themes in the general programme were normally introduced by a plenary session at OUDES. Appropriate material for background reading and follow-up activities was provided. Typically, such activities would be linked to a seminar at the school in which the appropriate member of staff would join the group to talk about the school's approach to an issue or about policy. Interns would carry out investigations related to the way aspects of this theme were being implemented at the school and later report back their findings to the rest of the group. Some of these investigations were extended later to form the basis of the final term's dissertation. In this way the interns, and also the tutors and the school, would build up a comprehensive understanding of the theme under consideration, with theory and practice being constantly related to a real situation. By this means the investigation and the seminar became a joint learning experience for all involved.

The central themes for the seminars in the early part of the year were the school's curriculum, the PSE (Personal Social Education) programme, IT (Information Technology) in the school, special needs provision at Park Hill, the role of the form tutor, school record keeping, school-industry links etc. In all, about ten other teachers contributed to this part of the Internship programme, teachers with real expertise who were willing to share openly with the interns not only their practice but also their plans and remaining problems. The level of maturity of discussion with, and between, the interns grew quite remarkably and they were quickly able to grasp the situation in 'their' school. There was never a sense of negative criticism by the interns of the school's practice though often an awareness and discussion of the weaknesses as well as the strengths. This was due both to the openness of the teachers, who shared the objectives of the Internship scheme and to the feeling - which the interns gained very quickly - of 'belonging' to the school. Thus any problems at Park Hill became 'their' problem too. The value of the advice that interns had been given in the opening two weeks of the course on learning from the craft knowledge of teachers was already evident.

As the year progressed the school seminar programme became more orientated towards the interns' agenda, with the majority of the sessions being devoted to debriefing the interns' own investigations and updating developments in the school curriculum and inservice programme. In the summer term the interns were able to spend some time working with a group of teachers who were reviewing and analysing the curriculum experience of the pupils in the lower school. A pupil analysis schedule was devised - an ideal opportunity for university and school to collaborate on a research project - and used by the interns across the school. Interns were thus able to help provide a systematic report on the variety of activities in which pupils were engaged in different subjects throughout the school. This material formed an important database for subsequent curriculum development in the school.

Interns also became fully involved with the life of the school in many other ways: helping with the planning and leading of school fieldwork and visits, accompanying trips abroad, taking part in the production of school plays and careers' days, developing resources for special needs provision, helping with games and sports, being involved with parents evenings and report writing, and helping with GCSE coursework assessment. To some extent such activities have always been part of a PGCE student's work, but under the Internship scheme the interns had become so much a part of the school staff that their contributions could be more significant.

One of the interns' formal assignments was to produce a dissertation on an aspect of educational practice or principle. For this project the interns were able to research aspects of the general programme as related to Park Hill School. The work produced here was of real interest and value for the school, who welcomed such critical, but sympathetic, analysis of their performance. Areas investigated included a study of, and recommendations for, a language policy across the school; an analysis of the strengths and weaknesses of the modular curriculum; case studies of emotionally disturbed pupils; a quantitative analysis of pupil performance as a function of their social background; and an in-depth study of the 'bottom set syndrome' and how the pupils in the underachieving bottom set had got there, and why. The school retains copies of these dissertations for its own use, as deemed appropriate by the professional tutor. Clearly such work may be of considerable benefit to the school and it is of unquestionable value to the intern in offering an opportunity to research and write under careful supervision and for a real purpose.

Perhaps the flavour of this whole-school work can best be captured by considering two particular themes; language and curriculum/special needs. The language theme was introduced in a plenary presentation by the English tutor at OUDES in which he gave the background to language as a tool for communication and also for learning. He was able to introduce the interns to the important literature and research in the field, and highlight the key issues. This presentation was followed up in OUDES by the special needs tutor, who was able to make the interns aware of the particular problems that language presents to some pupils with special learning difficulties and indicated the range of resources and strategies available. The curriculum tutors followed up the theme in their own areas, with examples of pupils' written work in their subject, research evidence available concerning their language difficulties in the spoken and written word, and the importance of active use of language for the pupils to write, or talk, themselves into understanding. The Background Paper provided for the language theme included suggestions for investigating pupils' writing in school and, in a seminar towards the end of the first term, the interns reported back in pairs to the group about aspects of written language in their own subject. It was a most impressive session, almost entirely directed by the interns themselves who confidently shared examples of the range of writing being produced in different subjects, provided a rationale, and offered perceptive criticism. The tutors' various inputs on the topic and the interns' own reading were integrated in the context of a real situation at an appropriate time with striking success. These insights sharpened the practice of the interns in their own subsequent teaching and observing, and informed their consideration of related concerns such as classroom talk, marking and recording.

The interns were introduced to the curriculum theme in the first plenary session of the year when the head of one of the more progressive Internship schools spoke to the interns about the rationale behind the changes being made to the pattern of curriculum in his school. It was a lively presentation, but in hindsight he would have been more helpful at a later stage in the course when the interns would have appreciated more what the problems were. A university-based seminar earlier in the term involving a simulation of a heads of department meeting more usefully highlighted the problems. Here, the interns each took the role of a head of department and decided how many periods from a 40 period week were required for their subject at the 1st and 4th form level, and whether their subject should be setted or mixed ability. They then found that when all the requests were brought together there were insufficient periods in the week to cater for them all. The subsequent discussion and horsetrading between the different subjects made the interns think much harder about what subjects should be taught, and why, whether all pupils should have the same curriculum or have options, what the balance should be between academic, recreational and vocational subjects, and whether a modular curriculum might solve some problems and cause others.

This simulation did not solve the problem but made the interns more sensitive to the issues. The professional tutor, and the deputy head introduced the interns to the curriculum pattern at Park Hill School on the induction day, and the mentors discussed with their interns the place of their own subject in the whole curriculum. (The curriculum tutors would have already set in train a continuing discussion within their subject of the philosophy of, and latest developments in, their curriculum area). At the beginning of the second term the professional tutor arranged a seminar on the option system at Park Hill School, and this was followed by school-based investigations to consider such factors as why the option system had been arranged as it was, how the pupils were counselled concerning their option choices, how the uptake of different subjects varied with sex, and how the pupils perceived their choices. There was a debriefing session concerning these investigations, in the school with the deputy head responsible for curriculum planning. A further open discussion with this deputy was arranged for the summer term, after sessions at OUDES introducing alternative curriculum patterns including a modular curriculum. The level of debate at the final school-based seminar reflected a deep appreciation of the relative advantages of different curriculum patterns, and the important constraints acting on any 'ideal system' in a real school. One of the interns considered the case for the modular curriculum in depth for her dissertation, and found that she had convinced herself of a view entirely opposite to the one she had held six months earlier.

4. Effects of the Internship Scheme at Park Hill

(i) Effects on the interns

One doubt about the Internship scheme was that interns would have detailed experience of only one school. To what extent might this limit their horizons and employment prospects? Some of the interns did express concern about this before the course started but it soon became clear that the advantages of a well planned and integrated course far outweighed the disadvantages. One of the aims of Internship was to enable interns to become involved with as many aspects of school life as possible throughout an academic year so that they would have a better understanding and more valid experience of what it means to be a teacher. Fragmented experiences in different schools could never have provided this most valuable aspect of professional development. The interns felt as if they 'belonged' to the school; partly because they had been made to feel so welcome and partly because they knew they would be working with the same staff and pupils for the whole year. They knew too that they had a valid contribution to make to the school and were not merely there as visitors or on sufferance.

As a result the level of professional commitment by interns to the schools was extremely high. Several of the interns took part in an overnight money-raising event when they had been in the school for only two weeks. One intern took over from the full-time teacher who was ill and unable to attend a parents' evening at the last minute. Fortunately they had been well-briefed about parents' evenings and she and the other interns who attended were well-received by the parents. Interns also became involved with a range of activities, a process which was assisted by the professional tutor who had found out about the wider interests of the interns and helped them to make links with PE, drama, music and other departments where their interest and talents were welcome.

The early sessions of the general programme at the school were conducted in a fairly traditional and formal manner with staff from the school providing information for the interns. Whilst we had no pressure to run these introductory sessions in any other way, the general and professional tutor soon decided that they wanted to vary the approach. We wanted the interns to experience some of the techniques which they were being encouraged to try in the classroom, so didactic methods gave way to investigations, discussions, active learning, self and peer evaluation. For example, interns were encouraged to think about the principles behind the Oxford Certificate of Educational Achievement by taking part themselves in activities to be undertaken by pupils including writing reports on their own progress and discussing the reports and how they felt about self-evaluation. The interns particularly appreciated this range of approaches and were able to apply some of the lessons learnt to their teaching.

One good example of the partnership between the school and university can be seen in the way that the investigations were conducted. The general tutor provided interns with some useful written guidelines and advice on the use of different research techniques. The interns then started their investigations and within a couple of weeks were asked to bring their preliminary findings and notes of any problems they had encountered to a session with the professional tutor. Each intern spoke about his or her work so far and the whole group contributed to discussions on ways of improving and developing the investigation. The level of discussion and the final investigations were most impressive showing a clear understanding of the links between theory and practice. In the past students have had few opportunities for such research and it has been the sole responsibility of the training institution to monitor and keep the studies.

It is too early to say whether the interns will use the techniques they have learnt in the schools where they teach or whether these small scale investigations will encourage interns to study for higher degrees but it is certainly true that the interns who are now teaching in Oxfordshire schools have an impressive awareness of wider issues and appear to be confident that they will be able to tackle some of them once they have survived their first year of teaching.

(ii) The effects on the school - organisation

Making Internship work well involves a great deal of hard work from everyone concerned. Good planning, co-operation, flexibility and good communications are essential. In order for the general programme to work well, certain basic matters need to be attended to. Firstly it is essential that the general tutor, the professional tutor, the mentors, the headteacher and as many of the staff as possible understand the principles of Internship and the differences between Internship and traditional teacher training.

The general tutor and the professional tutor need to allow time for planning and adapting the general programme. Many general and professional tutors contacted each other at home by telephone as well as holding regular meetings. It is possible to increase the effectiveness of the programme by paying attention to simple details such as ensuring that all the interns are available at the same time - and that mentors know when this will be before they plan their timetables for interns. A room, preferably the same one, needs to be available each week and interns need to have a written programme for each term.

Communications were dealt with in a number of ways. A key feature of the scheme is the close involvement of the general tutor, an induction programme was planned for him so that he would become more knowledgeable about the school and its staff. The general tutor was invited to and attended staff meetings, Inset days, and other school events. He followed a pupil round the school for a day, was introduced to everyone concerned with interns and attended meetings of mentors and tutors who were to be involved.

OUDES supplied the school with copies of all the briefing materials and background papers given to interns. These were made available to staff in the staff library. Regular mentors' meetings were held as well as occasional meetings to brief tutors, heads of year and the staff as a whole. Heads of department who were not mentors were sent copies of agendas and minutes. Some of the staff undoubtedly felt that they heard too much about Internship but everyone was certainly given every opportunity to be well-informed.

One area of communication for which we did not allow enough time was the briefing of teachers, other than the mentor, who were to have interns in their lessons. This briefing needs to be considerably more detailed than the general information given to staff so that the interns' time is well spent and they are given appropriate support.

(iii) The effects on the school - staff

Two-thirds of the staff of the school were actively involved with the interns by regularly working with them in lessons or tutor time; running talks and activities for the general programme or monitoring the effects on a year group or the school as a whole. The interns were highly committed to making a positive contribution as professional members of tutor teams and departments as well as working hard on their teaching commitments and this was greatly appreciated by the staff. Many of the staff found the contact with interns both enjoyable and professionally stimulating. The main difficulties related to the work of the mentors. The time commitment required of the mentors was extremely high, especially in the first two terms. This was particularly true for those who were having to give a great deal of help and advice to the two interns who were struggling. The mentors found the assessment procedures very stressful and the whole process has been revised. Two of the departments in fact decided to share the job of mentor between two people to reduce the pressure and involve more staff in the scheme. Despite the pressures in this first year it was clear that there were many possibilities for staff development provided by the Internship scheme. Staff who worked with interns or prepared activities and talks for them enjoyed opportunities for leadership and were pleased to be contributing to the professional development of new teachers. Finding and exploiting further ways of contributing to staff development provide a challenge for the future of Internship.

(iv) The effects on the school - pupils

One of the major concerns of the staff of the school was the possible effects of Internship on pupils. All of us had past horror stories to tell of classes running riot with students and ruining the examination chances of pupils but few had blamed these disasters on the schools and colleges for throwing students in at the deep-end without proper preparation and support. In response to such concerns, one member of staff was given a little free time to monitor the effects of the scheme on pupils, but even before the report was produced it was clear that any fears there may have been were largely unfounded. This was probably the most fundamental way in which it was realised how different Internship was from traditional courses.

Internship was given a high profile with the pupils from the outset and the professional tutor explained to all the pupils in assemblies about the scheme before the interns started to work in the school. Mentors made sure they introduced interns to their classes and worked alongside them in a range of activities so that pupils did not feel abandoned. Thus pupils had the advantage of two or three adults working with them and meeting their needs until such time as the interns were ready to work alone. The possibility of individualised learning became a reality and the additional time afforded to teachers to help individuals and groups in the class and to prepare materials was highly valued. In addition, interns helped provide continuity when their teacher colleagues were away from school on one or two occasions. It was felt that the help and support given to interns by their 'partner' lightened the load of the mentor.

From the research report it was seen that Internship had a very positive effect on the staff involved. They felt that their teaching had been improved by working with enthusiastic, energetic young colleagues. The pupils, for their part, quite enjoyed having younger teachers and few felt at any disadvantage. Pupils felt the lessons were similar to those taught by their normal teacher or more interesting and original - few were dull.

(v) Effects on the partnership

One of the best innovations of the Internship scheme for the schools and professional tutors was the creation of general tutors who had the time to build a proper relationship with the group of interns and the staff of the school. The joint planning of the general programme between the professional tutor and general tutor as well as the more limited joint planning of curriculum activities between curriculum tutors and mentors made the staff of the school feel that their contribution was really important and that they had something to offer new members of the profession which was likely to benefit schools as a whole as well as the individuals concerned. There is no doubt that it was very hard work for all concerned and it will be important to see if the level of commitment can be maintained. It should be easier for everyone concerned when all is not new and when some of the problems encountered first time round are resolved.

There is almost nobody who has been involved with Internship who would like to go back to the old system in spite of the work involved and this is perhaps the best recommendation there could be.

5. Relating 'Whole-School Activity' at Park Hill to the Theory of Internship

The goals of Internship as set out in Chapter II of this book were already familiar to the general tutor, mentors and professional tutor at Park Hill, for they had been promulgated in the Commissioning Paper which was produced to frame the work of the Development Group of seconded teachers. With small modifications, these goals and principles were agreed between the schools, OUDES and LEA and had been incorporated into *The Internship Handbook,* which was first published in the summer term before the Internship scheme began.

Foremost among these goals was the desire that interns should, on completion of their course, *"be able to cope effectively in the classroom"*. While the original intention was that this 'coping' should derive from the work done within a specific curriculum area, in practice many of the aspects of the 'whole-school activities' and general programme constantly reinforced the strategies which interns were acquiring within their subject disciplines, or widened their awareness of the possibilities of different methods which were effectively deployed in other subject areas. Group discussions in the general programme on issues such as gender, special needs, classroom management - to highlight but a few - generated ideas, both theoretical and practical, which interns could incorporate within their own teaching styles.

Secondly, analysis of trends within the school curriculum at local and national levels, helped to develop the interns' awareness of other school subjects, thereby attaining another goal of the Internship scheme. Practical simulation exercises were a part of the group work within the general programme, and these sessions featured subject pairs of interns vying with other pairs over the formulation of a workable curriculum model, thereby helping such interns to see the relative merits and demands of other subject areas, and to understand in part the constraints that lie within the planning of any school's curriculum. The general programme in this form took the interns outside their subject boxes and enabled them to have a wider perspective on issues ranging from pupils' choice of subjects to the design of the school timetable. Inevitably such analysis had to be relatively superficial, but it did allow key issues to be raised and to be tested against the interns' own personal background in education, and their widening awareness of education from the teacher's viewpoint. Increasingly, interns were able to weigh the evidence offered from a variety of different sources, and to interpret such data in a way that matched their current state of understanding. Often such issues as the curriculum would be revisited during the general programme so that interns would have the opportunity to revise their views in the light of the progress they had made during the year.

Reading through some of the investigations which the interns carried out at Park Hill, it is apparent that the Internship goal that required interns to *"appreciate the potentialities and the problems of achieving social justice in their own teaching"* was being addressed in a thoughtful and practical manner. Some interns focused upon the school's system for supporting less able pupils, or, in one case, the support given to 'travellers' where the study involved interviews with staff and peripatetic specialists to determine the culture and special needs of such pupils. Some interns prepared case studies of individual pupils to evaluate the kinds of needs which such individuals had, and the ways in which the school was able to meet them. Therefore, such issues of social class, gender and ethnic culture were taken up from the necessarily limited space given to them in the very full general programme, and were dealt with in a sensitive and extensive way by particular interns in a school which, by its nature, did not see such topics as matters of high priority.

A fourth goal of Internship dealt with the need for interns to learn to *"cope effectively with aspects of being a teacher which extend beyond the bounds of their own subject area(s)"*. The role of the form tutor, and PSE in general, were vital parts of the general programme across the whole year. Interns were attached to form groups, took an active part in the school's PSE programme, and explored the wider issues of 'tutoring' in a sequence of sessions which were based at the school, and involved the participation of a cross-section of tutors from the school with different experience and commitment to PSE. Once again a variety of views emerged from these experiences, which the interns, from their comments in interviews with the professional tutor, and their writing in dissertations and smaller investigations, seemed to assimilate and interpret in the light of their own experience. Thus, different goals of Internship were being met and were soon to be mutually supportive of one another. Theory and practice were merging.

This merging of theory and practice in the experience of interns was described in the goals of Internship as the interns' need to *"see schooling in relation to educational ideas, and to see the contrast between the practicalities of schooling, and such theoretical notions"*. The whole nature of the general programme reinforced this goal, in that interns were constantly being presented with aspects of theory, whether it came from the general tutor, visiting lecturers at OUDES, or school experts on a variety of subjects. In conjunction with this theory was the interns' observation of and participation in the complex life of one school across the whole of one year. From the interns' comments writings and actual experiences it was evident that they were aware of the tensions between theory and practice, and were receptive to the needs to resolve these tensions by means of compromise within the school system, and within their approach to their own teaching.

Very popular items on the general programme among interns were the discussions of school record keeping and pupils' special needs. Both of these topics related strongly to the Internship goal of making interns aware of *"pupil characteristics and the differences among pupils"*. The interns' extensive involvement with pupils in the school across the whole year made their understanding of issues related to these two areas much more incisive and pertinent. Again, the general programme could reinforce the treatment given to these topics in curriculum areas, and offer a forum for comparison and analysis across subject divides.

Problems and inconsistencies which were apparent in the previous PGCE course helped to define the goals of Internship. If, as has been suggested above, the whole-school activity and general programme helped to bring to life many of those goals, the same programme was also instrumental in eradicating many of the problem areas of the old system. By doing this, Internship offered new strengths and opportunities to all participants, and it is some of these that we wish to outline now.

Firstly, the general programme, in the regularity of its meetings, and the coherent pattern of its events, helped to bond the different subject pairings of interns, and from the start of the year a unique sense of identity and shared purpose arose within the twelve interns attached to the school. They identified with the one school, they supported each other in times of crisis, and celebrated each other's triumphs in ways which were independent of subject loyalties. Sharing this bonding were the general tutor and professional tutor, and thus the essence of partnership was exhibited in the meetings of the whole-school group of interns. At the heart of the scheme, as it seemed to us, lay the effectiveness of working relationships, and nowhere was this better demonstrated than in the purposefulness and conviviality of those weekly meetings. However, when problems arose with an intern, the close rapport between professional tutor and general tutor together with the group's sense of identity helped to direct support towards the intern involved in crisis. A system which before had largely relied upon long range contacts between OUDES and school, or the effective working of bureaucratic exchanges was now transformed into close working relationships, with regular points of contact, clear channels of communication and shared understanding of the goals of the course.

The general programme, its contents and concerns, also featured on the agenda of the regular mentors' meetings with the professional tutor and general tutor. Thus what could have easily been a divide separating curriculum issues from whole-school topics never occurred.

A variety of speakers and 'experts' from the school staff participated in the general programme sessions, and these staff were invariably not directly involved as mentors or departmental staff in Internship, so that wider elements of the school contributed and gained from the Internship scheme. Add to this number those staff who as form tutors had interns working with them throughout the year, and who were selected primarily because they had no direct involvement with Internship, and it is clear how extensively Internship, in one form or another, affected the whole school.

On some occasions the professional tutor was able, through the one day secondment scheme, to visit OUDES and participate in the whole-school discussions, and so break down even more the sense among participants of two distinct locations which could be invidiously associated with theory (OUDES) and practice (school). Moreover, the frequent presence of the general tutor around the school, and at school-based in-service sessions, helped to make the notion of partnership a credible reality in the eyes of school staff.

For the interns, the general programme offered a structure, sometimes overwhelming but usually constructive, for the analysis of a variety of issues which might receive uneven treatment in isolated curriculum areas. Gender, social class, the politics of education and so on, were topics which were given different or no emphasis at all in some subject areas, but which were very productive in stimulating awareness and often heated debate within the whole-school group.

Moreover, the general programme was flexible enough to allow scope for debating issues which were outside the planned structure of the 'whole-school' programme. There was space to focus on items which were special to Park Hill, such as the modular curriculum, or space to include open sessions where interns' concerns of the moment, on any topic, could be aired. Other items such as the discussion of interview techniques or meeting with probationers were much appreciated by interns, and obviously met needs which had not been envisaged in the original design of the programme.

From the whole-school point of view, the work which the interns did within the general programme offered valuable opportunities for curriculum review, for highlighting issues like gender and multi-cultural concerns which are usually submerged or not seen as priorities in the school, or simply providing school staff and senior management with vital data which could be used to evaluate aspects of the school system. After all, the interns at the end of the year were not merely casual visitors to the school, appearing for 'teaching practice' and then vanishing. The interns were very aware of the school system, the network of communications, problem areas within the school, and through being closely attached to the school, they could evaluate aspects of the school without posing a threat to established 'empires', and they had at their disposal the valuable commodity of 'time' which staff committed to a full timetable could not spare for such evaluative exercises. In addition the interns were energetic, were broadly accepted by staff and pupils, and were closely supportive, but not uncritical, of the school system.

These were just a few of the strengths and opportunities of Internship as exemplified through the 'whole-school activities' and general programme, which were apparent in the first year of operation at Park Hill School. Inevitably, with any new scheme, there were problems too. It should be noted, however, that these observations were written in the light of the first year of the scheme's operation and that the problems outlined have been addressed in the second and the subsequent years.

The initial design of the general programme was too ambitious, and involved the interns being overloaded with topics and having too little time for reading and reflection. Accordingly the interns were confused by switching rapidly from one topic to another, or felt, justifiably, that issues were dealt with in too shallow and superficial a manner. Individuals sometimes felt they had insufficient opportunity to report back to the full group with the general tutor and professional tutor and to gain adequate feedback for the efforts they had expended. Moreover, in its first year, the general programme did not always match the timing of its topics to the actual stages of development or awareness of the interns. The analysis of the curriculum, for example, appeared very early before the interns had the necessary vocabulary of technical terms to make much sense of its complexity. An extensive introduction to the school's PSE system was programmed before the interns had experienced directly any involvement with tutor groups. This was especially significant since most of the interns came from schools which had no PSE programme as such.

The assignments which were set towards the end of the first term also caused difficulty. The interns felt insecure and confused because the requirements for assignments were insufficiently clear and their completion dates overlapped with the dates for completion of curriculum tasks. A bunching effect was the result, causing stress to the interns.

Apart from problems linked to the interns' experience of the course, there were other difficulties which arose in connection with certain staff within the school. Whereas mentors had received some kind of training in their role and were readily in contact with curriculum tutors and the professional tutor, those staff with whom interns were placed to learn about PSE and the tutor role had little knowledge of what they should do, and how Internship had changed the kind of training which interns were to receive in the school. This problem raises the wider issue of how best to spread understanding of Internship throughout a school so that as many staff as possible may benefit from the experience.

Overall, the general programme and 'whole-school activity' aspects of Internship offered new challenges and possibilities to both interns and staff participants from school and OUDES. Teething problems were inevitable, but the preparation for the scheme's introduction had been so thorough and thoughtful, and the system of limited secondments which went along with the scheme's inception, ensured that problems were identified at an early stage, and that changes could be readily incorporated within the next year's programme.

Perhaps a final comment on the effectiveness of the absorption of a whole-school education in a particular school through the Internship scheme, can be made by the recruitment of staff in the school. Of the staff vacancies advertised at Park Hill, three were filled by interns who had spent the year there, and two by interns from other local schools.

Chapter VII

The Impact on the Schools
Hazel Hagger

The author has been Field Officer to the scheme since its inception and was herself a member of the Development Group of seconded teachers. She is closely involved with all of the participant schools as well as with OUDES and thus has a unique overview of the effects of Internship. She spends most of her time in the schools, talking with teachers and interns, and attending meetings concerned with Internship. All the comments by teachers in this chapter are taken from her conversations with mentors and professional tutors or from reports on aspects of the scheme written by members of the Internship Monitoring Group.

It was not difficult to find secondary schools in Oxfordshire eager to be involved in the new PGCE Internship scheme; indeed, such was the response to the university's invitation to join it in training teachers that a number of schools were left disappointed at not being among the 15 who were to work with the first intake of interns.

The schools, then, were willing partners; the teachers, volunteers not conscripts. As yet, however, Internship did not exist save as a complex set of ideas and principles, suggested practices, guidelines and a programme, and it was thus quite likely to mean different things to different people. Teachers' knowledge, understanding and expectations of the scheme were dependent on a multiplicity of factors, among which were the extent and nature of their involvement in the planning and development process; perceptions of OUDES tutors; conceptions of the nature of teaching and of the process of learning to teach; attitudes to the efficacy of their own teacher training; and, simply whether they had had the time and the inclination to read the handbook and the many other papers that had emanated from OUDES. For some teachers it was a radical, innovative and coherent scheme which held out the promise of clarifying the relationship between the theory and practice of teaching; for others it was an elaborated extension of the existing PGCE course, providing an opportunity to work more closely with individual tutors whom they liked and respected. Whatever their view, all teachers welcomed the much enhanced role of schools and teachers in the training of new recruits to the profession.

The induction conference in July 1987, attended by OUDES tutors, LEA officers and advisers, and representatives from the 15 schools, was marked by feelings of goodwill. Teachers were impressed by the rigorous thinking and hard work that had gone into the planning of Internship, and they were excited by the embodiment in the scheme of a recognition of their expertise as practitioners. They were willing to be part of this innovation, but commitment to the scheme could only come after they had experienced it in practice. In recent years teachers have been subjected to innumerable educational initiatives, and they are not unfamiliar with feelings of weariness when practice fails to match rhetoric. Thus, at this stage, they wished to reserve their judgments on Internship - they would wait and see whether it worked.

The plans, negotiated with and endorsed by the teachers, were in place, but there was no suggestion that they were perfect or complete. The need to improve them was the primary justification for setting up the Internship Monitoring Group comprising OUDES tutors and a representative - seconded for a day each week - from each of the 15 schools. The major task of the teachers monitoring the scheme in their respective schools was to find out whether the plans were clear, feasible and effective, and to explore the concerns of those involved in their implementation. It is on the basis of the meetings of that group and the reports written by its members, together with findings from my own work in visiting the schools as field officer, that I have drawn up the following account of how Internship was perceived in schools during its first year of operation.

1. The General Programme, and the Work of Professional Tutors and General Tutors

The role of the general tutor was a success. Schools welcomed the opportunity to forge a close relationship with a tutor who took an interest in the school as a whole, attending staff meetings, participating in social activities, etc. Such was their involvement in the life of the school, that many general tutors were regarded as honorary members of staff. This success can be attributed in part to the fact that it was a new and additional role rather than a reconceptualisaton of an existing one. For the tutors - although adding quite considerably to their workload - it offered new insights and new relationships, and they were not being asked to jettison established ways of working. The notion of a tutor being attached to a single school worked, and both sets of partners were enthusiastic about this close link between OUDES and the schools.

In each school the professional tutor was also the main link between the interns and the whole school, and between mentors within a single school working in different subject areas. The extent to which schools as institutions welcomed the interns and furnished them with a positive learning environment was, to a large degree, dependent on the energy and skills of the professional tutors in working with their colleagues. In those schools where the professional tutor held regular meetings of the mentors, the advantages of working as a school team were clearly in evidence. Mentors were able to learn from each other's strengths and to voice concerns, and the connections between the general programme and the various curriculum programmes were discussed - and subsequently exploited - to the benefit of the interns.

Teachers were not so fulsome in their praise of the general programme itself. While endorsing its recognition of the full professional role of the teacher, and the need for beginning teachers to be concerned with issues other than their subject specialism, they were critical of its structural complexity. The programme was both too full and too rigid, leaving little room for response either to the concerns of an individual school, or to the needs of individual interns; the latter were overburdened with assignments and investigations, and had little time in which to absorb and reflect on what they had learned. In response to a call for a programme of fewer issues and a structure which offered greater flexibility, a working party was set up in March 1988 to design a new general programme for the following year.

2. The Curriculum Programmes, and the Work of Mentors and Curriculum Tutors

Teachers were as one in preferring the role of mentor to that of supervisory teacher. Their responsibilities had been made more explicit, and they were now properly located at the centre of teacher training with a distinctive and equal contribution to make to the interns' learning. They were working with curriculum tutors, but they were not expected to see the complexities of teaching in the same way as did their university partners; their strength lay in the knowledge, perspectives and concerns they had as practising classroom teachers. They welcomed the training the interns had been given in learning from experienced teachers and found them quick to adopt a teacher's rather than a pupil's perspective when observing. They were excited by the discussions following observation when, in response to the interns' questions, they attempted to reveal the thinking behind the skills embedded in their day-to-day practice:

"The structure that is put upon the follow-up discussion and the whole emphasis of the observation is very different from the normal observation and follow up discussion. The perspective that 'whatever happens in the classroom is due to the teacher' not only values all the skills teachers have but which they tend to discount; it also focuses the interns' thoughts on what has been done, is being done, to achieve this present state. In the present climate of undervaluing teachers, this approach is a very useful one. The teacher will respond positively and the interns can learn the little tricks, basic assumptions and underlying philosophies that every teacher has but often forgets to communicate to others."

Mentors saw that their expertise was being valued, and this in itself was rewarding.

It soon became clear, however, that insufficient thought had been given at the planning stage to the constraints within which teachers work. They are busy people with many responsibilities, and the primary concern of schools is the learning of pupils rather than the learning of adults. Uninterrupted time and privacy are at a premium, and Internship demanded both. It is not easy to discuss one's own observed teaching; it is especially difficult to reveal the thinking underlying one's actions in the classroom, while in the staffroom or departmental office with colleagues close at hand.

Mentors were frustrated at not having time to discuss lessons fully with interns and to answer all their questions. They also found it difficult to ensure that all teachers within the school department had a thorough understanding of the scheme's principles and recommended practices.

Their departmental colleagues had neither a designated role nor any non-contact time for working with interns. They did not attend meetings at OUDES or have regular contact with curriculum tutors. They were encouraged to read the handbook, but it proved indigestible for many and was left unread. It was too long and too theoretical, and, as one of the professional tutors pointed out: *"Teachers are inundated with pieces of paper, and they have to absorb information when they can - walking down the corridor, taking a breather between lessons. If you want them to read about Internship, it has to be on one side of A4."* Knowledge and understanding of the scheme was consequently patchy, and it was not surprising to find teachers working with interns in ways very different from those envisaged by the planners. Assumptions had been made about the attitude of teachers to trainees and insufficient thought given to the difficulties that some teachers - used to seeing pupils as learners and adults as teachers - might have in understanding that the interns as adult learner teachers did not fit into either category. Collaborative teaching was proving especially problematical during the autumn term, the first term of the scheme. For some teachers - often those who had always worked alone with pupils - it was threatening or simply confusing. Others found it exhilarating and regarded it as a crucial part of the interns' learning process, but the joint planning it involved dug deep into the limited time available in a typically frenetic school day.

In the past, student-teachers, supervisory teachers and tutors had worked much more within the parameters of their subject disciplines. The way in which teachers were trained in subjects other than their own was of little interest, and there was no desire to pull down the hedges of the many secret gardens of teacher training. Now, in each school, as the 8-12 interns shared ideas and concerns - both formally in the general programme seminars and informally in the staffroom - and as the mentors and professional tutors began meeting as a team, teachers became aware of, and disconcerted by, the differences among the curriculum programmes. Concern was expressed at the disparity in the number and nature of assignments to be undertaken by interns, for example, by the varying explicitness of the different published programmes, and by the different ways in which the principles of the scheme were being interpreted.

It was the work of the curriculum tutors in schools that came under the closest scrutiny. The role of curriculum tutor was a demanding one; s/he was both player and manager - 'the Kenny Dalglish model' as it was known during the development phase - with a distinctive part to play as well as having overall responsibility for the interns' learning. Perhaps the difficulties stemmed from the fact that the curriculum tutor's role - unlike that of the general tutor - was essentially a development of an existing one. Curriculum tutors had worked successfully with teachers and student-teachers in the past: they were used to going into schools to visit and assess students on teaching practice. Now, however, they were working within a scheme that not only embraced all seven curriculum areas in OUDES but made explicit their responsibilities and the nature of the partnership with mentors, and this involved developing new ways of working.

Most tutors were in schools for complete morning or afternoon sessions on a regular basis, discussing the work of the interns with mentors, working in classrooms alongside interns or teachers, helping teachers to understand, for example, ways of using the List of Important Abilities. Their energy, enthusiasm, knowledge and skills in working both with interns and teachers surpassed even the highest expectations, but it led to criticism of those tutors who were slower to give up established ways of working. While they came to appreciate that tutors too had a full workload and that their job in schools was not to provide model lessons for apprentices to emulate, many mentors felt they had the right to know *"what support they can expect and when"*. At the beginning of each term some tutors sent copies of their complete programme of school visits to all the mentors and professional tutors with whom they worked, and the professional tutors asked for all tutors to work in this way. The calls from the schools for a more collectivist approach from the curriculum tutors, and a greater degree of standardisation in the way that they worked in schools was the subject of much discussion at OUDES, touching as it did on the thorny question of autonomy.

Teachers' reactions to, and perceptions of, the scheme during its first year of implementation were full of surprises. Not least of these was their desire to work closely with the tutors in school. It had been anticipated that some mentors and professional tutors might well see the school-based elements of the course as their domain, preferring to work with tutors as distant partners in the university. On the contrary, teachers welcomed the tutors in school, recognising, for example, that while tutors were not practising school teachers, their extensive experience of helping others to learn how to teach was invaluable, and that there was much to be learned from them.

Mentors wanted more time in which to carry out properly what they saw as *"a rewarding and challenging role"*. They saw the need for more training in such skills as the diagnostic assessment of teaching, and they wished to increase their overall understanding of the scheme, but a number of them had not had the time to read the existing training materials or to attend all of the meetings in school or at OUDES. Clearer, more easily digestible training materials would help, but it was in working and talking with tutors in their visits to the schools that many teachers developed their understanding and skills. At the end of the first year, the most satisfied mentors were those who had worked most closely with their tutor partners.

3. The Shape and Structure of the Year
The shallow-end approach to learning how to teach - as opposed to the sink or swim initiation into classrooms which tends to accompany traditional teaching practice - was given substance in the shape of the year: an induction period, followed by two days each week in school, before the full-time experiential period in the schools. This gradual introduction to the complexities of classroom teaching was seen by the teachers as allowing interns to develop their confidence by concentrating

their attention on a few skills at a time before embarking on whole lessons. It also encouraged teachers to focus on specific skills when they were discussing their own or the interns' teaching, rather than talking in more general terms about a lesson being 'good' or 'bad'. Interns were able to observe teachers at work, teach alongside them, and begin to unravel the mysteries of the school's ethos, organisation and curricula - both overt and hidden - before taking on any real responsibility for pupils' learning. This also made sense to teachers - especially those who remembered vividly the horrors of their own training as they learned through trial and error, or those who could recall occasions while supervising trainees when they had had to rescue both pupils and student-teacher from drowning together at the deep end into which the latter had been thrown.

Mentors were hard-pressed in the initial batch of 'J' weeks, and felt that a third day in school for the interns would relieve some of the pressure on themselves, and enable the interns to have more opportunities of learning about the realities of school and teaching. They also recommended that 'S' weeks be extended from 9 to 12 weeks (as indeed they were for 1988/89), arguing that interns needed a more sustained period of concentrated teaching in order to understand the importance of such things as long-term planning.

For the teachers, the most rewarding phase of the course was the nine-week period of 'S' weeks when interns were in school all the time. As the interns became increasingly competent and taught whole lessons, the teachers had more time in which to help them. Moreover, the interns, now familiar with the department and the school, were seen more as colleagues than dependent trainees, and teachers delighted in their ideas, enthusiasm and energy. For the interns too, this was the most fulfilling period of school experience, made more so because they had already established themselves in the school in the preceding 'J' weeks.

Guidelines to help in devising timetables for the interns during the 'S' weeks had been distributed to the schools, and mentors were urged to ensure that interns continued to have opportunities to teach collaboratively - with teachers or with a fellow intern - and to observe experienced teachers. Mentors were not always successful, however, in persuading their colleagues to work in the ways suggested. Some interns were left undisturbed by teachers whose classes they took and became 'substitute teachers', relying on their mentor and tutor to give them feedback on their teaching. Once again, the need was apparent to enable *all* teachers working with interns to have a full understanding of the scheme and to develop the skills needed in working with trainee teachers.

The final period of 'J' weeks proved least satisfactory. It was felt that at this stage in their training, interns were in a position to make a material contribution to the school departments in which they were working, and that they would have particular interests to explore, or expertise to offer. Thus, the school element of the planned curriculum programmes was purposely much more open-ended, leaving room for mentors to negotiate schedules of work with their interns, taking into account the needs of the school and of the interns. Some mentors and interns seized the opportunity to devise full and varied timetables, and interns were busy doing many of the things that the teachers wished they had the time to do - visiting other schools, observing teachers in other subject areas, producing new materials on word processors, helping pupils to use film and video, compiling reading lists, cataloguing resource materials, helping teachers to exploit the use of computers, staging events such as 'Book Weeks', teaching a specific topic across a whole year group. There were other mentors and interns, however, who, having become used to following a coherent and integrated programme, felt a lack of direction. They were unclear as to who was to drive the programme at this stage of the course, and momentum was lost. It was evident that a great deal more thought needed to be given to this final part of the year - a time necessarily fragmented with interns away on interview and changes in the school rhythm due to external and internal examinations - if it were to be beneficial for all concerned.

4. Assessment

The most contentious feature of Internship was assessment of the interns' work in the context of school. It was not the case - as might be assumed - that the mentors and the tutors disagreed about the work of individual interns, or that the procedures for assessment were complicated. The root of the problem lay in the notion of Chartered Intern Status, the awarding of which signalled that an intern had achieved the competencies detailed in the List of Important Abilities and could confidently be expected to achieve Qualified Teacher Status at the end of the course. Once chartered the interns' task was to articulate their own criteria by which they would evaluate their teaching.

The perceived unattractiveness of the words 'Chartered Intern', coupled with the newness of the concept, tended to discourage the mentors, professional tutors and interns from attempting to understand the thinking underlying the title. Moreover, the scepticism of some of the tutors who felt that this issue had not been fully resolved during the planning and development phase filtered through to the schools, and added to the confusion. It was evident that a number of interns were unclear about the differences between rigorous, analytic self-evaluation, and the habit of reflecting on their work, as they had been encouraged to do from the first day of the course. Teachers felt concerned for those interns whom they saw as having been inadequately prepared for self-evaluation.

Mentors and professional tutors also rejected the notion of a single fixed point at which all interns would be assessed as competent, arguing that such a procedure failed to take account of the different rates at which interns progressed. They also disliked the assessment forms - designed specifically to save them from the chore of having to write lengthy reports - feeling cheated at not having a full opportunity to record an intern's achievements, strengths and activities.

The conferring of Chartered Intern Status served to free many interns from anxieties about their competence as teachers, and they became more adventurous and confident in the classroom. A few, on the other hand, took it as a sign that they had passed the course, and their commitment and energy dwindled noticeably during the summer term.

5. The Interns' Development

The interns were well prepared for entry to the profession. Teachers were impressed not only with their ability *to teach,* but with their knowledge and understanding *about teaching* and the teacher's full professional role. The general programme - though overfull - enabled them to adopt cross-curricular and whole-school perspectives so that they had a clearer idea about the place of their own subject in the school curriculum. Furthermore, the year-long association with one school - about which misgivings had been voiced during the planning and development phase - allowed them far greater insights into the realities of the profession and made it possible for them to make more informed judgments about their place in it.

It might have been expected that interns and teachers would be dismissive of the theoretical work undertaken at OUDES, regarding the increased amount of time spent in school as the single most important reason for the success of the scheme. On the contrary, it was the integration of philosophy and practice - made possible by the partnership between OUDES and the schools - that came to be seen as the key to the interns' successful development as teachers. As one of the teachers monitoring the scheme explained:

"Despite (or indeed because of) feeling overworked at times, many interns realised life at the 'chalk face' needed to be more than survival. Sense could only be made of this daily pressure if it were sustained or underpinned by a sound philosophical base. They were actively seeking and developing a rationale. Often, too, those who felt most overworked were actually reacting to the difficulty of managing their time; of balancing reflection and reading, with marking and preparation. This is a sophisticated lesson. Many practising teachers still have difficulty getting the balance right. That interns appreciated the need for a balance meant they had understood a great deal."

As active, critical learners, interns developed a conceptual framework for thinking about teaching that would enable them to continue learning throughout their professional lives.

The fact that Internship was an improvement on previous PGCE courses was not in doubt. The schools were well pleased with the products of this new way of training - the interns - and headteachers and their staff talked incessantly about the quality of their teaching and thinking. They were eager to employ them, and many teachers commented somewhat wistfully that they wished that they had been trained in this way.

There were, of course, a few interns who struggled in the classroom, but the partnership between the schools and OUDES and the emerging spirit of team work meant that their needs - and those of the mentors working with them - were quickly and effectively addressed. As one of the professional tutors commented:

"Mentors and interns felt well supported by the other members of the Internship network of professional tutor, general tutor and curriculum tutor. Channels of communication worked well, and when difficulties arose, the support system sprang into action very quickly, and worked to greater purpose in remedying problems than had ever been apparent before in previous PGCE schemes."

6. The Benefits for Schools

If it was evident that the interns themselves had benefited from this new scheme, what of the teachers, the schools and their pupils? It was mentioned earlier that teachers' reactions to the scheme were often surprising. Their enthusiasm for this planned enterprise which entailed considerably more work for them at a time when they were grappling with the demands of the new GCSE examinations, and having to face up to the implications of the Education Reform Bill was nothing less than astounding, and suggested that Internship also had much to offer to them and their pupils.

Mentors had access to new ideas and resources, both through the interns and the tutors. Working with the tutors and teachers from other schools within the same subject area to develop curriculum programmes encouraged mentors to reflect on the aims and corpus of their subject as well as to think about teaching strategies and classroom management. The presence of two interns in a school department throughout the year, coupled with the close relationship with a curriculum tutor, stimulated talk about classroom teaching and the exploration of philosophies. Interns assisted in the development of new courses and the production of fresh materials. The general programme served to heighten teacher awareness of educational issues such as gender, and, in one or two schools, the interns' investigations and dissertations became the basis for staff discussion and the development of new school policies.

Moreover, the presence in school for a year of a large group of lively graduates intent on entering the profession, and eager to learn from practitioners' expertise and skills, boosted teachers' morale during a period when the teaching profession was regularly being taken to task in the public domain for its inefficiency and shortcomings. Many teachers believed not only that their own teaching and thinking were better as a result of their participation, but also that the processes integral to the scheme gave an impetus to new ways of working with colleagues and provided models for their own professional development. The following comments of one of the mentors is typical:

"I was forced to think about my teaching in a way that I haven't done for years - as well as being surprised at discovering how much I know, it's made me reflect on my teaching, which must be a good thing. Having the interns with us made the department much more open - previously we taught behind closed doors, now we're trying to work together. The approach to observation in Internship would be of real use to heads of department when looking at members of their department - there's a lot we can learn from each other in school."

Members of the Monitoring Group were in no doubt that Internship was good for schools. As one of them asserted in her final report:

"Internship can mean that our learning environment never becomes static. As we all work to use interns imaginatively and develop the possibilities of collaborative teaching, we will be enhancing our own professional development and pupils' learning."

It is easy for those outside schools to overlook the needs of pupils when considering ways in which teachers should be trained. For teachers, however, pupils' rather than trainees' needs are paramount, and there were fears that the pupils might suffer from having so many interns in a school for a whole year. Such fears proved to be unfounded. The progressive nature of the course ensured that interns did not have responsibility for teaching a class until they were deemed able to do so by mentors. This, and the interns' familiarity with the school and classes, meant that they were not looked upon as student-teachers by the pupils. *"Internship seems to have broken down many of the barriers which have hindered pupil/student-teacher relations for many years"* was the comment of a member of the Monitoring Group.

Over and above the removal of such barriers were positive practical benefits. With the emphasis on collaborative teaching, pupils received more attention - there were extra pairs of hands in classrooms to help with such things as practical sessions in science, oral assessment, group work, computer-based lessons and simulations. Furthermore, during the course of the year, interns became full members of the school community, and many took the opportunity to become involved in the extra-curricular life of the school. When the end of term came, it was not only their departmental colleagues but also members of drama clubs, cricket teams, debating societies and so on that felt saddened by their going.

7. Recommendations from the Schools

Before looking at those aspects of the scheme which were generally felt to be most in need of improvement, it is important to note the spirit in which the many helpful suggestions were made: they were not the voices of complaint from outsiders, but were suggestions for modifications from people who now felt part of the scheme and wanted to make it better. Moreover, whereas in the initial months the teachers' questions had focused on their roles as mentors and professional tutors, and their anxieties on the impact of the scheme on the schools, as the academic year came to a close their concerns centred on the needs of the interns - a further indication that they had become committed to Internship.

From the long list of recommendations, four broad but overlapping strands emerged.

(i) First, was the call for all staff in the schools to have a wider and fuller understanding of the principles and practices of Internship. It was suggested, for example, that schools invite OUDES tutors to explain and answer questions about Internship at full staff and departmental meetings, prior to the arrival of the interns in school. Related to this was the recommendation that materials produced to help teachers should be more succinct and more immediately attractive in design and layout. Teachers wanted to work effectively with interns, but training and support had to take account of the hurly-burly of their working lives.

(ii) The second major area in need of modification - about which the professional tutors and some mentors had had a great deal to say throughout the year - was one that permeated all aspects of the scheme. The teachers monitoring it made a strong plea for greater standardisation, not only in the way Internship was implemented in the schools, but on the demands made of the interns both in school and at OUDES. They wanted *all* interns to benefit fully from what were seen as the rich learning opportunities offered by Internship. To this end, they wanted *all* teachers working with interns to use the List of Important Abilities, to be prepared to reveal their craft knowledge, to work collaboratively in classrooms, to carry out partnership supervision during the self-evaluation phase of the course, and so on. A degree of variation of practice in an innovation involving so many people and institutions was inevitable and acceptable, but the teachers believed that mixed messages from OUDES created unnecessary difficulties for them and for the interns, and the desire for greater uniformity - in the design of curriculum programmes, in the number of assignments demanded of interns, and in the work of tutors in schools - was widespread. In the words of a member of the Monitoring Group:

"The curriculum tutors should arrive at a more consistent approach to their role. Whilst there is value in the diversity of perception, there is also too much room for confusion. Closer liaison between the curriculum tutors is essential."

(iii) The third strand focused on the role of the interns in school. From every school came reports of the interns' sensitivity to their teacher colleagues: they were seen as *"unarrogant, respectful and eager to learn from teachers"*. The mentors, though approving of such attitudes, wanted the interns to take greater responsibility for seeking help in setting up activities in school. Teachers work under great pressure, and while they were always willing to respond to the interns' requests, they did not always have the time to take the initiative in setting up opportunities for their learning. They therefore recommended that interns be given a more thorough grounding in the principles and practices of the scheme, so that, for example, they could tell teachers what they wanted to do in a given week, rather than being dependent on the teachers' detailed knowledge of the interns' schedule.

(iv) Time - especially the lack of it - was the final cause for concern, and recommendations from schools were directed at the LEA and the schools' own senior management teams, as well as OUDES. The LEA was urged to continue its financial support of Internship, while headteachers were asked to ensure that mentors and professional tutors received the full benefit of each school's 0.5 enhanced staffing, with protected non-contact time falling on the days when interns were in school. Out of concern for the interns, whom many teachers felt were over-burdened during this first year, OUDES was encouraged to examine both curriculum and general programmes with a view to prioritising tasks, assignments, investigations and activities.

As suggested earlier, the four elements of Internship in need of modification overlap to a great extent. In its crudest form, teachers were arguing for greater commonality at OUDES which would lead to a greater shared understanding of the scheme among both interns and teachers, which, in turn, would enhance the interns' learning and enable teachers to work more effectively with them. Teachers had a highly developed sense of working within a scheme, and they were sufficiently confident and contented with it and the partnership to ask OUDES to be more directive;

they wanted to have a clearer idea of what to do and how to do it, not least because it would save them time. Any plans, however, had to take into account the nature of schools and of teachers' working lives, and be sufficiently uncluttered to enable the interns to experience and learn from the unpredictable realities of teaching that cannot be planned for in advance. The programmes - especially the general programme - should be detailed and clear, but not tightly packed, with unreasonable demands.

The original plans, inevitably, had been neither perfect nor complete; but the teachers, far from feeling weary or disappointed, were looking forward to the arrival of the second wave of interns when, in partnership with the tutors, they would work to make Internship even better.

Chapter VIII

A Headteacher's Perspective

Howard Green

Howard Green, Director of the UK's first Educational Assessment Centre for the development and selection of headteachers based at the Oxford Polytechnic, was headteacher of the Henry Box School, Witney, throughout the planning phase of Internship and during the first three full years of the scheme's operation. He was also the representative of the Oxfordshire Secondary Headteachers' Association on the University Certificate Steering Group responsible for overseeing the development and implementation of the scheme in Oxfordshire schools. In this role he was able to voice the various concerns raised by staff and fellow heads with regard to the scheme and to mediate developments to them.

When the Internship scheme was formally launched in June 1987, these words appeared in *The Internship Handbook*, the document setting out the key ideas of Internship and the roles and responsibilities agreed by all involved:

"At the heart of the scheme is the idea of a close partnership between OUDES and the secondary schools and teachers of Oxfordshire."

For the partnership to become established in the first place and then to flourish, Oxfordshire's headteachers played a key role. There are two reasons why this should be so. Firstly, heads would inevitably be directly involved in the negotiations about exactly how a scheme of initial teacher training as radically different as Internship would be implemented in their schools. Secondly, at the time secondary schools were already going through a period of unprecedented change which was exacerbated by the most difficult and often bitter period of union action by teachers. As well as the possibility of launching the Internship scheme, schools were facing the implementation of new Education Acts affecting fundamental aspects of their life and work, including teachers' conditions of service, a completely different pattern of public examinations at 16+ (the General Certificate of Secondary Education) and numerous other apparently worthwhile developments like the Technical and Vocational Education Initiative and the government's Low-Attaining Pupils' Project.

All these changes were making immense demands on the commitment of teachers, the atmosphere in schools and the attitudes of parents and governors. It is some measure of the excitement and interest that the notion of Internship created that despite these demands, headteachers and their colleagues in Oxfordshire's secondary schools were willing to discuss the scheme and then move ahead, in partnership with OUDES, to develop it. I was privileged to play a part in the management of this process in two ways. Firstly, as the representative of the Oxfordshire Secondary School

Headteachers' Association (OSSHTA) on the University Certificate Steering Group (UCSG) which planned the Internship scheme; secondly, as head of one of the 15 schools that eventually took part in the first full year of the scheme (1987-88). In what follows I shall look at these two headteacher perspectives in more detail.

A. A Collective Perspective: the Role of the Oxfordshire Secondary School Headteachers Association (OSSHTA)

I have often reflected on why an idea as auspicious as Internship should have become a reality at such an inauspicious time. There are at least four reasons.

In the first place Internship was a model for initial training long overdue. Ever since the ill-fated James Report on teacher training, and probably well before that, both teachers and their trainers had yearned for a model that brought theory and practice, experience in education department and in school, into juxtaposition.

Secondly, in establishing the University Certificate Steering Group, OUDES brought together a key group of people including teachers, trainers, advisers, LEA officers, HMI, Union representatives and those with experience of initial training in other public services like health. Their chairman, Richard Aplin, was a teacher (Head of Languages at Henry Box School). The Director of OUDES, Dr Harry Judge, was a driving force behind the Internship scheme, a member of UCSG and perceived by the schools as a practitioner, having been head of Oxfordshire's largest secondary school.

Thirdly, the Local Education Authority was forward looking, innovative and expert at maximising available resources (whether provided centrally or locally). It had generally good relationships with the teacher unions and the Chief Education Officer, Tim Brighouse, enjoyed a close professional relationship with the Director of OUDES.

Finally, the secondary heads in Oxfordshire had developed a strong collective voice through OSSHTA which had a constructive dialogue with both the LEA and OUDES. Of course, individual schools had worked closely with OUDES for many years to maintain the existing, traditional pattern of teacher training. However, for a radical shift in this pattern a collective voice was essential. So Oxfordshire heads working with their staff teams represented one corner of a triangle of relationships that was centred on a good idea.

How then did the good idea become a reality, what was the role of OSSHTA and what were the main issues that had to be resolved?

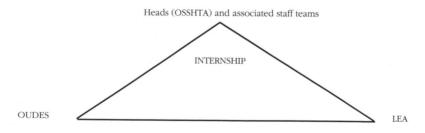

Heads (OSSHTA) and associated staff teams

INTERNSHIP

OUDES

LEA

1. Dissemination of Information
Throughout the process of development OUDES kept heads well-informed about the Internship scheme. It was introduced to the University Certificate Steering Group in a paper from the OUDES staff in February 1985. Then on 5 June 1985 the Director gave a presentation to OSSHTA about the proposals and asked a simple question: *"Will you as heads enter into partnership with OUDES in the development of these proposals?"*. The answer was in principle an emphatic *"Yes"*.

From that point on to the launch of the scheme in September 1987 heads were fully involved in the subsequent modification and refinement. I was able to provide regular feedback from the UCSG at termly full OSSHTA meetings, the OUDES organised several further meetings about the developing scheme specifically for heads, there were regular visits by OUDES staff to Oxfordshire schools to provide up-to-date information and to answer questions. Several schools had teacher representatives on the UCSG and the Internship Development Group, which did the final detailed planning during 1986-87, consisted mainly of full-time secondees from Oxfordshire schools. In all these ways there were frequent informal exchanges with heads about the progress of the scheme. The heads were fully informed and were therefore able to keep their colleagues in the schools well informed.

2. Resources
It was clear from the outset that the Internship scheme would make increased demands on schools' resources. In particular the school staff who would be directly involved with the training of interns as professional tutors and mentors would need time to properly fulfil these roles. As I have mentioned in the introduction the wider context for the development of the scheme included widespread union action, often bitter conflict over the imposition of new national conditions of service for teachers and a heightened sensitivity among teachers about any additional demands on their time. Because Internship was such a new idea it was very difficult to quantify the likely time requirement. However OSSHTA agreed that we should ask OUDES and the LEA for 1 full-time equivalent (FTE) teacher additional to each establishment's staffing to allow time for the professional tutor and the mentors to operate their side of the scheme (assuming 10 (or 12) interns working in 5 (or 6) school departments). But where was this resource to be found? There appeared to be two main possibilities: either the LEA (via the INSET budget) or a national agency interested in teacher training (and in particular the DES). Despite much effort, including a visit by the Director of OUDES and Oxfordshire's Chief Education Officer to the DES, the second route proved to be fruitless. In the end, 8 LEA secondments for the Special Diploma course were allocated to the Internship scheme in 1987-88. By this means, each partner school received 0.5 FTE. Of this 0.2 had to be used to release one of the mentors on one day each week to attend Special Diploma seminars at OUDES. This group of mentors used the opportunity to review and evaluate the scheme in their own schools as the basis for their dissertations. The remaining 0.3 FTE was used by the schools to give a little additional non-teaching time

to staff directly involved with the scheme. In my own school the extra time amounted to only one extra (70 minute) non-teaching period for mentors. Clearly this level of resourcing is quite inadequate because a conscientious mentor is usually spending several hours each week working with interns. OSSHTA continues to press for further staffing resources for the Internship schools.

3. Non-Internship Schools

Before the Internship scheme most Oxfordshire secondary schools had taken some student-teachers from OUDES. One of the implications of the new model of training was that fewer schools would have more interns. As it happened in 1987-88, 16 secondary schools (from a total of 35) were directly involved with the scheme taking between 8 and 12 interns each. There was a legitimate worry, particularly among the non-Internship schools, that this would lead to a 'them' and 'us' situation. Rather like the higher status conferred on teaching hospitals, the Internship schools would be regarded by a wider audience as having been selected to undertake the training of teachers and therefore as being stronger institutions. A number of schools were very keen to be involved with the scheme but felt that, for several good reasons, they could not join the first cohort of Internship schools in September 1987. They probably felt most keenly about this particular issue.

These fears were expressed at various meetings during the planning phase and the department made every effort to keep *all* Oxfordshire secondary schools fully informed about the scheme. There are three or four schools waiting to join the scheme and it has been agreed that they will be able to enter the scheme after three years in September 1990. At that time three or four of the existing Internship schools will drop out of the scheme for one year only, to be replaced on a cyclical basis by the remaining Internship schools.

Another concern raised by the non-Internship schools, including Oxfordshire's primary and middle schools, was that an unfair slice of the LEA's secondment 'cake' was going to the relatively small number of Internship schools to provide for the 8 FTE secondments at OUDES. This is a fair criticism, made more pointed by the recent substantial reduction in the total number of LEA secondments, and puts further pressure on OUDES to find the staffing resources for Internship from elsewhere.

4. Chartered Intern Status

The Internship scheme that was eventually launched in September 1987 envisaged two phases to the interns' training year. At some point during the year, which might be different for each intern but would normally be around Easter, and after discussions between interns, OUDES staff and the professional tutor and mentor in the school, the interns would be given Chartered Intern Status to signify that they had acquired and demonstrated a predetermined range of teaching skills and competencies.

The label Chartered Intern Status created some concern amongst heads partly because they felt it implied rather anachronistic notions of 'Pass' or 'Fail' and did little for the confidence of those who were not awarded this status early in the year. However a deeper worry was that once an intern had become a Chartered Intern the school might be tempted to give them more responsibility than their legal status allowed. For example, if a Chartered Intern had an accident during a science lesson with the normal classroom teacher off the school site then the school would take the blame in any subsequent legal action.

During a review of the first year of the scheme in November 1988 this issue was fully discussed. As a result, the notion of two phases to the interns' year remains but the label Chartered Intern has been dropped.

5. A Collective Overview

I am sure that I write on behalf of all my headteacher colleagues in Oxfordshire when I say that the Internship scheme has been a great success enriching both the training of teachers at OUDES and the life of our schools. Difficult issues have been faced openly and honestly, at times the debate has been heated and clearly the scheme is still at a relatively early stage in its development. However there is a commitment on all sides to make the Internship scheme a permanent feature of the educational landscape in Oxfordshire.

B. An Individual Perspective: Internship at Henry Box School

1. Preparation

On 11 July 1985 the Director of OUDES wrote to all Oxfordshire's secondary heads asking them to consider whether or not they wanted their schools to have a representative on the Internship Development Group in 1986-87 and so make a positive commitment to join the first group of Internship schools in September 1987. On 16 July, just before the end of the summer term, I sent a detailed memo to the relevant heads of department at Henry Box who were already aware of the broad outlines of the Internship scheme. I encouraged them to discuss the scheme with colleagues and to give me an initial response early in the autumn term. This response was positive and Richard Aplin, head of languages, indicated his interest in joining the Internship Development Group.

By the following autumn Richard Aplin had started work with the Development Group on a full-time secondment (1986-87) focusing on the implications of the scheme for the assessment and accreditation of the interns. It was most helpful to have a colleague directly involved with the Development Group as he was able to provide regular feedback to the Henry Box staff on all aspects of the scheme as it developed. During this period Bill Berry, professional tutor and also a deputy head, was having discussions with our heads of department. The purpose of these discussions was twofold. Firstly, to find out if each department was willing and prepared to receive two interns the following September and secondly, what were the departmental questions and concerns about the scheme.

2. Concerns

In December 1986 I wrote to the chairman of the UCSG summarising the School's concerns but indicating that we were committed to full involvement from the launch in September 1987. At that time, I made the following key points based on the views of my colleagues. Firstly, time must be made available without strings attached for the professional tutor and the mentors to do their jobs properly. The total time required would be closer to 1 FTE rather than 0.5 FTE per school. We rejected the idea of cash payments to professional tutors or mentors for their extra work on the Internship scheme. Within the context of widespread Union action over pay and conditions of service and bearing in mind the fact that many colleagues beyond those officially designated as mentors would be helping with the scheme, cash payments seemed to be an unwise way of offering additional resources to the Internship schools.

Secondly, we felt that 10 or 12 interns in a school the size of Henry Box (6 forms of entry, 1,000 pupils) might be excessive. Certainly we believed that it would be excessive with the traditional pattern of initial training that involved a block of teaching practice. Some classes would inevitably have several student-teachers working with them for a substantial part of the year. If the student-teachers were not strong then the pupils would be disadvantaged and parental anxieties raised. Perhaps we had not yet fully appreciated that the Internship scheme was qualitatively different from traditional patterns of training: with interns in the school throughout the year they would be able to establish much more gradual and, hopefully, secure relationships with classes. They would be able to move step by step from working with small groups and assisting the normal teacher to taking responsibility for the whole class. As it turned out we had 8 interns at Henry Box in 1987-88 and increased this to 10 in 1988-89, so my fears were not substantiated!

There was also a concern that with 10 or 12 interns from OUDES we would have to break our teacher training links with the local college of education, Westminster College, Oxford. In fact this link has been weakened as now I will only have student-teachers from Westminster College specialising in Religious Studies and not English and Modern Languages as in the past.

We suggested that, where there were two schools close together (as we have in Witney with our neighbouring secondary school, Wood Green, only a mile or so away), then pairs of schools might take 6 interns each and organise joint programmes of professional development with the 12 regularly meeting together. Interestingly, although this idea did not gain acceptance at the time, it has recently resurfaced as a way of involving new schools in the Internship scheme without existing schools having to drop out.

Our third concern was that OUDES should not expect the regular release of the professional tutor and the mentors during the school day to attend Internship planning meetings. These would inevitably be some of our most experienced teachers and they should not have to be released from their classes. Such release was already reaching unacceptable proportions because of the demands of GCSE and other in-service training. Thankfully this warning was heeded by OUDES.

Finally we expressed the view that the Internship scheme implied the frequent and thorough involvement of the general tutor from OUDES with the life and work of their link school. It was most encouraging to see Dr David Phillips, our general tutor in 1987-88, at the first staff meeting of the year on 4 September 1987! I am glad to say that, from that point on, our expectation about the high level of involvement of the general tutor has been fulfilled.

The Development Group did an excellent job during 1986-87 and without their hard work on the detailed aspects of the scheme it would have had a much less auspicious start. Most of our concerns were allayed, apart from the amount of time given to the Internship schools which remained at 0.5 FTE with 0.2 spent at OUDES. I should add that after further discussion and review the whole 0.5 FTE will be available for use in the schools from September 1989 and OUDES continues to seek additional resources from national agencies.

3. The Launch

In September 1987 Henry Box became one of the first 16 Internship schools. The school was allocated eight interns (a pair in each of four departments). The scheme at Henry Box was very ably co-ordinated by Keith Geary, head of English, acting as assistant to the professional tutor with specific responsibility for the Internship scheme. This particular strategy had several advantages. As a deputy head the professional tutor had many other responsibilities in the school including overall staff development and, in particular, the monitoring and support of probationary teachers. Keith Geary was able to direct all his attention to the interns, he had been a student-teacher at OUDES himself and (dare I say it) he was somewhat closer to the interns in age! The mentors included three heads of department (Biology, Languages, Geography) and one second in department (English). The second in English, Valerie Parkes, had the one day a week (0.2) secondment at OUDES and completed an excellent dissertation for the Special Diploma which reviewed the first year of the Internship scheme at Henry Box. Perhaps necessity is the mother of invention because this secondment was turned into a good opportunity for further professional development.

During the school year (1988-89) we had 10 interns. Keith Geary remained the co-ordinator of the Internship scheme at Henry Box. Of the five mentors two were heads of department (Biology and Modern Languages) and three were members of departments with considerable teaching experience (English, History and Mathematics). It is worth emphasising the fact that involving colleagues other than heads of department as mentors has at least two advantages. It broadens the opportunity for professional development that mentorship offers and it takes the additional pressure away from heads of department who have more than enough on their plates at present.

Last but not least, when describing the launch of Internship at Henry Box, I should mention that both governors and parents have been kept fully informed about the development and implementation of the scheme. I believe that it has their full support.

4. Some Positive Reflections

Internship at Henry Box has been one of the most successful and positive innovations among many over the last few years. I should thank my colleagues, both at school and also at OUDES, for their very hard work. Without it the scheme would not have produced such worthwhile results. From conversations with many of the interns I know that they have found the Internship scheme a thorough, practically-based and stimulating form of initial training. It really does begin to integrate the theory and practice of teaching far more effectively. But what have been the key benefits for the school? Four stand out as the most important.

Experienced teachers realised that a model of initial training like the Internship scheme was long overdue. Many of us within education had been talking about models like this for years. At last we had the opportunity of actually implementing a good idea whose hour had come! I am quite sure that it was this feeling that made my colleagues willing to make the extra effort to introduce Internship when they already had agendas that were over-full. So the first benefit for the school is that we now know that we are helping with the initial training of teachers in a far more effective way. The frustration of a job less well done has receded.

Secondly, the Internship scheme has provided many excellent opportunities for the professional development of my colleagues, some of which I have outlined above.

Thirdly, it has created extra 'pairs of hands' and more space in the school day, certainly later in the year, which helps to offset the substantial time given to the scheme by professional tutor and mentors.

Finally, it has brought into the staffroom a group of young teachers with energy, enthusiasm and lots of good ideas. It may occasionally bring an additional permanent member of staff but that is an unexpected bonus!

C. Final Thoughts

Internship is a young plant that still needs care and attention to ensure that it matures and develops its full potential. I would in closing this chapter sound two notes of warning.

I know that many of my colleagues, both at Henry Box and in other Internship schools, feel that the scheme is yet another good idea which is being introduced on a 'shoe-string' of resources. There remains an urgent need to increase the level of resourcing to the Internship schools because teachers will be less and less willing to have their goodwill exploited. And this is not just another example of teacher 'whingeing', it is an honest and realistic response to the next huge wave of change that approaches us in the wake of the Education Reform Act. An effective mentor who is spending three or four hours each week with a pair of interns (which is not unusual) and gets only one, or at most two, hours each week to do the job may eventually stop doing it. I know that OUDES realises this need but do those in places like the DES who have responsibility for initial training at national level?

Secondly, it has been both encouraging and gratifying to see the positive response to Internship outside Oxfordshire from many educators at both LEA and national levels. However, it is neither a model for initial training that is easy to establish nor will it be a 'cure-all' for the problems of teacher supply facing the DES. The partnership between the OUDES and Oxfordshire's secondary schools that I mentioned in my introduction and which has resulted in the successful launch of the Internship scheme took about three years of careful planning to set up. It seems unlikely to be a suitable model for introducing 'licensed teachers' to the profession and coping with their initial training without a huge input of resources.

To end on a positive note - my involvement with the Internship scheme, at both institutional and LEA levels, has been one of the most rewarding experiences in the 20 years of my professional life. Long may it flourish!

Chapter IX

The LEA Engagement

Tim Brighouse

As Chief Education Officer of Oxfordshire during the planning and adoption phases of Internship, Tim Brighouse had a crucial role in the development of the scheme. The partnership between schools and university could flourish as it did only with the close involvement and the support of the LEA. A generous programme of LEA secondments to OUDES for several years preceding Internship had prepared the ground. In the planning stage, the unique and imaginative decision to second certain key teachers to form the Internship Development Group and, later, the Internship Monitoring Group, were clear statements of the CEO's belief in the scheme and of its value to the schools. Tim Brighouse is now Professor of Education at the University of Keele.

There has been something very unusual in the partnership between the Oxford University Department of Educational Studies and the Oxford Education Service.

To understand the Internship scheme fully it is necessary to gain a feel for that relationship. It has a long history. It probably started in a special way with the appointment of Harry Judge from the principalship of Banbury School in the early 1970s: his story is elsewhere but there appeared to be a clear determination from the first on his part to build on the networks of support he naturally inherited from the outstanding leadership of one of the country's leading state schools.

There were two features of the relationship which picked themselves out for me in 1978 when I arrived in Oxfordshire from London. First OUDES had already made a significant contribution to the quality and development of Oxfordshire's comprehensive schools by the simple expedient of arranging teaching practice not, as was the custom and practice, at a school negotiated by an alchemy of student whim and tutor connections at the many corners of England and Wales mainly in grammar and independent schools. At once and logically OUDES linked with nearby comprehensive schools, mainly within Oxfordshire, for the bulk of their teaching practice schools. There were other built-in advantages to the links thus created. Banbury along with two or three other schools had in effect become flagship schools for comprehensive education not merely within the county but nationally. They had in their staffrooms that sense of intellectual curiosity which is the hallmark of thinking schools where teachers were buzzing with ideas of curriculum development and change. They had become magnets for aspiring young professionals keen to forge an interesting, even a rapid career. Frequently such teachers had the talent to justify their high aspirations and many went on to leadership positions in other Oxfordshire comprehensive schools as well as elsewhere. So the teaching practice schools for the students from OUDES were often staffed by teachers and led by someone with a connection with these flagship schools. Success was begetting success and the quality of teaching and children's learning was much influenced for the better by this factor.

The second change was the forging of the closest links through the partnership of the Oxford Education Research Group (OERG), a vehicle Harry Judge created to bring together practising teachers especially the professional interest groups, the LEA represented through its advisers and officers and the university's other departments. Project and research schemes of national and international importance followed and there was a real sense in which, because the research was grounded in Oxfordshire schools, the dissemination at least within the county, caused teachers to reflect more than averagely about theory and evidence as well as to rely on their hunch and intuition. In these two important ways, namely the many years of school-based teaching practice and the research tradition, the ground was favourable for the introduction of the Internship scheme. There were other individually less significant but collectively as important ways in which the soil was propitious.

For a complex and muddled set of reasons, Oxfordshire schools in 1979 had been launched on a process of collective review or 'school self-evaluation', as it was known. The complexity and muddle is best explained elsewhere but one of the unexpected bonuses of the scheme, newly introduced to meet and divert into a more acceptable way political imperatives for accountability, was the realisation by the senior staff leading secondary schools or departments within the school, that they had externally imposed on them a process of collective review which had a number of merits: indeed the scheme required the fashioning of the highest common factor of collective agreement among staff about the aims and objectives of the school or departmental processes and activities. Early practice suggested that the best next step was to identify and describe in a non-judgmental way, existing ways in which the processes were carried out and, more daringly, consider alternative ways of carrying them out. In the ensuing collective discussion and debate about the comparative advantages and disadvantages of the different ways, for example, of teaching a foreign language, the advocates were forced into a consideration of evidence - a necessary factor but one unfortunately all too rarely considered in the busy interchanges of the classroom and the everyday crises of school life. The process of school and/or departmental review which school evaluation emphasised made schools at once sensitive to the need for a development plan - the format actually required a section of 'future directions' - and conscious also of the need for time to review more thoroughly evidence when pursuing curriculum development or school change.

An apparently disconnected series of events conspired to promote that change. Providentially at about the same time the LEA faced a crisis of a super-abundance of teachers. Commentators of a different age both retrospectively and prospectively will wonder there could ever be a problem of 'too many teachers'. It is important to remind ourselves that the combination of the oil crisis and disillusion conspired to make falling rolls and over-investment in teacher supply a real problem in the late 1970s and early 1980s as there were successive reductions in public expenditure. Initially the political thought turned to redundancy: this would not have been too helpful to teacher morale given that a couple of years earlier there had apparently been such a crisis of employer/teacher relations that it led to strike action, not about pay but about the level of resourcing of the service.

It was eventually possible to persuade the politicians and the county treasurer, that a more favourable financial route to the problem of too many teachers was to embark on a large scale programme of teacher secondment. Obviously it had considerable educational advantage too, not least because it supplied that follow-up time to individual schools to enable them to find the collective energy to look at issues thrown into sharp relief as part of their collective intent by the process of school evaluation referred to earlier. It also had the promise, properly organised, of enabling the LEA on a county wide basis to overcome the isolation of individual enthusiasts about a particular issue (eg parental involvement, school libraries, school professional development, professional tutor policies) and to gain the intellectual stimulus of working together for a common goal at LEA level. Indeed many LEA policies and practices were forged through the use of such secondment.

An acceptance of such a programme involving the equivalent of 100 full-time equivalent teachers immediately and 210 full-time equivalents in a year or so was helped by the County Council politicians' respect for Harry Judge and the teachers' high regard for OUDES and the majority of its staff. It is perhaps necessary to add the qualification 'majority' because the interpersonal chemistry of particular individual lecturers and how they are perceived by individual teachers within schools is crucial to the reputation of institutions of higher education in the local community of schools. Ideal of course is a harmony of high regard for a particular subject adviser/inspector and the lecturer in OUDES and their joint empathy with teachers seeing their respective and complementary roles in teacher development: all too often there is a mismatch either in the perception of the teachers of one or the other of the adviser and the university lecturer or sometimes even disastrously both. It had been of critical importance to the development of the partnership of the LEA and OUDES that the exceptions in the Oxfordshire case have been so few that, where they have existed, they haven't either compromised the collective harmony of the relationship or, as individuals, campaigned actively against change and development but merely got out of the way and occupied themselves energetically with another part of their busy agenda. Or at least if they have campaigned they have not been successful.

Soon we jointly developed 'clusters' of interest around particular subject areas involving seconded teachers, advisers and lecturers: some teachers were taken on secondment for two years, exploiting a loophole in the regulations which allowed consecutive secondments on the pool of advanced courses provided different courses were used. The 'two-year' secondees became a means of supporting the development of LEA wide initiatives and in some cases they were linked with a simultaneous development of secondment to Oxford Polytechnic where there was a focus of positive collective review at the level of the individual school rather than the LEA. After two or three years' experience of this large programme of secondment, there were predictable changes in the climate of the educational debate within Oxfordshire. Given time, recognition and support, teachers never fail to rise to the bait of intellectual dispute, creativity and idealistic challenge.

A number of educational ideas began to be canvassed and to be taken forward enthusiastically. There were two principal ventures. First there was the development of the Oxford Certificate of Educational Achievement (OCEA) in 1982 which turned out to be a crucial first step in the development of national policy on records of achievement. Second was the development of the Internship scheme on a time scale which is outlined elsewhere in this document. In effect they were balancing although not entirely contemporary developments for Harry Judge and myself. Personally I invested considerable time, effort, finance and organisational collective effort into the development of OCEA because I believed records of achievement (and ideally OCEA within that movement which it started) to be one of the key factors in enabling secondary schools to change. I hoped they might become places where more youngsters might develop their talent simply because the framework for assessment would be changed into one which more overtly valued progress and achievement across a wider range of human talent and across the whole curriculum rather than a narrow part of it. You could hope to change the climate in which schools operated, for example, in the way in which they reported pupil progress to parents so that the youngster had a stake in the process of assessment and gained a more precise map of their progress through rigorous and acknowledged self-review. I elaborate simply because the venture mattered to me in a way that Harry Judge could easily see and respect. As a result of the long association between the LEA and OUDES and most importantly because of a mutual respect, trust and friendship, I could be sure of the support as well as an investment of time and energy at critical times in that complex venture, involving as it did, the bringing together of four LEAs, the Oxford Delegacy of Local Examinations and a multitude of interests from industry, the community and the professions too complex to enumerate here.

When Harry Judge therefore, from the vantage point of guaranteeing the best quality in the supply of trained teachers, talked from time to time of the model of the medical profession and of the teaching hospital as a means of improving the link of theory to practice and of involving teachers as the lead agents in the selecting and training of the next generation of teachers, I was inclined to listen attentively and sometimes to debate, as we did all such possibilities, in a lively fashion. Indeed about four years before the Internship scheme was launched there was brief talk of making Cherwell School in north Oxford an observation school - an in-depth school if you like, to accept the bulk of the PGCE trainees. I was impatient to get on and remember one of our advisers at that time being particularly enthusiastic. Harry Judge thought it premature: he was in a good position to assess the situation as one of the governors who had just appointed an exciting new headteacher, Martin Roberts, who was to transform the school's reputation and more importantly its actual performance - not always the same thing - for the better. It was however only a matter of time before some such scheme would be tried because it was clear to me that the scheme mattered to Harry Judge.

When Harry therefore announced in due course that he was about to start, I gave him the same assurances of support whatever cropped up, that he had given to me over the OCEA. There were however some LEA difficulties, not in terms of money, but of changing personnel and of an advisory service which initially was being led, not merely strategically, but on a day-to-day basis by myself, as a result of the absence through ill-health of the senior schools adviser. When a new adviser, Bill Laar from ILEA was appointed, with the help of the Director of OUDES, I vacated my role on the Committee for Educational Studies - the Department's governing body in effect - in his favour as part of a deliberate attempt to ensure that in any new team spirit he developed as part of the advisory team, he would see the centrality of the close co-operation between OUDES and the LEA.

Ben Kerwood, later to be general adviser in Wiltshire, took on the difficult role of overseeing the project in its planning year, when the disputatious planning phase chronicled elsewhere took place. I attended two only of the regular meetings of the senior teaching staff from 15 or so of our schools. They were among the cream of the Oxfordshire senior teaching profession in their skill, reputation and intellectual curiosity: they argued and fashioned the scheme, testing it so far as I could see, to the point of destruction. There seemed to me to be particular doubt in the minds of some of the OUDES staff at this stage. Ben Kerwood would tell me from time to time, when parts of the LEA organisation either were clearly resentful of the priority of funding being given to the scheme, or when some practical obstacles were to be encountered on route. The two cumulatively compounded each other as the level of Central Government inservice grant (GRIST) was reduced from its initially relatively high level caused by Oxfordshire's heavy use of the pool, prior to the introduction of the scheme, to the lower level demanded by the formula. This reached its new level - a drop from x - y - in three years to 1989/90: as pet schemes of advisers were cut back, albeit many of them only recently created, the covetous nature of their glances naturally increased. They took some persuading that the scheme was worthwhile, as it called for quite a high commitment of funding through GRIST to sustain the in-school support for general tutor and mentor. It was fortunate that when Ben Kerwood departed as general adviser for Wiltshire, the responsibility passed successively to two pairs of hands the owners of which, in their different ways, could also see the value of the scheme.

Ben Kerwood had seen the turbulence of the planning year when at times it seemed that OUDES tutors themselves would not be able to discuss their way to consensus and agreement about their new role, especially in the face of some fairly searching criticism from the senior staff planning group who were on full-time secondment to plan it with OUDES.

In retrospect he comments on the intellectual excitement and sheer quality of the debate and about the relative absence of advisory interest or input caused as I have implied earlier, by their preoccupation with other things after the interregnum during Bill Laar's first months as he was creating a team spirit. Kerwood gave way to David Church an educationalist whose advice I valued highly. He was dependable: he had taught in a comprehensive school for many years, had been an area education officer for longer, a senior assistant education officer in charge of secondary schooling and was by that time a general adviser in charge of planning and implementing the pastoral cover of schools. He was key to Bill Laar's plans for the advisory team. Above all he was a safe pair of hands: someone who could be relied upon to keep a weather eye open for trouble and defuse or divert it before the scheme was threatened. At this time, both their impressions and mine, confirmed concerns that some subject departments within the designated schools would not be among the LEAs strongest in that particular subject and there was concern that this might affect the quality of the training of the students. Moreover there was a worry that the designated schools requiring large numbers of trainee teachers would lead to parental complaints of youngsters being subjected too greatly to inexperienced teaching. There was concern too that the 15 or so designated schools would be the target for jealousy from schools not participating. Among the designated schools there was a concern that they might be overwhelmed and that there might be inadequate back-up from the LEA or OUDES.

It was about the time of the launch of the scheme that Ann Carter, a new general adviser for inservice training took up the responsibility for the oversight of the scheme from the LEAs viewpoint. New to the authority from ILEA where she had worked as a Teacher Centre warden she represents serendipity. For it was only later that I discovered that she had taken her PGCE at Sussex University which was later to claim that it had been doing the same thing for 20 years. The Sussex view was represented by the following letter to the *Times Educational Supplement (TES)*:

"Sir, In a context where some politicians, pundits and journalists seem to have convinced themselves that PGCE courses generally teach the theory of swimming to students who aren't allowed near a swimming pool, it is important that the educationists should not collude in developing this myth.

*Oxford University's Department of Education, having finally caught up with development in PGCE work, launched a school-based PGCE course in 1987. Following an HMI visit, this course is now publicised (*TES, *November 11; also* Times Higher Educational Supplement (THES)*, November 11) as "novel", "barely lifted from the drawing board", "a new form", "imaginative", "exemplary" (HMI).*

In fact, the Oxford scheme is extremely similar to the Sussex school-based PGCE. This has been established for 20 years and has been independently evaluated on three occasions and in every case the evaluation has been published. It is also the subject of a published HMI report. Other PGCE courses have been developed along similar lines to the Sussex course over the past decade.

While I would not want to discourage my colleagues at Oxford from extolling the merits of this form of initial training, I would like to correct a damagingly misleading impression they create about what the rest of us have been doing for some time."

Ann Carter's experience of the PGCE at Sussex certainly saw attractive similarities between the two schemes but sharp distinctions. The Sussex scheme involved the payment of honoraria to teachers in different schools to take on the mentor responsibility at the school level. At the university level, departments other than education took a role in the teaching of the subject of methodology. The scheme was much less firmly coupled and it has to be argued that there was not the same coherently thought through programme of matching general tutors and subject mentors which is the feature of the Oxford scheme.

So the scheme eventually came to fruition after a careful year's planning in September 1987 with the first graduates emerging from the profession in 1988. If that is the unexpurgated story of how and why the scheme came to fruition in 1987 from the viewpoint of the LEA, this piece would be incomplete without some attempt at evaluation of how well it has gone from the LEA's viewpoint and what its prospects might be for the future.

First the best testimony is probably to be found in the unsolicited follow-up to the Sussex letter quoted earlier in an opinion article in the *TES* of December 16 1988, from John Claydon, deputy head of Wood Green School, Witney. He writes as follows:

"The enthusiasm with which HM Inspectorate has received the innovatory Postgraduate Certificate in Education course at Oxford University's Department of Educational Studies is mirrored, without exception, in the participating schools. The suggestion (TES November 25) of Oxford being 20 years behind Sussex University is laughable and does no justice to what is being developed here, nor to the impact that the Internship scheme, as it is locally known, has had on our schools. OUDES staff spend most of their time in schools, either as curriculum tutors or general tutors for a group of interns in a particular school. Weekly school-based seminars thus have both a university and a school input. School staff regularly attend OUDES as a matter of course, not as visitors.

My task is to co-ordinate the scheme in my own school. Ten interns are bound to make a substantial difference to a staffroom of 60 and to the amount of contact pupils have with them. It still seems remarkable to me that, despite being very open about the experimental nature of the first Internship year, I received no complaints whatsoever from anyone - teachers, governors, parents or pupils. In fact we were mildly surprised to find that the benefits we had predicted, such as more one-to-one time with individual pupils, genuine team-teaching, stimulation to teaching strategies and real help with the preparation of handouts and resources, actually happened. Interns are not 'played up' or 'tried out' as student-teachers traditionally are. By working with the teacher in the classroom, often in pairs, and gradually assuming responsibility, they are accepted as teachers in their own right.

We are also pleasantly surprised that interns are able to teach us so much about our own school. In carrying out their school-based investigations and research for dissertations, they bring freshness, intelligence and knowledge of the most recent research to so many of the issues which trouble us and on which we have too little time to reflect. We have excellent surveys, for example, of option choices, primary/secondary liaison, special needs provision, sixth form pressures, research on 16 to 19 year olds and equal opportunities.

On a sophisticated plane we find that the age-old gap between theory and practice has disappeared. Four out of five probationer teachers at my school were interns in Oxfordshire schools last year; again and again at interview they demonstrated the maturity, practical awareness and confidence usually associated with more experienced teachers.

Teachers have enjoyed working with interns, and universally not resented giving up some of their own time to plan and evaluate. The reason is that they can see and feel the value of what they are doing as the confidence of the interns grows. The interns have awakened in our teachers what attracted us most to the profession in the first place. There has been a huge stimulation of teaching technique and varied, ambitious approaches.

Judged against other initiatives, Internship has been outstandingly successful. It has been so strongly welcomed in the schools because the staff at OUDES have sacrificed their autonomy for true partnership. All of us who are involved know in our bones that we have hit on something very special and that we are reshaping the future of teacher training nationally."

It is worth noting that of all the schools in Oxfordshire, the Wood Green senior team would be among those most necessary to persuade of the virtue of externally imposed change: properly their plaudits for those in authority are hard won and their criticism, which can be very pointed, unhesitating. The article implies a number of benefits which can be readily recognised including the increased assurance and maturity of the interns, the fillip to good practice for existing teachers and the potential of interns as gatherers of evidence to support processes of school review. In short the presence of the scheme seems to encourage habits which are associated with school effectiveness, for example collective review, professional development, improved classroom pedagogy and intellectual curiosity. As Ben Kerwood remarked:

"If the value of the ordinary student-teacher is high, how much higher was the value of these new interns with the mutual support and team approach planned with their mentors and tutors in school. I was left in no doubt as to this by the experience I had of Pat Ashton's work at Leicester on the IT/INSET Project. Much of the Oxford scheme is based, I believe, on that IT/INSET thinking. I don't think enough acknowledgement was made of that indebtedness...Where the University Department scheme gained was in its commitment to and preparation for team work. It is working successfully now, I suspect...in large measure due to the sense of ownership for the scheme among the teachers in the schools. The same must be true of the University tutors - always likely to be the weakest link in the chain, but equally likely to be one of the greatest beneficiaries of the scheme. In this sense, one of the values of the scheme to the LEA was the updating

and bringing into the heart of our schools of the tutors at the Department. I think this is a particularly interesting aspect, as it again emphasises the mutual gain from an enterprise of this kind. I suppose it is another aspect of the gains from school-based secondments which we used so extensively under GRIST. Teachers seconded into responsible roles in projects became both providers of INSET and beneficiaries of it themselves. One of the best ways to learn something is, of course, to teach it."

A second and invaluable bonus is the quality of recruits to secondary schools in Oxfordshire: not merely appointments in the designated schools but through the linked networks of headteachers in other schools have added to and multiplied the advantage already enjoyed since the day that Harry Judge amended the location policies for teaching practice on his arrival at OUDES and referred to earlier in this chapter.

Longer term prognosis and assessment of innovation is hazardous at the best of times. How far is innovation dependent on the creativity and personal investment of the originators? How high up the agenda of those who have to sustain and adjust the innovation are the principles and aims which were shared by those who created it - often a different group with much less vested interest in its survival?

The Oxford Internship scheme would probably pass those first fitness tests not least because the change involved a root and branch change to a way of working in OUDES, which, in any case, had to change its working habits to meet some of the CATE criteria regarding course length and taught hours. In that sense there is no going back. As I have argued earlier, there were other factors in its favour - the close relationship of the Director of OUDES and the Chief Education Officer and, although it will be quickly appreciated the initiative was one of the last acts of partnership before both departed to new jobs, the fact was probably important only in the planning stages, when the unconvinced voyagers, either in OUDES itself or among the LEA officials, might have been tempted to turn back to port. In any case this close relationship was merely a factor among many others, the key feature of which was that colleagues among advisers, tutors, teachers and headteachers had worked closely together in a proliferation of educational ventures. No, the partnership was always likely to outlive any two individuals who might be leading it.

In normal circumstances therefore, the obvious challenges to the scheme withstand examination. So probably do the subtler ones such as whether there is there an 'Oxford factor' at work in the quality of the PGCE/intern intake and, for that matter, in the quality of the schools, which might make the scheme less transferable. The quality of the OUDES student intake is no different from that of many other departments of education and the quality of Oxfordshire schools, while I believe exceptional, lies within the reach of all, given the right leadership and support. An example of schools just as good can be found in all parts of the country. Moreover, I could argue that participation in the scheme, as the John Claydon extract earlier showed, is a real spur to school effectiveness.

Subsequent press attention, ministerial interest and requests for information from other university and polytechnic departments, suggests that many people believe the idea, or at least the guts of it, is exportable to other areas. Indeed from the LEAs viewpoint with an eye to prospective teacher shortage, the thought of having a captive interest in the training of the best of the profession, is particularly attractive and therefore any distortion of Local Education Authority Training Grant Scheme (LEATGS - the acronym that succeeds GRIST) is easily balanced by the direction of equivalent resources into the paths of other schools not participating. In any case the extra funding for staffing was something which probably was necessary only to pump prime and keep goodwill. The benefit to a particular school, given the long-term certainty of the interns' presence year after year, far outweighs any disadvantage or extra work for those already on the staff.

In normal times one could stop there. Other events however in the short time since the scheme's inception, cast shadows over its future. Consider.

The 1988 Education Reform Act introduced Local Management of Schools (LMS) which requires LEAs to fund schools not on an historical basis with detailed control over separate headings but on a simple formula basis in one form with no strings attached. Simultaneously secondary schools have been encouraged to consider grant maintained status 'opting out' as it is known - which, if attractive to large numbers of secondary schools, would destabilise the LEAs' finances. The argument is analogous to that which led ILEA fatally to call the government's bluff by saying that if more than three Inner London Boroughs opted out it would be impossible for them to operate without costly and wasteful overheads. The answer to that argument is now history as they say - and so is ILEA. Similarly, the LEAs are wary of leaving within the aggregated schools budget too large a central resource of overheads, whether in the mandatory or discretionary exceptions, for fear of their loss in the unwanted event of schools opting out. Put simply, this means that the facility of LEAs to fund special schemes such as the Oxford Internship model is circumscribed. Were it not for the move towards articled teacher status, that perhaps need not be a serious issue because the extra LEA cost involved could be seen as a starter cost only. Moreover, there is a countervailing argument: that the idea of putting extra resource legitimately into targeted schools when the general ability to do that is diminished by LMS should be attractive to some LEAs, namely those who appreciate the shortcomings of the government's general principle of formula funding which diminishes the importance of human judgment in management and hinders the ability to treat schools differently which is the hallmark of translating a policy of equality of opportunity into successful practice.

Nevertheless LMS represents a turbulence factor which renders predictability of the lasting nature of the scheme more than usually hazardous.

So too, but on a larger scale, is the government's response to the gathering crisis in teacher availability. (It is incidentally proper to redescribe teacher shortage in this way as the problem facing the profession is unprecedented and unique since it is not so much a problem

of insufficiency but of unattractiveness to those already trained). To deal with this problem the government has a battery of tactics but no discernible or at least declared strategy, partly one suspects because to acknowledge the existence of the problem is unacceptable politically. Included in that battery are:
- The proposal for licensed teachers aimed at more mature entrants either from other countries or in mid-career - those who formerly might have enrolled for a PGCE course as a mature student, either on a full or part-time basis;
- The articled teacher initiative which sees teachers training on a school focused but HE institution linked course over two years during which the trainee teacher will be paid a bursary by the host LEA.

Both these developments have at their heart the notion of the school as the focus for development, the second in particular may be a prelude to the break up of the quota of places and the exposure of the system to the vagaries of market forces which in the end may shrivel the expertise of research, reflection and renewal which has always been the strength of the university or polytechnic departments.

It goes against the grain to be alarmist - but the outcome may be the total transfer of the process of education and training of would-be teachers from the HE institutions to the schools themselves. If it were to be so, these 'teacher training' schools would have considerable advantages in recruitment and in public perception unless the LEA acted through its paymaster role (which is envisaged in the preliminary details of the articled teacher proposals) as a quality control agency, switching about the privilege of training in a ceaseless quest to make all schools enjoy the spur to effectiveness which the Internship scheme has clearly proffered to those schools enjoying it. But it is important to point out the link with the HE institution in the model as being perceived by the school as an important and vital ingredient in it. The preferred option therefore lies in a combination of rotating designated schools, LEA and HE institutions. One hopes people will stop to consider the evidence before disturbing such a triangular model. The Oxford Internship scheme provides a powerful example to those who care to pause for thought and whose objective is not short term expediency but the long term goal of bringing within reach of every child the possibility of successful learning within a successful school.

Chapter X

An Evolving Course

Terry Allsop and Graham Corney

Terry Allsop and Graham Corney have been joint tutors for the PGCE Course at OUDES since 1988, the second full year of Internship. Curriculum tutors for Chemistry and Geography respectively, each is also a general tutor with a particular responsibility for a general group of interns in one of the Internship schools. As expected, the first year of Internship suggested that some things had been overplanned, others underplanned; some aspects of the new roles proved problematic, others were to be unexpectedly rewarding. Nonetheless, although there were necessary adjustments to be made, the fundamental model had proved itself and had sufficient flexibility to adapt.

At the time of writing the course is only mid-way through its second operational year. Even so, the innovative nature of the programme has generated its own momentum for further development, and this has been supplemented by evaluation of the course in practice. This chapter begins by summarising how the course is being monitored and evaluated, and then records some of the main changes being implemented.

1. Evaluating Practice

The course is monitored and evaluated in a number of ways. Continuing evaluation and development is a feature of the regular meetings of each curriculum subject group and the professional tutors' group, each composed of school and OUDES staff. It is also carried out in schools in meetings of mentors from different subjects and their school's professional tutor, and at OUDES through termly staff development days.

During the first year of operation, each school nominated a representative to monitor the introduction of the course, receiving a one-day secondment from Oxfordshire LEA. These teachers and members of OUDES formed the Internship Monitoring Group (IMG). At the end of the year, the group's written reports highlighted achievements and noted areas of concern. During the second year of operation, each school was again able to nominate a representative to support the course, receiving one day's secondment from the LEA. These teachers and members of the university formed the Internship Support Group (ISG), their work being based on concerns identified by the IMG.

The work of these two groups has been invaluable, providing the beginnings of longitudinal reflection on the course. A major review day meeting was held on 9 November 1988, involving headteachers and staff from 16 schools along with representatives from the LEA and all OUDES tutors. The deliberations of that day gave us enormous encouragement for the future of the course, and a great deal of evaluative material.

In these ways, all school and OUDES staff have been able to draw on evaluation, to share experiences with one another, and to reflect on their own practice and experience. An additional source of evaluation and support has been effectively provided by the field officer, an experienced teacher seconded full-time by the LEA for the period 1986-90.

The remainder of this chapter highlights the agenda for development resulting from these ongoing discussions.

2. The General Programme

The General Programme in the 1987-88 course consisted of a number of themes which recurred at several points during the year. Thus any theme, for example 'Pupils with Special Needs', consisted of several presentations at OUDES, investigations by interns in school, and school-based seminars reporting on the results of these investigations. In practice the interns were therefore involved in studying a number of themes at one time, and general and professional tutors reported that the programme was over-complex. A working party devised a programme for 1988-89 based on themes treated in blocks of time, usually of two weeks' duration, covering the weeks up to the first 'S' week. The themes included in 1988-89 were:

- Learning and teaching
- Pupils and their learning (special needs, language, rights of groups)
- Curriculum and assessment
- Information Technology
- Personal and social education

The make-up of one typical theme is given in *Figure 1* below. It shows the inter-weaving of the different elements of the theme, identifying the different activities and their different locations.

Figure 1
Education for a multi-ethnic society

Introduction to multi-ethnic policies and practice	-	Presentation, and follow-up seminar with general tutor in OUDES
Multi-ethnic considerations in a particular school	-	Investigations and seminars in school organised by professional tutor and general tutor
Multi-ethnic considerations in a specific subject	-	Activities in OUDES and school teaching organised by curriculum tutor and mentor
Education for a multi-ethnic society	-	Assignments carried out by the intern based on OUDES and school activities together with individual reading and reflection

---

In addition, for the second half of the year, a number of Access Topics have been developed, to be incorporated in the programme of each school, but planned by general/professional tutors to suit their schedule. The topics, which are supplemented by occasional whole-course presentations are:
- Education and industry
- School and community
- 16 - 19 education
- Education after the 1988 Act

3. Phases of the Year

In the scheme as originally planned it was envisaged that interns who had achieved a basic level of proficiency related to the List of Important Abilities should be awarded 'chartered intern status' at the end of the second term. The intention was that this would alter the relationship between successful interns and their mentor/curriculum tutor, thereby encouraging them to adopt a more self-evaluative approach and take on greater classroom responsibility.

In the first year of operation, chartered intern status was not understood by all participants, and practice varied considerably: the IMG reports identified it as an area of concern. During the second year, a group of ISG members took account of the previous year's experience, developed more clearly the principle of two phases in the year, and discussed this with staff in schools and OUDES. An interim report from the field officer suggests that their work has helped interns, mentors and tutors to understand the ideas more clearly and to develop more effective practice.

These can be summarised as follows:
(i) In Phase One of the year, the focus is on helping each intern to achieve a basic level of classroom proficiency.
(ii) In Phase Two of the year, each intern is encouraged to take greater responsibility for identifying and developing aspects of their own teaching which most concern them. This is carried out in partnership with their mentor and curriculum tutor. During the last few weeks of the year, each intern is asked to contribute to a particular aspect of the work of the school department identified in discussion with the mentor.
(iii) In the past the transition from Phase One to Phase Two has been recognised by the award of chartered intern status but there is a resolve in the future to make this process more sensitive to the needs of individual interns.

4. Reporting on Interns' Progress

During the first year of operation of the scheme, it became clear that, in a situation where four professionals were involved in monitoring the progress of each intern, an effective system for recording was essential. A working party developed a new set of reports which are completed three times during the year by the mentor and curriculum tutor, and by the general tutor and professional tutor. An example of one of these is given in *Figure 2*. These reports have clarified the process of monitoring intern's achievements: this is likely to lead to the development of an intern profile in the near future.

Figure 2
Postgraduate Certificate in Education

Intern's Name ——————————————

ASSESSMENT REFERENCE POINT 2

The following form to be completed by
Curriculum Tutor and Mentor

Please indicate your judgment of the intern in relation to each of the
following:

	Satisfactory	Unsatisfactory
Attendance		
Attitude		
Completion of required tasks and activities		
Completion of appropriate written work		
Classroom performance as described in the list of important abilities		

A satisfactory answer to each of these is necessary for the intern to
move from Phase 1 to Phase 2 of the year and sufficient if in agreement
with the judgments made by the General Tutor and Professional Tutor.

If you consider the intern unsatisfactory in any area, please give
further details. If you would like to comment positively on any aspects
of the intern's progress, please do so, overleaf if necessary.

Signed_____(Curriculum Tutor)
_____(Mentor)

5. Interns' Assignments
Assignments carried out by students before the introduction of the
Internship scheme differed in nature between curriculum and general
work. For curriculum assignments, it was common practice for students to
be asked to prepare assignments which related school practice to a more

general understanding of issues related to particular aspects of the teaching of a subject. General assignments, however, had tended to be very theoretical in nature. The introduction of the new course has allowed both curriculum and general assignments to relate practice to theory. Two innovations deserve specific mention.

(i) Throughout the year, both General and Curriculum Programmes generate small scale investigations to be carried out in school, some taking as little as 30 minutes of observation, others representing a week's work. Findings are routinely reported back after an agreed time to the relevant group. Exceptionally, data has been used in presentations to faculty or whole-staff meetings, and in one case in the formal evaluation report of a school to the LEA. One group, at Gosford Hill School, was asked to prepare a report for a school working party on equal opportunities.

(ii) Each intern is asked to prepare, for submission in the summer term, a dissertation of between 5,000 and 10,000 words. In the world of Internship, this too has to have an empirical element based on work done in the intern's school, along with some critical reflection based on reading. In at least one school, the professional tutor has created a list of themes which the school would like looked at! No wonder, then, that the engagement with the task and the quality of the product have been enhanced. In the second year of operation, interns have been encouraged to begin work on their dissertations immediately after Christmas in order to allow time for serious empirical work. It was fascinating at the 9 November review to find headteachers seeking access to the findings of the dissertations done in their schools, recognising that it was unusual for such work to be done in schools except occasionally by researchers, and that such work was bound to have an impact on their own staff who were frequently involved in the development of the study.

6. The Role of Curriculum Tutors

During the 'J' weeks where there is strong interaction between university and school elements of the course, the curriculum tutor now has the crucial task of maintaining the rhythm of Topic Introduction - School Experience - Debriefing and Reflection most often on a weekly or two-weekly cycle.

There was a notion abroad in the early days of the scheme that a major part of the work of curriculum tutors was being transferred to the mentors. With experience of the scheme, it is now being realised that the partnership of mentor and curriculum tutor provides the interns with a far greater measure of support, critical reflection, and encouragement than the separate roles did in the past. While mentors contribute their expertise as experienced teachers, the role of curriculum tutors has had to be rethought. In the first year of the scheme, a meeting of mentors at Lord Williams's School, Thame, indicated the following areas of concern relating to the role of curriculum tutors:

- That minimum expectations of the number of visits to each pair of interns should be established
- That planning of visits should be carefully co-ordinated with mentors as well as interns

- That brief visits are ineffective, longer visits of perhaps half a day are required to fulfil the idea of partnership in Internship
- That tutors need to have a clear function in each lesson in which they participate

A discussion paper produced by curriculum tutors during 1988-89 suggests the following guidelines:
- Normally, a useful visit to a school is likely to be of half-day duration
- Visits following prior planning between curriculum tutor and intern(s) are likely to be particularly profitable. The regular involvement of both curriculum tutor and mentor in the planning of the work of the intern is an important aspect of creating coherence in the Internship scheme
- Curriculum tutors' active participation in lessons may take a variety of forms (eg group work, work with individual pupils, assistance with GCSE assessments, assistance with oral work, neutral chairing of debates/ simulations, helping to organise and carry out field work). The notion of curriculum tutors deliberately setting up 'demonstration lessons' is not thought generally appropriate in Internship
- Curriculum tutors will normally try to engage in three-way discussions of interns teaching. Crucially, the curriculum tutor will ensure that discussion of the intern's work with the mentor takes place before leaving the school
- Curriculum tutors will continue to develop the idea of partnership supervision, particularly during the second part of the year
- Curriculum tutors and mentors will continue to use their meetings to discuss the nature of curriculum tutor visits
- All of this takes us well along the road to a reconceptualisation of the curriculum tutor's role in schools, perhaps taking over at last from the basic view of 'recent and relevant experience' propagated by CATE.

7. Professional Development of Teachers
Two areas of interest are noted in this section.
(i) Evidence from a number of sources, including the field officer, suggests that mentors are very positive about the scheme. Two typical comments are:
"It has helped me to reflect on my own teaching"
and
"It has given me personally a tremendous boost".

However, it is not surprising that among the 70 or so mentors, understanding of the scheme varies, and this affects their practice with interns. An important part of both the curriculum group meetings and informal mentor-curriculum tutor discussions is to help mentors and tutors increase the effectiveness of their work with interns.

One means by which their effectiveness can be increased is through mentors' participation in a new course on Internship leading to the award of a Special Diploma in Educational Studies. This two-year, part-time programme allows mentors and professional tutors opportunity to study in depth six modules related to Internship, to carry out extensive practical work related to their role, and to write a reflective report about their work.
(ii) Evidence from informal discussion and the reports written by members of the IMG suggests that teachers involved in the Internship

scheme benefit professionally. More recently, a small group of ISG members have taken the professional development of teachers as their focus. An early task for the group was to identify the potential for professional development arising from Internship. Opportunities were listed at three levels - individual teachers, school departments, schools. The list was discussed by representatives of school and university staff at ISG meetings and in the November 1988 review meeting. Amendments were made where appropriate, and the finalised list is reproduced as *Figure 3.*

Figure 3

Potential professional development opportunities at individual teacher level

Potential Professional Development: Individual Teacher	Internship Activities
1a. Mentors and other subject teachers' increased awareness and reflection about their own teaching strategies and overall approach to teaching.	1.1 Mentors/other teachers' collaborative lesson planning, teaching and reflection with interns, and curriculum tutors on occasions.
1b. Mentors and other subject teachers implementing new ideas and approaches.	1.2 Mentors/other teachers collaborative lesson observation and reflection with interns.
	1.3 Mentors/other teachers involvement in assessment of interns.
	1.4 Mentors involvement in planning and reflection about the overall curriculum programme for interns with other mentors and curriculum tutors.
	1.5 Mentors/other teachers discussion about current issues affecting them - with curriculum tutors.
2a. Form tutors, increased awareness and reflection about their own 'teaching' strategies and overall approach to PSE.	2.1 Form tutors, collaborative planning, observing, teaching and reflecting about PSE work (both individual lessons and units of work).
2b. Form tutors implementing new ideas and approaches.	2.2 Presence of interns enabling different kinds of work to go on in PSE.
	2.3 Form tutors' involvement in assessment of interns.
3. Professional tutors increased awareness and reflection about school policies and cross-curriculum/whole-school issues.	3.1 Professional tutor leading seminars on cross-curriculum/whole-school issues; and collaborating in joint seminars with general tutors.
	3.2 Professional tutor planning and reflecting about the overall programme for interns on cross-curriculum/whole-school issues - with general tutor.
	3.3 Professional tutors involvement in assessment of intern.
	3.4 Professional tutor involved in cross-school networks - with other professional tutors.

Potential professional development opportunities at department level

Potential Professional Development: Department	Internship Activities
1a. Increasing awareness and reflection about departmental teaching strategies and overall policies. 1b. Implementation of new teaching strategies and policy.	1.1 Collaboration between mentors/other teachers and interns in planning, observing, teaching and reflecting about lessons acting as a catalyst to departmental developments. Curriculum tutor also involved in this process at times. 1.2 Presence of two interns enabling different kinds of work to go on in a department (eg small group work). 1.3 Interns' subject expertise as recent graduates. 1.4 Interns releasing subject teachers (especially in second half of the year) for departmental development. 1.5 Interns developing resources for departments. 1.6 Curriculum tutors asked to advise on current issues affecting department. 1.7 Mentors' involvement in a curriculum network with mentors from other schools and curriculum tutors.

Potential professional development opportunities at school level

Potential Professional Development: School	Internship Activities
1. Professional tutor's increased awareness and reflection about school policies: input to staff meetings and working parties.	1.1 Professional tutor leading seminars on whole-school/cross-curriculum issues, and collaborating in joint seminars with general tutor.

1.2 Professional tutor planning and reflecting about the overall intern's programme on whole-school/cross-curricular issues - with general tutor.

1.3 Professional tutor involved in assessment of interns.

1.4 Professional tutor involved in cross-school networks - with other professional tutors.

1.5 Interns carrying out investigations related to school priorities.

1.6 General tutor acting informally in an advisory capacity, and more formally contributing to school INSET programme. |
| 2. Year tutors influenced by form tutors. | 2.1 Form tutors working with interns to plan, observe, teach and reflect about PSE work (both individual lessons, and units of work). |
| 3. Induction of probationers. | 3.1 Probationers joining interns seminars. |

Having prepared this list, the group then collected evidence of professional development in practice. The example of mentor development is taken as illustrative. Evidence was initially collected through a questionnaire for mentors in four schools, and this was then supplemented with selected interviews. A summary of the questionnaire sections is shown in *Figure 4*.

Figure 4
Mentor Professional Development   (n=17)

1. How long have you been in Internship?
(i)   in planning, pre 1987   13
(ii)   in 1987-88   13
(iii)   in 1988-89   16

2. How have you as a mentor worked with interns?
(i)   Joint planning of lessons   17
(ii)   Joint teaching   17
(iii)   Joint reflection after joint teaching   17
(iv)   Observing an intern teach   17
(v)   Helping an intern with diagnostic assessment
        (phase 1 of the year)   14
(vi)   Helping an intern through partnership supervision
        (phase 2 of the year)   13
(vii)   Intern observing a lesson you taught, with
        follow-up discussion   17
(viii) Others mentioned:
        Help with written assignments/dissertation   4
        Help with job interviews   1
        Help with evaluating new teaching materials   1
        Joint preparation for an open evening   1

3. Which of these have helped you develop your own skills as a
teacher?
        Reflection on my own teaching   13
        New ideas from interns/OUDES   7
        Improved teaching strategies   10
                                                                        includes
                                                                   group work:3

4. Are there other aspects of Internship from which you feel you have
benefited?
        Working with curriculum tutor/field officer   2
        Increasing department resources   2
        Meeting other mentors in OUDES   3
        Increased job satisfaction/morale   2
        Mentor meetings in school   1
        Affecting the staff of the department as a whole   5

---

8. Structural Issues

The symmetry of the initial Internship model, 15 participating schools each with ten interns, was appealing but ignored a number of issues, several of which were discussed in a session with participating headteachers at the 9 November meeting. From the outset it had been stated that all Oxfordshire secondary schools were members of the scheme, but that only some were actively involved at any one time. We were much exercised by the existence of a queue of schools wishing to work with interns. Two approaches have been agreed, after discussion with the Oxfordshire Secondary Heads Association and the LEA. Firstly, in order to allow up to five more schools into the scheme, schools may, after three years involvement, be asked to rest for one year. Secondly, for the 1989-90 year, schools were invited to consider working in pairs.

Throughout the development of Internship, a fundamental principle has been that of the engagement of the interns with the life of one school throughout almost a complete school year; it is perhaps the sense of belonging thus engendered that has marked the scheme as so successful for the interns. Some adaptions are clearly appropriate and would include:
- Interns working in 11-16 schools need to experience sixth-form work.
- Interns working in 13-18 upper schools in Oxford city should spend time teaching in the 9-13 middle schools.
- Interns working in single-sex schools should see other approaches.

The pairing of schools is therefore not problematic if it allows the kinds of extensions of experience listed above. What is much less clear, and arguably much more doubtful, is whether the essentials of Internship can be retained when smaller numbers of interns in two schools are brought together only for certain aspects of the course, chiefly the General Programme. Initial responses from the schools suggest a lack of

Ed. The three suggestions above that interns in 11-16, 13-18 and single sex schools should have wider experience have all subsequently been adopted.

The scheme continues to grow. For the academic year 1990-91 there will be 18 internship schools in the secondary sector, aided by one tertiary college and links with several middle schools. There will be 186 interns. Nearly 100 mentors and 19 professional tutors will thus be directly involved.

Chapter XI

Internship: A View from Outside
Paul H Hirst

How does the Internship course compare with other English teacher
education programmes which are substantially school-based? Four such
programmes were recently evaluated in a Cambridge-based project
directed by Dr John Furlong and Professor Paul Hirst. We therefore asked
Dr Furlong to be Internship's first external examiner, and we asked
Professor Hirst to write one of the final chapters for this book. Since
Internship is not only a practical development but also a contribution to
theoretical thinking about teacher education, we were interested too to
know how Hirst, whose own theoretical position is radically different,
would react to Internship ideas.

We have not been disappointed. His judgment about how our own
practice compares with that of others is certainly interesting. We accept the
implication of his chapter that we need to express some of our ideas more
clearly and in more detail. Most especially his arguments about
inadequacies in our theoretical rationale will contribute, we hope, to a
useful ongoing debate; a parallel critique from an Internship perspective is
being contemporaneously published in another book on partnership in
teacher education, edited by Paul Hirst's Cambridge colleagues.

To anyone concerned with the development of initial teacher education
courses and searching for a programme that begins to do justice to the
complex demands of the enterprise, the preceding accounts of the Oxford
Internship scheme, its rationale and its practical development, make
fascinating and rewarding reading. It is very doubtful whether any
previous initiative in this area undertaken in the UK has been so
thoroughly deliberated in its planning, so carefully implemented and so
extensively monitored. What has been achieved is indeed most impressive
and for some time to come other UK courses are likely to be appraised at
least in part in relation to this particular 'paradigm'. Manifestly those
responsible for its evolution were working in the wider context of a
certain amount of research and considerable experiment undertaken in
numerous universities and colleges over the last 25 years. There was too
the impetus of increasing national and international concern to securely
ground teacher education in the realities of the day-to-day practical
demands of teaching and schooling. As a result, the outcome can be seen
as very much the embodiment of the present 'state of the art'.

Central to that 'state' is the explicit rejection, expressed clearly in this
volume, of two previous 'models' of initial training. First there is the model
of 'apprenticeship', rejected primarily because its limited and limiting
'imitation' is quite inadequate for the complex professional demands of

contemporary teaching. Yet it had to be recognised that at the heart of professional practice of the most sophisticated kind, there lies a body of knowledge, judgments, skills, dispositions, activities and relationships that can only be developed in the actual doing of the job. They must be learnt at the feet of a 'master' if each generation of students is not to start from scratch.

The other model explicitly rejected is that of 'theory into practice'. With the development of educational psychology and then in the 1960s, particularly, of sociology and philosophy of education, a new concept emerged of educational practice rooted in the achievements of these and other disciplined studies of education. The basic idea was simple: the inadequate 'commonsense' of teachers handed on in apprenticeship training should be replaced by the rationally defensible knowledge and understanding which the disciplines alone can provide. It was considered that only on that basis could truly professional judgments, skills and so on be developed. Initial training on this view is seen as the acquisition of certain bodies of academic theory which students then learn to apply in practice. But again the inadequacy, even the impossibility, of professional practice in these terms has become only too obvious. For all its ambitions, the understanding available in the disciplines does not begin to provide, and maybe in principle cannot provide, the basic knowledge necessary for the complex tasks of teaching. And if professional practice cannot be so conducted, training cannot possibly be satisfactorily constructed in these terms. Yet it has to be recognised that work in the disciplines has indeed progressively shaped many areas of educational practice, making those practices more rationally defensible and thereby more professionally acceptable. Worthwhile initial training must therefore prepare teachers to engage seriously in the proper critical, rational appraisal of what they do in the light of developing knowledge and understanding in the disciplines.

But if neither of these extreme models is adequate, on what model exactly can courses properly be based? Indeed where are we to look for such a model? There being no readily acceptable articulation of what professional practice, and hence professional training, actually involves, the repeated answer in recent years has often been to look to the pragmatic development of courses rather than to some theoretically justified rationale. Indeed if the most defensible practices of teaching itself cannot be simply derived from prior theory, those of teacher education would seem to be equally unattainable by that procedure. In that case, why not look for the most defensible model in successful practical experimentation? Let us progressively adapt initial training courses by critical rational reflection in the light of experience, being prepared to modify both ends and means in the process. The best emerging model for courses will then at least have the pragmatic justification that it successfully prepares students for the practical business of teaching. Just such pragmatic development has been the hall-mark of changes to many PGCE courses over the last 15 or more years and the Oxford Internship programme is surely the most sophisticated example to emerge in the UK to date.

Looking at this course in the context of previous experiments, it is immediately apparent that almost every element in the programme has been tried elsewhere. Against the background of the wide ranging courses validated by CNAA, the possibilities considered by UCET working-parties (1) and the characteristics of the school-based PGCE courses examined in a recent DES project (2), what stands out about the Oxford course is not the novelty of its overall approach or of its major elements. Rather it is the way that its approach and its elements have been so systematically and self-critically worked through. As a result, the programme capitalises more than any other on the most successful features of current practice. One has only to read the formulation of the goals, the problems and the principles of Internship here set out to recognise in these what many others have set out elsewhere. The concentration of students in particular schools, working in pairs, was successfully exploited even 20 years ago, particularly in London. The involvement of students in sustained 'internship' working under the aegis of a 'mentor', even if those terms were not employed, was built into the University of Sussex course in 1964, and its impressive achievements have been widely attested.(3) The varying strengths and weaknesses of patterns of serial practice, with students working in school one day, two days or even three days a week when not in full-time block school experience are now becoming generally recognised.(4) Successful attempts at tightly relating work in school and in a training institution on both subject teaching and wider professional concerns have become almost commonplace. And no one can doubt that the greater the degree of joint planning and co-ordinated execution of a course by teachers and tutors working in collaboration, the greater is the likelihood of producing effective training. Roles almost identical with those of the Oxford 'university general tutor' and the 'school professional tutor' have been introduced to excellent effect elsewhere. Other parallels could readily be drawn by moving down into the finer detail of the Oxford course. But none of this is surprising, for though little or no mention is made of developments in other places, the world of the PGCE tutor is relatively small and the formal and informal contacts of those involved are quite considerable.

The point being made here, however, is that the Oxford course has been able to build confidently on an emerging body of successful practice. On that basis, with great determination and single-mindedness and by exploiting to the full a sympathetic context, there has been forged a tightly formulated and structured programme that others have almost despaired of achieving. Indeed others approaching so tight a scheme of collaboration and agreed procedures have had to retreat to less effective organisation in the face of decreasing resources and growing pressures on schools. All the more then are the achievements of the Oxford course to be applauded.

Others seeking to develop highly collaborative schemes in current circumstances will probably envy above all the opportunities provided when an LEA is prepared to second 12 teachers and an LEA officer full-time for a year, then to give to each school in the programme resourcing of 0.5 of a teacher and release of one teacher a day a week for two years. When that support comes after years of close working, during which many teachers have taken advanced courses in the training department, the opportunities for sustained joint creative planning and effective implementation really do exist. But such opportunities have to be well used and the organisation of the various planning and implementation groups in ways suited to the circumstances of all concerned is critical. Crucial too is devising procedures that will release the initiative and enthusiasm of all those concerned. The practical 'nous' of those responsible for the detailed work, the drive of tutors and teachers alike and the dynamic leadership and support of 'those at the top' were clearly vital elements in pushing this complex development though in the face of every difficulty.

The key feature of this, as of so many other educational developments can perhaps best be seen as centring round three kinds of issues; those concerning the structure of the course, the roles of the personnel involved in implementing it and the teaching methods and styles used throughout. Where the course structure is concerned, the pattern of periods of serial and block school experience sets a framework that makes possible or impossible certain forms of collaboration between teachers and tutors and thereby the inter-relation of the kinds of training each group provides. If teachers are to take over from tutors more of the training than has traditionally been the case, they manifestly need more time with students. But the issue of the patterning of serial and block experience turns above all, on the relationship envisaged between students work with teachers and that with tutors. 'Apprenticeship' training demands sustained school experience and little else. 'Theory into practice' training tends to distinguish sustained periods for the mastery of difficult theory at the hands of tutors from periods for the mastery of skills of practical application primarily under the supervision of teachers. Alternating blocks of theory and practice thus seems the inevitable pattern if anything is to be thoroughly undertaken. But if certain forms of theoretical work with tutors are seen as in some sense necessary elements contributing to students' practical training itself when that is fully professional conceived, then a serial pattern of work becomes critical. If even basic professional activities require insight that tutors rather than teachers can best provide, serial experience has a crucial role.

How many days per week must be spent in school will of course depend on exactly what theoretical work is considered important and how far it is judged that teachers can or cannot undertake it. In the Sussex course, much of theoretical work considered necessary for practice is placed in the hands of teachers where both subject teaching and wider professional matters are concerned. As a result, three days a week are spent in schools for a very substantial part of the course. In the DES-sponsored study of school-based work in four different PGCE courses it seemed clear however that unless very special arrangements are made, teachers are happier with a somewhat less demanding theoretical role.(5) In the Oxford course, two days a week in school prior to a major block experience would seem to harmonise well their notions of the significance of different types of theory for practice and realistic expectations of what teachers rather than tutors can best undertake with students.

The idea of a return to serial practice after block experience of some 12 weeks in which students come to take over full teaching responsibilities is much more questionable however. In the DES study many students found a return to a seemingly less responsible role in a now well known school difficult and frustrating.(6) Opportunities for more specialised work or wider experience in another context seem to have proved more successful in other courses. A change of school or another teaching institution for the last practice can also help to overcome the otherwise narrow range of experiences that work in only one school provides.(7) In the light of the difficulties already voiced at Oxford, modification of the programme along these lines might be worth serious consideration. The issue of serial or block work at the period, as at any earlier stage, is again related to questions about the significance of theoretical work in relation to practice. Once basic professional competence had been established, it could be argued that more sustained attention to theoretical questions begins to have a place, making serial practice less significant. Be that as it may, it is surely clear that the coherent development of the structure of a course presupposes some view of the kinds of theory students must master, its relationship to practice and how mastery of the theory in proper relationship to practice is best achieved. Though the presuppositions of the Oxford course on these matters have been spelt out to some extent, teasing them out further would no doubt help solve some of the remaining uncertainties about the course structure.

The same clarification could surely also help to sort out certain ambiguities that still seem to hover around the central question of the roles of teachers and tutors. The roles of mentors and school professional tutors are clearly seen as rooted in their possession of situational knowledge of schools, classes and pupils. They have thus a sharp grasp of the criteria for practical effectiveness, bearing in mind the political, resource, expertise and the time constraints of the context. By contrast, university tutors are seen as possessing a knowledge of research evidence, general ideas of good practice, being able to grasp issues of theoretical cohesion and the educational and social values implicit in practices. They thus can bring different criteria to the assessment of practice and therefore have a different role to play in teacher training. When it comes to the relationship between these two forms of expertise and thus the proper relationship of the related roles in training, what is said is both more debatable and less decisively helpful. That knowledge of both kinds and the use of both kinds of criteria in understanding practice are important for students' professional development is strongly maintained. And it is clearly recognised that each of these two convenient categories itself contains very diverse forms of knowledge and criteria.

But it is also asserted that none of this knowledge is totally reliable or universally applicable and that 'wise beginning teachers will take none of it on trust, but will carefully examine and test it for themselves'. Students must therefore approach learning to teach in a realistic, rational and exploratory way, having access to different kinds of knowledge about teaching whilst realising that tutors and teachers will often employ quite different and even conflicting, if equally valid, criteria for practice. Knowledge from university sources especially needs testing with the help of mentors against practicality criteria in the schools. Knowledge from school sources especially needs testing with the help of tutors against more academic criteria in the university. By these means interns are to be encouraged to develop their own personal thinking, synthesising knowledge acquired from various sources and testing it against diverse criteria. In the end, students should have learned to monitor their own teaching, not only in relation to criteria specified by others, but they should also have articulated their own criteria for personal self-evaluation and have both justified these and have generated valid ways in which evidence could be collected and evaluated in relation to these criteria.

If that is the relationship of various kinds of knowledge and theory to practice, then the proper roles of teachers and tutors in training are not going to be marked by consensus or even consistency in either their theory or practice. The course is then one in which students are to find a coherence between university and school elements because of the dialogue and mutual respect between the parties and the co-ordinated and integrated programme they provide. In the earlier part of the course however, for pragmatic reasons, students must find effective ways of meeting certain specified necessary demands of competent teaching. It is later that they must come to articulate and explore their own criteria for important facets of their teaching and gather evidence for looking critically in these terms at what they do.

Such a view of the relationship between different kinds of theory and practice is certainly generous to all would-be contributors. It frees tutors and teachers of any real responsibility for reconciling their views and contributions to training except at the earliest stage. But it manifestly makes huge demands on students by giving them each the responsibility for forging a way through to a coherent personal view of what teaching for them involves. Faced with diverse criteria and partial knowledge, they are enjoined to test things for themselves, and that to the extent of articulating their own criteria for examining their own practice. The collaboration of tutors and teachers in such a training enterprise demands first that they agree on this model and its presentation to students as the rationale for what they will encounter. Beyond that, each party can exercise its own autonomy whilst procedurally agreeing to co-ordinate the timing of work on topics on which both parties can contribute. It seems to demand too, collaboration in promoting students' testing of ideas and practices they encounter so that they can find a personal view. At the earliest stage however such an open-ended approach is recognised as practically impossible and basic competence is seen as achieved by engaging in activities satisfying criteria laid down by teacher and tutors.

But is this need for specific 'laid down' criteria simply a pragmatic demand in the early stages of learning to teach? Is it perhaps not rather the case that all practical judgments, skills and relationships however sophisticated, implicitly if not explicitly, conform to certain criteria which are being accepted, for such criteria are in fact constitutive of those judgments, skills and relationships? Calling into question the criteria of any practical activity or testing those criteria is then a procedure necessarily incompatible with the actual exercise of the practical activity itself in a rational way. At all stages of their teaching, in the development of their practice, students must then at least provisionally employ criteria they have acquired or developed from somewhere or somehow. At the very start students of the Oxford course, like all others, if they are to achieve practical success acquire the criteria they employ by taking on board understanding, activities and skills that are objectively enshrined in the actual school practices they encounter. Tutors and teachers clearly wish students to be thus initiated into practices they consider thoroughly professional, and a significant consensus by all parties on the criteria of these practices is necessary for students' coherent development. But must such consensus progressively give way to diverse views and practices through which students find their own way, formulating their own criteria and testing things for themselves as they go?

Does not truly professional development demand a more positive and substantive role from tutors and teachers? On the account given, consensus on the contributions from the two parties seems unattainable, indeed almost ruled out in principle. And even the search for consensus as a basis for professional practice seems to be dismissed. Each individual student, like each individual teacher, is seen as left without the support of even an emerging consensus on what practices in any general sense are professionally justified. A personal professional stance, individually tested seems to be all there is.

Clearly in the contributions of a number of tutors and teachers in earlier chapters there is a hankering after the provision for students of a much more far reaching consensus in both the theoretical and practical parts of the course than the rationale of the course considers legitimate. And what is more some of the well developed parts of the course are shown to have been jointly produced on the basis that there is an evolving body of practices for which public rational defence is to be expected and should be pursued by those professionally involved. What is thus supported is the view that teachers should not be trained to see themselves as primarily developing a personal professional stance. Rather they should see themselves as part of a professional group working towards an ever increasing consensus about practice. Students are then to be trained by initiation into the most defensible practices to date and into the search for the further development of these.

Of course there is one sense in which students must individually find their own coherent and defensible practices, for they alone can make appropriate judgments in the particular unique circumstances they face. But that can only be a rationally defensible procedure if it is in the light of knowledge and principles that are justified by wide ranging professional experience. Professional practice is no such thing unless it is based on a body of knowledge and generalisation which has public rational defence way beyond anything individuals can personally synthesise and test. As researchers and experimenters, tutors and teachers play vital roles in the formation of general principles for educational practice. But in teaching itself, and in training others to teach, such general principles are being used in the immediacies of practice to make the most defensible judgments possible. In these circumstances a teacher or student comes to formulate hypotheses for handling particular classes and these hypotheses are individually formulated and tested, but not directly against a chaotic world of conflicting knowledge and views. No individual teacher is capable of such a procedure, nor is it rationally defensible. A band of justified principles relevant to the situation alone can make the individual enterprise coherently intelligible and rationally manageable.

If this is so, then training throughout requires firstly the development of personal understanding and individual practice in the light of the best available professional knowledge and general principles. Secondly it requires that students learn to seek constantly more justifiable knowledge and principles and to contribute in their own way to the investigation and experimentation that can in rational debate and criticism generate such an expanding basis for professional practice.

If this view of theory, practice and the relationship between them is correct, then the Oxford programme is in its articulated principles aiming at an ideal which is in the end, not only impossible but mistaken. It follows that in the end, the roles of tutors and teachers must fall apart rather than cohere. In practice, things seem to work on a more acceptable basis at least in some, and perhaps in many, elements. Tutors and teachers then work towards an emerging consensus throughout. In other places, ambiguity and uncertainty about roles is to be found. What seems now to be needed is a sharper, more detailed elucidation of just how theory of various kinds must operate if practice is to be adequately professional, and in the light of this, a more detailed formulation of the roles of tutors and teachers. Separating a first level of theory as this operates in the immediacy of practice, from other levels of theory would surely help to sort out that training which is necessarily personal, individual and experiential from that which is necessarily more general if equally crucial to the enterprise. Getting clearer about such levels of theory would then surely pay off in sharper characterisation of the roles that teachers and tutors can best undertake and the relationship between them.

The same clarification of the theory-practice relationship would also seem to be the key to resolving ambiguities about the methods and styles of training that tutors and teachers should employ. In the course details relatively little is said explicitly on these matters though certain general features of the approach are clear. At the start, training might be described as primarily a process of initiation with much to be learnt and assimilated under the guidance and instruction of tutors and teachers. The process is to be developmental, moving from relatively simple practical situations to the complex situation of sustained whole-class teaching. Learning is seen as a guided and analytical process in considering particular aspects of teaching. Yet in this, learning by the modification and evolution of students' existing ideas and commitments, through the formation and testing of new hypotheses, is seen as the prime procedure. If, then, one aspect of training is through the analysis of objectively given situations, another is through critical self-analysis. At the early stages of training, it seems that agreed practical principles and criteria must lie behind these procedures in terms of which students develop their personal capacities. Later, however, it being taken that there are no agreed general principles and criteria that can be relied upon, students must autonomously develop in critical reflection their own personal practical principles and criteria.

But how exactly are students to be trained beyond the early stage? They can be constantly encouraged in analytical reflection and constantly faced with new evidence and new possibilities. But there seem to be no agreed principles or even criteria for this reflection. Coming to be fully professional thus seems to be not only a somewhat daunting task, but in the end a strictly personal and subjective matter for which no clear training can be given.

From what has been argued earlier on in this chapter, it is highly questionable whether this is an adequate account of what practice and training in that practice demands. Maybe the change from the early to later stages of training is not to be seen as a shift from forming personal practices against given agreed principles and criteria to forming them via personally generated principles and criteria. Maybe rather it is a shift from forming personal practices against given criteria to engagement in the public world of ongoing professional critical reflection that seeks ever more adequate and more objectively grounded principles and criteria for one's personal practices. At all stages of enlightened professionalism, students and teachers are then constantly involved in critical reflection on, and reformation of, their personal practices. What marks out different stages is the extent to which the principles and criteria such personal development employs are or are not also being subjected to ever more sophisticated public rational examination.

In that case, once students are initiated into the development through critical reflection of their personal professionalism based on a set of practical principles and criteria, they need to learn to engage in critical reflection at 'higher' levels, examining the general practical principles and criteria they employ in the light of the rationally defensible general principles and criteria progressively emerging from research and wide ranging experience within the profession. At the early stage, professional development involves merely critical reflection on practice in relation to given principles and criteria. At later stages these principles and criteria are also the objects of critical reflection. And then not subjectively, but in objective, rational enquiry. These later stages thus involve not only critical reflection on particulars of personal practice, but critical reflection of a quite different kind, an altogether more general and abstract theoretical consideration of principles and criteria. In the Oxford programme teachers and tutors are clearly encouraged to agree on their training methods and styles at the early stage. What previous chapters indicate is that different groups of trainers have devised different methods and styles and it is not obvious what these are seeking to achieve or that they do train students in conducting critical reflection on their own efforts at teaching. In the interests of more consistent and effective work some more fully elucidated notion of what this kind of critical reflection on practice involves is desirable. Where the later stages of training are concerned little or nothing is indicated as to how students may be trained to critically reflect on general principles and criteria. But, indeed, unless this kind of critical reflection is more explicitly recognised as part of a public rational debate, its nature and the kind of training it requires cannot be clearly set out. What this second type of reflection is not, however, is another form of reflection on individual personal experience. What is more two such radically different forms of critical reflection will be likely to require quite different methods and styles of training.

Without a sharp distinction between the two kinds of reflection, that on personal experience and that on general principles and criteria, uncertainty can also readily arise about the desirability of training following students own individual concerns. The Oxford programme rightly asserts that effective professional development comes by the modification and evaluation of students' existing ideas and commitments. It does not however follow from that that training should follow their individual immediate concerns. Starting from where students are and their ideas of where they consider they should go next does not of itself necessarily provide a valid judgment of where indeed they should next go. At the early stage the Oxford course is not seen as simply, or even primarily, a following of students' own concerns. But beyond that stage, at least in principle, it has no other clear basis for students' development other than their direct provocation by uncertain knowledge and generalisations. If however personal professional development at all stages is seen as taking place against an external body of rationally developing general principles, then following immediate personal concerns is never an adequate basis for personal development. There are always the external demands of the best available general principles. As has been indicated earlier, without the acknowledgement of such a domain of principles it is extremely doubtful if the notions of professionalism and professional development are intelligible. Again uncertainty about the exact significance of such a body of general principles and criteria raises ambiguities in the course: by whom exactly and on what grounds should the agenda of the course at its different stages be determined?

These comments on the structure, roles and training procedures of the Oxford course have concentrated on ambiguities that seem to need further consideration if the impressive achievements of the programme are to be followed through into a truly coherent form of training. Just what kinds of theory does professional practice require, how in fact are different kinds of theory properly related to practice and how then can we best train students so that these forms of theory and practice develop in proper relation?

On these questions the message conveyed to all parties in the enterprise is in the end, it seems, too open-ended for a fully integrated course to emerge. The machinery for integration is there but just what training demands of all the parties is as yet uncertain. Maybe practical experience will pragmatically settle some of the issues involved. But their rational solution will surely require a further analysis of the relationship of theory to practice. In previous paragraphs it has been indicated that perhaps the best way to approach these questions is by distinguishing a number of different levels of theory which are different in form and in their relationship to practice.(8) In such a scheme the practice of an individual can be seen as requiring the use of a structure of concepts, understanding and principles in terms of which personal practice is justified. This constitutes a level of practical theory in terms of which the individual makes particular judgments and develops a pattern of practice. Critical reflection on particular situations and activities on the basis of this practical theory enables the individual's practice to develop coherently and defensibly. The early stages of professional training then surely demand the mastery of practices embedded in just such a body of practical theory. And that mastery comes by critical reflection on one's own and other practices in increasing use of the terms of that practical theory.

But if practice is to have adequate rational defence, the practical theory it employs must itself be rationally defensible. That theory must therefore itself be subjected to critical examination so that its understanding and practical principles are known to have appropriate justification. There must therefore be a level of theoretical work in which the principles of practical theory are examined as generalisations from practice. The professional development of any given individual will then require that the practical principles being used are constantly reviewed and revised against the achievements of the second level of concern with theory. In adequate professional training students, even early on, should come to realise that the practices they are beginning to master are only as good as the practical principles on which they rest. They need then to be introduced to that form of critical reflection on their practice that concerns not primarily the justification of particular events, but the justification of the general principles on which they are operating. In this form of critical reflection, different principles including their own are being examined and assessed in the light of their practical significance with a view to possible change in the principles that are personally accepted.

But still further questions need to be raised if practical principles are to be adequately justified, questions concerning the very framework of general beliefs and values within which the professional practices of education are taking place. There is then a third important level at which practice is linked to theory. Here it is the theoretical work in many well established disciplines which has been developed to provide the fundamental knowledge and understanding we have of human beings, society, and the physical world. If practical principles of education are to be rationally defensible, then the wider knowledge and understanding of philosophical, psychological, sociological and other kinds that they presuppose must be defensible. Professional development then requires that practical principles be kept constantly in review in the light of work in relevant fundamental disciplines. Not because these disciplines can provide new practices or principles directly but because in the light of new understanding, new practices and principles need to be pragmatically devised. In professional training the significance of critical reflection at this third level of theoretical concern needs to be adequately introduced even if there is no opportunity for its systematic pursuit.

Some such account as this of the kinds of theory that are significant for professional practice and how they are differently related to practice would seem necessary to determine more adequately course structure, the roles of different participants and appropriate training methods. At present the Oxford programme rather than sort out these questions at any depth relies on a simple recognition of two categories of different contribution to professional practice that students most take on board - those of teachers and tutors. How these differ is sketched in crude terms and any pursuit of clarifying further their relationship to each other is eschewed. Beyond this recognition there is reliance primarily on procedural agreements recognising these contributions as largely parallel and of equal importance. But what place these contributions should properly have and their relationship to each other is surely a matter of their nature and their precise significance in the development of professional practice. It is not a question of simply giving time and organisational recognition to diverse elements. For instance what role should tutors have in relation to students' practical school experience? On the approach suggested here, the answer turns in part on what they can best provide for students' mastery of the immediacies of personal practical professionalism. But it turns too on the need tutors have for understanding students' individual practical professionalism if they are to help them critically reflect on the principles they currently accept in their own practice. Again, the precise significance for students of what has happened in their personal experience depends crucially on whether they are in the process of reflecting critically on that experience in the light of certain accepted principles or whether they are subjecting those principles to critical review.

The approach here suggested in terms of levels of theoretical concern is itself only one step further in analysing the nature of professional practice, each of the suggested levels being capable of much further exploration. And what is being primarily argued here is not for the detail of this approach but for the necessity of some such more detailed articulation of the theory-practice relationship. It is however difficult to see how one escapes the notion that professionalism rests on a recognition of the central role of a publicly defended, rationally justified body of general practical principles. Of course such principles will vary in their levels of generality. Their justification in relation to practical experience and in relation to fundamental work in academic disciplines may be difficult so that we have to make do with the most justifiable we have at present, recognising the very provisional nature of that judgment. But if the nature of professionalism demands reliance on principles with public backing rather than merely personal judgment, training must be true to the business and make the best of what we have got. It is in this respect that I think that the Oxford course is at present in need of some reconsideration in both its rationale and its practice.

There is at present much interest in initial teacher education in the English-speaking world with research and experiment taking place in many places. The prospects for improved courses are good. Where we have got to in the UK is, at least in its organisational principles and the general direction of its rationale, well expressed in the Oxford course. They may have been more fortunate than some in the particular circumstances they have been able to exploit. But for other course planners there is here a programme and a story of course development worth detailed examination. It has much to offer and that not only in principle, for, in the UK context, there are many particulars that are well worth emulating elsewhere. Oxford must therefore not only be congratulated on what they have achieved but be thanked for presenting it so fully for the consideration of others. What is more, like all good projects, they leave us not only challenged by what they have done, but provoked to consider 'and where do things go from here?'

References

1. Universities Council for the Education of Teachers: *The PGCE and the Training of Specialist Teachers for Secondary Schools,* 1979.
Universities Council for the Education of Teachers: *Post-Graduate Certificate in Education Courses for Teachers for Primary and Middle Schools,* 1982.
2. Furlong, V J, Hirst, P H, Pocklington, K and Miles, S: *Initial Teacher Training and the Role of the School* (Open University Press, 1988).
3. Lacey, C, Hoard, P and Horton, M: *The Tutorial Schools Research Project 1964-73* (SSRC, 1973).
Furlong, V J et al, chapter 3.
4. See Alexander, R: 'Innovation and Continuity in the Initial Teacher Education Curriculum' in Alexander, R, Craft, M and Lynch, J (eds): *Changes in Teacher Education: Context and Provision Since Robbins* (Holt, Rinehart and Winston, 1984).
Furlong, V J et al, chapters 2, 3, 5 and 6.
5. Furlong, V J et al, pp. 34-35, 82-84, 169-170.
6. Furlong, V J et al, chapters 2, 3 and 5, pp. 168-169.
7. Furlong, V J et al, chapter 3, pp. 167-169.
8. For further discussion of different 'levels' of theory see Hirst, P H (ed): *Educational Theory and its Foundation Disciplines* (Routledge and Kegan Paul, 1983).
For a related notion of 'levels of training' see Furlong V J et al, especially chapter 4.

Chapter XII

Internship: A View from Abroad

Judith Warren Little
University of California, Berkeley

Although Internship is a local development, the concerns underlying the Oxford scheme are shared by educationalists in many other countries and related approaches have been considered and sometimes tried elsewhere. It was with this cross-national dimension in mind that we asked Judith Warren Little, Assistant Professor in the School of Education at the University of California, Berkeley, to comment on Internship in Oxford. Judith Warren Little was formerly director of the Professional Studies Group at the Far West Laboratory for Educational Research and Development. She has a long-standing interest in initial teacher education and has written on the role of the mentor in American teacher induction programmes.

These remarks have been in the making nearly as long as the Internship itself. They arise from curiosities and enthusiasms that were first sparked when I visited Oxford in the summer of 1987, just as the planning for the Internship had reached fruition and implementation was due to begin. In the US, as in the UK, the latest experiments in teacher education respond to the litany of recommendations for linking university-based teacher preparation more productively with work in schools. Perhaps the most provocative and potentially consequential set of reform recommendations of this decade in the US have been those promulgated by the Holmes Group, a consortium of approximately 100 research universities, in their 1986 report *Tomorrow's Teachers*. Prominent among the Group's recommendations is a call for Professional Development Schools to be organised as analogues of medicine's teaching hospitals. (1) A wave of optimism surrounds the present push toward these 'professional development schools'. Such optimism would be both bolstered and tempered by the experience of the Oxford Internship scheme in its first two years.

Three themes in these chapters illuminate the way in which the Internship scheme might inform experiments elsewhere. The first theme highlights the characteristic values, norms, and relations required by the Internship. In the struggle to work out structural details and formal institutional arrangements, many of which are revealed here in helpful and persuasive detail, persons often tend to overlook the essentially 'cultural' aspects of the scheme they are pursuing - the way in which it relies on shared values, beliefs, and accepted ways of working together. A close reading of these accounts brings those features nearer to the surface. A second and related theme underscores the magnitude of this undertaking. Others are likely to underestimate the breadth of this conception and the scale of the implementation task because of a superficial structural similarity between discrete elements of this programme and comparable elements of programmes elsewhere. Many programmes in the US, for example, make use of a position titled 'mentor', but I know of none in which that role is embedded in a principled scheme of the scope attempted here. Third, the scheme satisfies what might be termed a 'standard of mutual benefits'. It yields a range of individual and institutional benefits that are felt both in the immediate present and in the longer term; it embraces goals that reach beyond the preparation of individual teachers.

1. Beyond Programme

The Internship is distinguished first by its attempt to join university and school in a fully interdependent system of teacher preparation and induction. The basic principles of the Internship are collectively determined and collectively held; its central elements are institutional, not personal and idiosyncratic. The framework is built around the obligations and benefits of mutual support across roles and institutions. Throughout there are mechanisms for establishing shared perspectives and agreements (for example, the use of the Development Group at the outset, the broad participation of school and university representatives in planning the specific subject curricula, and the monitoring responsibilities that are widely shared). This is more than a 'programme'; rather, it is a way of seeing, a way of pursuing the work of teaching and the professional preparation of teachers. I underscore this point because of the tendency to rely on structural responses to problems and possibilities that reside in large part in the culture of educational organisations and the general norms of the teaching occupation. In consequence, change is often confined to the margins, exerting little lasting influence on prevailing policies and practices. For example, I found it instructive to contrast the Oxford scheme with an attempt made at the University of Utah some years ago. (2) The Utah programme linked a pair of student-teachers with a classroom teacher and university subject specialist (supervisor) in a school that was nominally part of a 'career ladder' scheme. In principle, such career ladder arrangements foster precisely the kinds of teacher-to-teacher support and consultation envisioned by the teacher preparation programme. In practice, however, the experiment in teacher education foundered on problems associated with smallness of scale, a rapid pace of implementation, and a very narrow base of understanding and support. Its rationale and structure were understood and supported by the immediate participants, but not by the staff at large. The staff therefore interpreted the new arrangements in terms of past conventions, seeing in the placement of two student-teachers with a single classroom teacher a case of 'hoarding' of scarce resources. The Internship relies for its success on the existence of shared norms that favour mutual support among teachers and the 'public' discussion of teaching. To achieve or sustain such norms, it seeks participation on a large enough scale in each school to form a meaningful presence, and seeks explicit commitment to the kinds of relationships and interactions consistent with its aims.

Through its extensive and intensive university-school collaboration, the Internship is organised to achieve a rare degree of breadth and depth in teacher socialisation. Virtually all teacher education programmes supply beginning teachers with classroom experience; few supply them with an equally potent introduction to the organisational life of departments and schools. In this regard, the available research mirrors common practice; in the words of one critic, studies of teacher socialisation *"have focused almost exclusively on the individual characteristics, conceptions, skills, and dispositions that students bring to teacher education programmes and have ignored the collective aspects of socialisation into teaching"*.(3) So, too, do teacher education programmes concentrate on familiarising prospective teachers with classroom life. The Internship requires action and enquiry in a broader arena. In cohorts of ten or twelve, interns serve as short-term, inexperienced members of a staff - but members nonetheless. They are attached to a school and a department, not to an individual teacher. The school and departments, therefore, are charged with providing interns adequate opportunity to learn. Although the mentor takes charge of organising opportunities and monitoring progress, the department at large is home to the intern's activities. Interns come to be acquainted with the whole range of the department's curriculum offerings and pupils. The mentor is responsible for direct guidance of individuals and pairs, for monitoring programmatic issues, and for organising opportunities that involve others on the teaching staff. I contrast this arrangement with the increasingly familiar one in the US, where individual mentors are paid a stipend to supply the individual support and guidance for individual student-teachers. In one large scale reform initiative in California, for example, nearly all resources were devoted to training classroom teachers in the techniques of clinical supervision and to a modest increase in individual stipends; the assumption underlying the programme was that measurable improvements in teacher education could be achieved by adding to the supervisory skill of the individuals to whose classrooms student-teachers were assigned. The programme had uncertain effect overall, but may have achieved its greatest impact in the context of a few 'partnership' schools in which university and school personnel were already closely involved in the joint operation of the schools and the teacher education programme.(4)

The Internship is further distinguished by its explicitly intellectual and dynamic conception of teaching, teachers, and teacher development. It is not unusual, perhaps, for programme leaders to espouse principles that honour the complexities and subtleties of teaching, the dignity of teachers, and the dynamic aspects of teacher development. In one recent collection of essays by American researchers, virtually all contributors seek opportunities for 'reflectivity' in the goals and curricula of teacher education programmes (even though they are at odds about other matters of governance, form, and content).(5) The Internship scheme is not alone in proffering a view of intending teachers as persons who arrive at their professional training with their own beliefs and models of teaching and learning; who are capable and sensitive learners; who, under supportive conditions, can begin to make (various) senses of the complexities of teaching. Nor is this programme unique in seeking 'reflectivity' in the teachers it prepares. I find such premises and aims congenial, and fully consistent with the rapidly growing body of research on teachers' thinking. I am also accustomed to finding the link between premise and practice rather tenuous. It is especially likely to be tenuous, or at least problematic, in the absence of any certainty about what teachers know and how they come to know it, or how teachers make their knowledge both explicit to themselves and accessible to others.

Insofar as it can be revealed in these pages, the link appears sturdier here. The Internship attempts to make good on its claims for 'reflectivity' mainly through its emphasis on interns' own investigations. In their university seminars the interns work at making sense of their own and others' work in classrooms, but also discuss the assumptions, beliefs, and policies reflected by patterns of school practice. The interns' assignments and opportunities thus reflect a multi-faceted conception of the teacher that has the teacher-pupil relationship at its heart but that also extends beyond the classroom. The multiple dimensions of a teacher's work are demonstrated in a way that is not possible with programmes centred exclusively on 'practice teaching'. The interns work in classrooms but are also expected to know and contribute to the departments and the school. Through their investigations of school-wide issues, the interns are asked to consider issues that transcend individual classrooms and to do so in a manner that might inform school policy and practice. The schools, in turn, are expected to support and contribute to these investigations. Intending teachers acquire both the capacities and the inclinations of continuous study. 'Learning by experience' does not, in this context, become an exclusive warrant for privately held prerogatives, but informs and is informed by other modes of enquiry.

Nor do the obligations and opportunities for enquiry and experimentation fall only to those learning to teach. Throughout, and for all participants, the programme appears to require and reward efforts to re-examine the taken-for-granted aspects of teaching and schooling. The Development Group began with action research projects. The interactions between interns and mentors are given the flavour of consultations. And to the reflectivity of individuals, the Internship adds a commitment to institutional learning. The programme itself is made subject to serious scrutiny, as are the policies and practices of the schools. Here we have an effort to build a 'community of inquirers'.(6)

The investigatory stance of the programme, and the joint development of its curriculum goals and activities, make possible some treatments of teachers' knowledge and beliefs that would otherwise be problematic or even controversial. I was struck by the courage of the English team in this regard. Together, at least for purposes of the teacher education curriculum, the team abandoned assumptions of a 'consensus-based version of the subject'. They thereby created a powerful set of possibilities for interns, and a powerful set of challenges as well. By exploring their own histories as students of English, their own beliefs and assumptions, their pedagogical and curricular preferences, and their emerging practices, the interns discover the fluid interplay of subject matter and pedagogy.

They are prepared to be more deliberate in their own curricular and instructional choices. By investigating the policies and beliefs operating among teachers in the departments of their own schools, they become attuned to the existence, character, and intensity of commitments (and disputes) within disciplines and within schools regarding subject philosophy and subject pedagogy. They are, as a consequence, perhaps more conscious of the contexts in which their personal preferences are shaped and exercised. They are also, perhaps, less likely to be taken unawares by the 'political' dimensions of department life. (An issue not addressed here is the extent to which the possibility of such queries is compromised or constrained by the development of the National Curriculum and by the government's increasing control over teaching and teacher education. This is an issue of increasing import in the US as well, where the burgeoning policy presence of state governments is making itself felt in claims on the form and content of teacher education).(7)

We would no doubt err in overstating the nature and extent of consensus that undergirds this programme, or the degree of intellectual adventurousness that pervades it. Pupils and classrooms have an immediacy that requires resolution in the moment; teachers' own sense of competence and confidence comes in part from a sense of certainty and stability that suffers under constant scrutiny. And we would err as well by placing all our faith in the carefully-crafted set of roles. This is, after all, a human enterprise. It will encounter the predictable array of triumphs and troubles, large and small. People will sometimes find delight in each other, and sometimes not. Donald McIntyre and his colleagues have examined the difficulties in rendering the largely private and certainly intricate knowledge of teaching in terms that are accessible. Our own experience with teacher-adviser programmes and other forms of teacher-to-teacher consultation suggests that the first stages of such encounters feel clumsy as persons they learn how to talk in persuasive and meaningful detail, and to avoid inadvertently offending one another. In the effort to avoid offence (or in the effort to honour traditions of autonomy), teachers may talk to one another in ways that simply reinforce conservative precedent. Personal predilections remain unexamined. The spirit of 'investigation' that is at the centre of the Internship favours a different kind of exchange, and supports a norm of informed discussion, debate, and innovation that is difficult to achieve and sustain amidst the press of daily practice. Such a scheme will thrive in schools where a generalised norm of continuous improvement prevails - such things can't be dredged up only for the preparation of newcomers.

2. Magnitude of the Task

The challenge and the promise of the Internship reside in the degree to which principles, policies, and practices are interwoven and interdependent, and to which they represent a substantial departure from most present practice. These detailed accounts reveal precisely how difficult it is to pursue a venture that is this tightly linked at the levels of concept and strategy. At the same time there is nothing mysterious about what was required to get started. In the planning and in the actual attempt, such a scheme proves both difficult and do-able. On this point the messages of this book seem inescapable.

The setting for this experiment was favourable in a quite ordinary way - that is, in a way well within the reach of many institutions. Without denying the importance of the leadership provided by Judge and Brighouse, or the way in which their personal and professional history helped to supply vision and secure resources in the early stages, I want to highlight the ways in which Oxford's circumstances were neither more nor less favourable than those of other universities and schools. Because leadership looms so large in accounts like these, it is important to de-mystify leadership and to place it the context of a wider array of players. Getting started is in large part simply making the pitch: stating the principles publicly, and publicly calling for participation. But these leaders did not and could not single-handedly supply all the intelligence, inventiveness, energy, patience, courage, goodwill and good humour required to convert a good (but not new) idea into practice. Indeed, one or more of the key leaders was absent for large periods of formative discussion and debate. Leaders acted to concentrate resources on the programme, but the material resources were modest in relation to the task.

The leaders were crucial but not unique in their character, their resources, or the strategies they pursued. Nor were the other participants unusually favoured by character or circumstance. The university and the schools were not strangers to one another. Their dealings had more often been congenial than not. Their history disposed them toward a joint venture, though it could not have prepared them for the demands and dilemmas of this one. Indeed, this arrangement represents a direct challenge to many of the usual ways of thinking and acting together. In other ways, too, the setting was not trouble-free. Heads and teachers were preoccupied with other matters. The Internship was introduced at a time of multiple and increasing external demands on teachers and heightened labour conflict. Overall, the message appears to be that we need not (must not) wait upon perfect circumstances and flawless performances to begin on important work together.

The first stages (at least) of these ventures proved to be turbulent. The planning phase was, in Brighouse's recounting, 'disputatious'. Each idea was tested near to 'the point of destruction'. The risk, of course, was that this 'good idea' would make relations between the university and the schools worse, not better. Persons and groups are asked to tolerate the assaults and criticisms of others, to reconsider and perhaps to alter closely held beliefs and personal identities. The account of the Internship's beginnings echoes Lanier's record of similar joint efforts to construct an elementary teacher education programme in the US.(8) Reviewing that record, one is left with the conclusion that the tension and dissonance that arise from differences in purpose, circumstance, and history are both inevitable and productive - that to seek the smooth path may be to weaken the enterprise.

3. The Mutual Benefits Standard

The Internship begins as an argument about the improved preparation of teachers. Nonetheless, it seems clear that the programme has the prospects for increasing the broader collective and institutional resources that support teaching and its improvement. Indeed, the original conception of the Internship model anticipated that *"all parties - teachers, students, tutors, school pupils, LEA - should benefit from the operation of the schem.".* One might argue that such a resource-intensive enterprise will only be sustained by benefit that is widely felt.(9) I find it a useful exercise to attempt an inventory of the present and future gains that are plausibly felt by each individual, group, and institution, and to assess the demands associated with participation. On the whole, present and direct benefits sustain participation in ways that longer-term abstract promise cannot. Innovative projects of various sorts (not restricted to teacher education) seem to fare better when they preserve a reasonable equilibrium among demand, support, and reward.

The elements of the Internship programme (and the specific cases of Park Hill School and Henry Box School) suggest some of the ways of anticipating and assessing the individual and institutional benefits. For the interns, a principal benefit resides in their enhanced employability. Graduates of the programme may have an unusual command over classroom teaching and an unusual grasp of departmental and school-level obligations. For the mentors and other teachers who devote time and give up a measure of control over their classes, the potential benefits lie in an expanded pool of ideas, the 'extra hand' in the classroom, the companionship of a colleague (even if less experienced), and in an easing of daily time pressures. Teachers can be expected to support the programme to the extent that their own investments of time early in the year are offset by the contributions the interns make over time. By the second term, the interns may help ease the classroom workload or contribute new ideas. Where interns progress rapidly, they may add to a mentor's or a department's stature in the eyes of the head or other peers. They thereby add support (or ease the burdens) in the daily round of teaching. Through investigations and dissertations on issues of schoolwide interest, interns expand the supply of information that feeds institutional learning. Although these investigations and dissertations are almost certainly of variable utility, even one or two a year deemed valuable by a department or a school may be sufficient to fuel support for the programme.

It seems clear that the schools (or at least those we find described here) experience benefit in the present; the programme does not rest on the shoulders of altruism, on abstract conceptions of 'service to the profession'. This is crucial in light of schools' immediate obligations to the pupils who now attend them. For the system, the return must be in the present. In the longer run, the promise of the programme lies in its ability to influence the quality of the teacher workforce. We learn that many of the vacancies in the secondary schools in Oxfordshire are filled successfully with OUDES interns. As the number being retained in the county is large and increasing and turnover among beginning teachers is reduced, there is a good long-term return on the investment.

4. Partial Glimpses, Missing Voices, and Emerging Curiosities

The Oxford Internship scheme is not unique in its premises, principles, or practices, but it is nearly so. This book celebrates the beginning of an ambitious experiment and exemplifies the programme's own capacity for learning. This latter element is crucial because the present rendering of the story is incomplete in some important ways. The Internship was only midway through its second year when these pieces were written. Some questions and curiosities are well satisfied, while others are necessarily held in abeyance. This book portrays with considerable detail, insight, and rich imagery the planning of the Internship and its resulting architecture; the stories that are told here confirm much of the accumulated wisdom about institutional change, and offer some new insights as well. As observers we are well positioned to anticipate the kinds of benefits the scheme may yield, but less well positioned to say precisely and comprehensively what the yield turns out to be. Further, we glimpse relatively little of the day-by-day realities of the Internship. I find myself wishing for a chapter, or a second book, in which the daily work of interns with mentors and tutors is portrayed in closer detail and in which the voices of the interns, mentors, and tutors are more prominent.

In many ways the Oxford experiment flies in the face of precedent in its treatment of the knowledge and practice of teaching, the development of teachers, and the relationship among educational institutions. The Internship has been launched in a period of increasing experimentation in a climate of both greater public urgency and greater governmental interest and control. This book, therefore, represents an important contribution to the debates over purposes, principles and practice; it is, crucially, a contribution grounded in detailed descriptions of work in progress.

References

1. This and other recommendations of the Holmes Group have spawned considerable controversy, some of which was recorded in special issues of the *Journal of Teacher Education* (July-August 1986) and *Teachers College Record* (Spring 1987). Nonetheless, the recommendations have also spurred widespread activity. Progress on specific initiatives is reported in the Group's quarterly newsletter, *The Holmes Group Forum*.
2. Reported in A W Hart & G V Adams (1986). Preservice socialisation for teacher career ladders. *Journal of Teacher Education,* (November-December), 59-64.
3. K Zeichner & J Gore (in press). Teacher socialisation. In W R Houston, M Haberman, & J Sikula (ed.), *Handbook of Research on Teacher Education* (New York: Macmillan).
4. The premises and first stages of implementation of this initiative are reported in J W Little, (1987), *Improvement of preservice teacher education through clinical supervision of student-teachers*. Programme evaluation report to the Office of the Chancellor, California State University. San

Francisco: Far West Laboratory for Educational Research and Development. The demonstrable successes associated with partnership schools are reported in M Berg et al, *Enhancing university and school-district relations through the collaborative supervision of student-teachers,* a 1988 conference paper describing an experimental programme at San Diego (California) State University.

5. The book is Woolfolk, A E (ed.) (1989). *Research perspectives on the graduate preparation of teachers.* Englewood Cliffs, N J: Prentice Hall. It is the result of a conference organised to explore issues and to examine the research agenda surrounding graduate preparation of teachers.

6. I have borrowed this term from Carol Witherell and Andra Makler, who use it to sum up the organising principles of collaborative teacher education they are pursuing in the Master of Arts in Teaching Internship Programme, a co-operative project of Lewis and Clark College (Portland, Oregon) and two neighbouring school districts. These principles - and the familiar difficulties of putting them into practice - are described in their paper "Giving each other reason: Building a community of inquirers through collaborative teacher education".

7. For one revealing case example, see N Prestine (1989). The struggle for control of teacher education: A case study. *Educational Evaluation and Policy Analysis,* 11(3), 285-300.

8. Lanier, J E (1983). Tensions in teaching teachers the skills of pedagogy. In G Griffin (ed.), *Staff development: Eighty-second yearbook of the National Society for the Study of Education* (pp. 118-153). Chicago: University of Chicago Press.

9. This argument parallels one developed by Michael Zey to explain the conditions under which informal mentoring thrives in private sector corporations. See M G Zey, (1984). *The mentor connection.* Homewood, Ill: Dow Jones-Irwin. For a discussion of the most common treatments of the mentor role in American teacher induction programmes, see also J W Little (1990). The mentor phenomenon and the social organisation of teaching, *Review of Research in Education,* volume 16.

APPENDIX A
The Definition of Roles

Chapter IV offers some sense of the roles of the professional tutor, general tutor, mentor and curriculum tutor. It has, of course, been essential to negotiate these roles and to achieve common agreement as to the responsibilities of each of these four significant people in the interns' experience. The following section attempts to clarify what each of the four undertakes and to provide a blueprint for their responsibilities within the scheme. It is necessarily fairly detailed but anyone wishing to set up a similar scheme would be well advised to negotiate a similarly detailed package if it is to be successful. The minutiae are important if roles are to be properly understood, perceptions shared and the possibilities for confusion minimised. What follows draws largely on the role descriptions which were agreed by all participants before the scheme was launched and which were published in *The Internship Handbook*.

The Professional Tutor and the Internship Scheme
The professional tutor's responsibility within the Internship scheme is essentially to do with co-ordination. Firstly, the professional tutor has an overview of the activities and involvement in the school of the whole group of interns. In particular, the professional tutor shares with the general tutor the co-ordination and delivery, where appropriate, of the whole group of interns' experiences in the general programme. Secondly, the professional tutor co-ordinates specific experiences for the general tutor so that s/he becomes integrated within the life of the school. Thirdly, the professional tutor remains in touch with the school's mentors, and provides any necessary co-ordination of their departmental programmes to keep the needs of the whole school in perspective, and to preserve a balance in the opportunities being offered to the whole group of interns.

The professional tutor has an especially close partnership with the general tutor who has been attached to his or her school. The professional tutor shares with the general tutor in setting up the general programme within the school, and in organising specific activities for the interns within the framework provided by the general tutor and OUDES. The general programme is flexible enough to be adapted by the professional tutor, working alongside the general tutor, to the special circumstances of each school. Indeed, the professional tutor has scope to initiate open-ended meetings with interns throughout the year and to discuss issues which arise spontaneously from the experiences of the interns in that particular school. The professional tutor receives, where necessary, resources devised within OUDES to support the programme. Although the professional tutor is closely involved in the general programme, the overall responsibility for the delivery of that programme rests with the general tutor.

The professional tutor is closely involved in the induction to the school of the general tutor and the group of interns. Such induction involves the professional tutor in providing information about the school and in making organisational arrangements to set up experiences relevant to the induction process. The professional tutor works very closely with the general tutor in the planning of the induction programmes, and establishes regular contacts with the general tutor throughout the year to follow up such programmes and to devise an overall strategy for the year's work in the school. It follows that meetings in the summer term to plan the following year's programme are essential as are meetings with mentors and staff generally in the weeks immediately before the arrival of the interns. The professional tutor facilitates the general tutor's engagement with the school at all levels, including making many seemingly small but absolutely vital links such as ensuring that the general tutor is known to all staff, has a mail box in the school, receives relevant papers, is invited to staff meetings and so forth. The professional tutor has the responsibility of devising a programme which introduces the general tutor as fully as possible to the working of the school and ensures that the general tutor is fully informed about the school's ethos, policies and methods of operation.

The Professional Tutor and the Induction of Interns to the School

The professional tutor and the general tutor work out a structured programme for the introduction of the interns to the school and for the interns' integration over a period of time into the ethos and workings of the school. This induction programme includes a range of activities such as:

(a) The professional tutor provides interns with background information on the school during the induction period. Such information might include: the school 'handbook', information on school procedures, timetable, school calendar of meetings and extra-curricular activities etc.

(b) The professional tutor informs interns about lunch, coffee arrangements, and any relevant staffroom procedures. The professional tutor makes the necessary arrangements for interns to have lockers, pigeon holes etc, so that the interns may be fully integrated within the staffroom.

(c) Making a guided tour of the school.

(d) Following a pupil, or perhaps several pupils of different ages on different occasions.

(e) The professional tutor arranges for the interns to meet 'key staff' - including the Head, Head of Year etc.

(f) Following a member of staff, or perhaps several members of staff occupying different positions (eg senior teacher, Head of House/Year, relatively new member of staff) on different occasions.

(g) Attending a staff meeting (decisions will need to be taken regarding attendance by interns at staff, faculty and department, meetings through the year, and their role in those meetings).

(h) The professional tutor arranges for the placement of interns with House/tutor groups (at whatever stage the professional tutor deems appropriate).

(i) The professional tutor may wish to invite interns to take part in any programme which the school has organised for Probationers - either by inviting interns to attend relevant meetings or by inviting interns to informal social functions planned for Probationers.

(j) Observing procedures and events in the school office for part of a day.

(k) Going on a school excursion, not necessarily related to interns' own subjects.

(l) The professional tutor may set up opportunities for interns, if they request this, to observe subjects other than the interns' main curriculum area. For example, the professional tutor might arrange for interns to view/ take part in practical subjects (CDT, Drama, Art etc), and provide them with observation tasks and the opportunity to discuss the experience.

The professional tutor and general tutor plan observation tasks for interns as they follow activities of the kind described above. The professional tutor and general tutor also agree how to share the early induction sessions in the school with the interns and how to debrief interns after each of their induction activities.

The Professional Tutor and the General Programme

The general programme involves a partnership between the school and the university. For the professional tutor this implies particular responsibilities:

(a) The professional tutor and the general tutor jointly plan the implementation of the general programme for interns at the school. Who does what, when and where need to be clarified at an early stage by the professional tutor and general tutor in each school. It is the general tutor's overall responsibility to ensure that this planning takes place.

(b) The professional tutor is kept informed, on a regular basis, by the general tutor of what will be happening in OUDES in connection with the general programme, and how activities in the school and the Department interlink.

(c) The professional tutor and general tutor monitor together the general programme tasks undertaken by the interns. In particular, the professional tutor ensures that adequate arrangements are made within the school for the interns to conduct their studies, while both professional tutor and general tutor share, as appropriate, the debriefing of interns when those tasks are completed.

(d) The professional tutor and general tutor make available to interns, in planned sessions, their own special expertise, and different and shared viewpoints on issues arising within the general programme, so that the interns may react to and learn from as wide a range of perspectives as is possible.

(e) The professional tutor and general tutor set up experiences (connected with the general programme) whereby the interns can test their responses to the wide range of perspectives offered to them, both in school and in the university.

(f) The professional tutor and general tutor offer opportunities in school and in the university for interns to discuss the results of their experiences, as developed from (d) and (e).

(g) The professional tutor and general tutor will need to meet on a regular basis across the year to review the entire programme being offered to interns and seek to make adjustments where necessary in the light of experience and of the opportunities available within the school and in the university.

(h) The professional tutor and general tutor jointly ensure, through communications as appropriate with mentors and curriculum tutors, that the general programme is co-ordinated, as intended, with the various curriculum programmes.

The Professional Tutor and Assessment of Interns

The professional tutor, if s/he wishes, may have access to the written assignments produced by interns in connection with the general programme, but s/he will have no obligation to assess such work.

The professional tutor and general tutor consult together, at appropriate times, concerning the overall progress of the interns and together assess the interns' involvement in the general programme and their contribution to the professional life of the school. There are three formal assessment points in the course of the year.

The Professional Tutor and Mentors

Channels of Communication

(a) The professional tutor involves the mentors in the interns' and general tutor's programmes of induction to the school at the beginning of the year, so that essential contacts are established.

(b) The professional tutor may wish to liaise with Heads of Department and mentors to discuss with them a department's proposed programme of induction for interns, or to offer suggestions for activities where appropriate.

(c) The professional tutor keeps mentors informed concerning the general programme, so that cross-curricular and curriculum-based activities may be integrated in the most effective manner within the school.

(d) The professional tutor and mentors set up appropriate procedures, in the light of procedures negotiated between the university PGCE tutor and professional tutors, to cater for increased visits to the school by university staff, and ensure that information is easily and effectively transmitted across the network of responsibilities.

The Professional Tutor's Overview Of Mentors' Programmes for Interns

(a) The professional tutor discusses the mentors' programme for interns at an early stage, so that:
(i) the interns' timetables can be checked to avoid specific pupils or classes being overloaded with interns;
(ii) departments, such as Special Needs, are not swamped by demands from interns at any one time;
(iii) the spread of classes, in terms of ability and age, used by interns, is appropriate;

(iv) the range of activities and teaching styles made available to interns is comparable across curriculum areas;

(b) The professional tutor reviews, with mentors, the progress of the scheme within their departments. Such reviews may be on a regular basis or according to need, and progress and problems may be minuted to help with the future development of the scheme in the school, and to pass on useful information to OUDES. Such review meetings could be open to Heads of Department, if they wish to attend. These meetings could offer support to inexperienced mentors, and celebrate successes which might then be transmitted from one subject area to another.

(c) The professional tutor periodically ensures that the mentors are continuing to give full support to interns throughout the year, and that mentors are effectively analysing interns' work in lessons. This monitoring may be conducted at an informal level and be dependent upon the time available to the professional tutor.

(d) Together the professional tutor and the whole team of mentors will:
(i) monitor the effect of the Internship scheme on the whole school, especially ensuring that pupils are benefiting from the experience, and that no undue discontinuity in pupil learning is taking place;
(ii) ensure that the interns are being fully integrated within the school, and that all opportunities are being made available to them to explore their talents and potential.

The Professional Tutor Supporting Mentors

(a) The professional tutor may be called upon, at the request of a mentor, to act as a neutral observer for an intern who is experiencing difficulties, and to pass on comments to the university via the general tutor.

(b) The professional tutor may from time to time arrange, or ask the Head of Department to arrange, for the release of a mentor from teaching, so that the mentor may be free to join other colleagues' lessons when interns are involved, or to meet university staff for consultations. This facility will again depend upon the time and opportunities available to the professional tutor and other staff.

The Professional Tutor's Involvement in 'Welfare of Interns' and Assessment

(a) The mentors, while largely being responsible for the day-to-day pastoral welfare of the interns, may need to refer specific problems to the professional tutor so that appropriate action or consultation may be arranged between professional tutor, general tutor and interns.

(b) The professional tutor co-ordinates, where necessary, the mentors' involvement in the assessment of interns, acting as arbiter in any dispute within subject departments over this issue.

The guidelines outlined above stress the main functions of the professional tutor, within the Internship scheme, and these may be summarised in the form of six key processes which span the professional tutor's involvement in the Internship scheme across the year: Induction, Integration, Co-ordination, Support, Monitoring, Evaluation. These vital processes may be carried out at two levels by a professional tutor. Firstly, at an informal level, which involves the professional tutor keeping in touch with the progress of the interns and mentors throughout the year, and picking up vibrations which call for a response from the professional tutor or require the professional tutor to call in another member of the Internship network to satisfy a need. Secondly, at a formal level, the professional tutor will be involved in the general programme, and in the activities and learning that are at the centre of this part of the scheme.

The General Tutor and the Internship Scheme

Each general tutor is closely associated with one of the schools involved in the Internship scheme, and is the main link between that school and the university department, having an especially close partnership with the school's professional tutor.

The general tutor is responsible for co-ordinating the general programme activities for the interns attached to that school. This general programme is about issues which are not peculiar to one curriculum area (eg Science or Humanities) and which impinge on schools as a whole. It addresses the characteristics of the learners whom schools serve, the organisational structures which they adopt to enable them to carry out their functions, and their relationship to the society in which they operate.

The overarching theme for this programme is 'The School Curriculum' - taking the notion of the curriculum in its widest sense. Thus the programme is concerned with the content and organisation of the curriculum, aspects of delivery in the classroom, and the factors which shape it - professional, political and social.

The framework for this programme has been constructed by a working group and resources for it (for schools, tutors and interns) have been prepared by individuals who have accepted responsibility for particular topic areas. There is flexibility built into this programme. The general tutor and professional tutor have the task of adapting and developing the framework in a way which takes account of its internal coherence and of the circumstances of the specific school.

Although the programme is to be shared by professional tutor and general tutor, it is the general tutor who has primary responsibility for its delivery.

In order to fulfil these responsibilities, general tutors need to take steps to familiarise themselves with the school; to help with the induction of interns; to maintain an active involvement with the school throughout the year; to undertake planning and review activities in connection with the programme; to be involved in the assessment of interns; to develop their 'personal role' in relation to all those concerned. The practical implications of these responsibilities are given below.

The General Tutor and the Induction of Interns to the School

The general tutor and professional tutor together work out a structured programme for the introduction of the interns to the school and for the interns' integration over a period of time into the ethos and workings of the school. It is hoped that this induction programme would include a range of activities such as:

(i) making a guided tour of the school;

(ii) following a pupil, or perhaps several pupils of different ages on different occasions;

(iii) following a member of staff, or perhaps several members of staff occupying different positions (eg senior teacher, Head of House, relatively new member of staff) on different occasions;

(iv) observing procedures and events in the school office for part of a day;

(v) going on a school excursion, not necessarily related to interns' own subjects;

(vi) attending a staff meeting.

The general tutor and professional tutor plan observation tasks for interns as they follow activities of this kind. (Generalised versions of these observation tasks, ready for possible adoption and adaptation for each school, are planned centrally in the university.) They also agree how to share the early induction sessions in the school with the interns and how to debrief interns after each of their induction activities.

Maintaining an Active Involvement in the School

The programme of planning meetings between the professional tutor and general tutor is continued across the year. Where time allows, the general tutor may wish to become involved with other activities such as school working parties concerned with issues related to his or her interests or expertise. S/he may also visit the school for various purposes, such as working with the interns, finding more out about the school, or attending staff meetings.

The General Programme

As noted earlier, the general programme involves a partnership between OUDES and the school. For the general tutor this implies particular responsibilities:

(i) The general tutor and professional tutor jointly plan the implementation of the general programme for interns at the school. Who does what, when and where need to be clarified at an early stage by the general tutor and the professional tutor in each school. The general tutor ensures that this planning takes place.

(ii) On a regular basis, the general tutor keeps the professional tutor informed of what will be happening in OUDES in connection with the general programme, and how activities in the school and the Department interlink.

(iii) The general tutor, jointly with the professional tutor, organises and monitors the activities experienced by the interns in connection with the general programme. Both the general tutor and professional tutor should, in their work with interns, bring to bear their distinctive experience and expertise. The debriefing of interns when activities are completed is also a shared responsibility. How these responsibilities are to be shared will be negotiated as in (i) above. The general tutor has the responsibility to ensure that all these things are done.

(iv) The general tutor ensures that s/he and the professional tutor set up regular meetings to review the entire programme being offered to interns and seek to make adjustments where necessary in the light of experience and of the opportunities available within the school and the university. (v) The general tutor ensures that interns work on the programme in ways which take full account of theoretical issues and of a range of alternative practices.

Interns: Assessment of Work

The general tutor has the responsibility for assessment of interns' written work connected with the general programme in collaboration with the professional tutor when the latter so wishes.

The general tutor and professional tutor consult together, at appropriate times, concerning the overall progress of the interns and together assess the interns' involvement in the general programme and their contribution to the professional life of the school.

The General Tutor: A Personal Role

The general tutor and professional tutor share the oversight of the pastoral welfare of the whole group of interns within the school.

In addition, an important part of the general tutor's role is to act as the main personal link between the school and the university. The availability and effectiveness of this personal linkage is of considerable importance to the success of the scheme. For example, general tutor and professional tutor should exchange information and consult if any pastoral problems arise. Furthermore, the general tutor could facilitate links between the school and the university eg by dealing with administrative, personal and operational matters between the school and the university department.

The general tutor thus has a general responsibility for keeping in touch with the school and being seen in the school for activities with teaching colleagues as well as with interns. The normal expectation is therefore that the general tutor will be in the school for about half a day each week during both the joint university/school weeks and the period when the interns are full-time in school.

The Role of the Curriculum Tutors and Mentors

Introduction

The spirit of the partnership between curriculum tutors and mentors is of fundamental importance. It is not the existing form of co-operation renamed. At its best, the old relationship between Tutor and Supervisor in supporting students was one of an organiser/provider with a voluntary agent and supporter. At its simplest, the new relationship is now one in which curriculum tutor and mentor each has a distinctive and equal contribution to make: the curriculum tutor from a base in the university, and the mentor from a base in a school. The quality and equality of the relationship must be clear to interns. Together, the curriculum tutor and mentor are concerned with the professional development of interns in relation to classroom practice. This will include distinctive aspects of teaching their own subject as well as more comprehensive classroom issues.

The Curriculum Tutor

The curriculum tutor - though attached to one school as general tutor - works with a number of schools in which s/he has pairs of interns. This guarantees a breadth of knowledge about local practice. The curriculum tutor also contributes an overarching academic and theoretical framework for the work of the interns. The curriculum tutor enjoys a broader perspective through national contacts and subject Associations. Over the year, curriculum tutors aim to assist interns to develop two closely related skills:

(a) the ability to cope effectively in the classroom.

(b) the ability to develop a critical understanding of the curricular and pedagogical possibilities inherent in various approaches to teaching.

In relation to Internship, the main executive responsibility of the curriculum tutor is to co-ordinate all aspects of the programme devised to help interns become effective and reflective teachers in the secondary school. This responsibility entails the activities noted below:

(i) agreeing with mentors on the criteria and process for selecting interns for the course;

(ii) pairing interns and arranging for their placement in schools;

(iii) collaborating with mentors to plan and implement a coherent programme for interns in schools and in the university, and to modify this programme in the light of experience.

This programme allows interns opportunity to explore issues which they identify in addition to those planned by mentors and curriculum tutors, and it takes account, wherever practicable, of issues in the General Programme which can be investigated through curriculum activities.

(iv) leading sessions in the university. Through such sessions, curriculum strategies, development and materials are placed in their various contexts (eg historical, philosophical, psychological). Interns will be introduced to a range of perspectives on each key issue and encouraged also to examine each issue in the light of other perspectives which they will encounter and experience in schools. Similarly, interns will be encouraged and helped to reflect from diverse perspectives on the ideas and practices which they learn in schools;

(v) contributing to and supporting the activities of interns in schools. The curriculum tutor does not make 'student assessment visits' to schools, but works with interns and mentors in developing specific aspects of the interns' teaching (including projects devised and planned collaboratively between interns and curriculum tutors in the university during 'J' weeks). Curriculum tutors are able to work alongside interns in classes as part of the process of providing mentors with some time to pursue their own professional concerns. They also contribute their expertise to developing with mentors collaborative modes of working;

(vi) helping interns structure their self-evaluation during the second phase of the year;

(vii) providing career guidance for interns;

(viii) helping mentors implement the principles of assessment, and moderating such assessments on a cross-school basis;

(ix) undertaking, and enabling others to undertake, research that will be of direct benefit to classroom practice.

The Mentor

The mentor enters into a voluntary partnership with a curriculum tutor and other mentors in order to contribute to the development of interns the experience of an established professional teacher and the perspectives rooted in that experience. The contribution made by the mentor differs from that of the curriculum tutor, which it must complement, because it starts from a different place. The mentor's contribution helps the interns to understand, from the school base, both the issues investigated by all interns; and also the unpredictable day-to-day realities of teaching that they each encounter.

The mentor's responsibility entails among others the activities noted below:

(i) arranging for interns to plan activities; to teach individual pupils, small groups of pupils, and whole classes; and to help interns evaluate these experiences;

(ii) working with interns to implement the school-based part of the agreed programme, and enabling them, through focused observation, practice and discussion, to test their developing ideas against the realities of school life;

(iii) helping interns develop effective self-evaluation skills;

(iv) developing a variety of modes of collaborative working, to include;

(a) Focusing on the teaching of the mentor and discussing it later.

(b) Working with individual pupils and small groups.

(c) One person teaches, one observes the teacher, one observes the pupils and the team discusses it later.

(d) Experienced teacher 'leads' the lesson and interns participate as 'classroom assistants'.

(e) The intern teaches a part of a lesson with the help of a plan outlined by an experienced teacher.

(f) Planning a lesson together with each member of the team teaching a part of it.

(g) Splitting up a class into three small groups and each person works with one group.

(h) Following up lessons by marking the work together.

(i) Producing resources to be used in lessons.

(j) Interns jointly plan and lead a lesson, using the teacher as a classroom assistant.

(k) One intern teaches the class while the other meets individually with the mentor.

(l) The interns teach the class while the teacher works with individual pupils.

(m) The interns prepare learning and teaching materials to help resource the school department.

(v) assisting the interns to make the maximum use of the opportunities afforded by observation in order to learn about teachers' qualities, strategies and achievements in the classroom;

(vi) assisting the interns to achieve sufficient mastery of the agreed qualities;

(vii) enabling the interns to analyse and evaluate their own teaching particularly during Phase Two;

(viii) liaising with the professional tutor, in particular
(a) to incorporate into the intern's programme general issues which can be investigated through curriculum work;
(b) to timetable an hour per week when interns from all subject areas in the school can meet;
(ix) providing career guidance for interns;
(x) assessing the competence of interns in the school setting;
(xi) contributing to university-based sessions, where this is practicable and organised by the curriculum group.

APPENDIX B
List of Important Abilities

> Sections A-E relate specifically to class teaching and will normally form the focus of discussions between interns and mentors, and interns and curriculum tutors.

> Section F relates in part to class teaching but more generally to the *attitudes* necessary for working as a member of a school staff. This section may have inputs from interns, mentors, professional tutors and university tutors.

Does the intern generally or regularly perform in the following ways?

A Planning Work
a1 Plans each lesson thoroughly, within the context of a sequence of lessons
a2 Selects learning activities which take account of pupils' different needs and potential
a3 Arranges for the equipment and materials required to be available at the appropriate time
a4 Considers the class management implications of planned lessons
a5 Takes account of evaluation of previous lessons
a6 Specifies how the lesson is to be evaluated

B Class Control
b1 Achieves ordered pupil entry to and exit from the classroom
b2 Maintains an environment where pupils are aware of acceptable levels of talk, movement, etc
b3 Begins and ends lessons effectively, and gains pupils' attention in a variety of ways when required
b4 Effectively disciplines pupils when necessary
b5 Effectively praises and encourages pupils as appropriate

C Clear Communication
c1 Speaks with a clear and distinct voice
c2 Ensures that instructions given are received without ambiguity by the class
c3 Makes judgments about language usage appropriate to the age and ability of the class and individuals in it
c4 Develops questioning skills which allow dialogue with her/his class
c5 Communicates enthusiasm for her/his subject

D Management of Learning Activities
d1 Carries out the planned learning activities effectively
d2 Responds to unanticipated situations
d3 Shows competence in explaining basic concepts of her/his teaching subject to pupils of a wide range of abilities

d4 Relates personally to pupils in a way which maximises their learning
d5 Establishes a safe working environment

E Evaluation of Pupils' Work
e1 Provides pupils with oral and written feedback on their written work
e2 Records the achievement of pupils, using the school's assessment procedures
e3 Adjusts his/her teaching in the light of work assessed

F Recognition of the Teacher's Role
f1 Establishes good working relationships with colleagues in the school
f2 Learns from the observation of, and discussion with, colleagues and from personal experience and reflection